ADDRESSES OF THE RICH & FAMOUS

How to Reach the World's Movers and Shakers

by

Cynthia Mattison

ODYSSEY PUBLICATIONS
A Division of Collectors Universe, Inc.
NASDAQ: CLCT
www.AutographCollector.com

Publisher: Odyssey Publications
             A Division of Collectors Universe, Inc.
             NASDAQ: CLCT

Cover Design: Jackie Floyd, Type "F"
Author: Cynthia Mattison
Edited By: Ev Phillips

Printed in the United States of America
First Edition, First Printing
10 9 8 7 6 5 4 3 2 1

ISBN# 0-9669710-4-3

Library of Congress Catalog Card Number: # 2001117218

Odyssey Publications
A Division of Collectors Universe, Inc.
510-A So. Corona Mall
Corona, CA 92879-1420

1-800-996-3977 or
(909)734-9636

www.AutographCollector.com

Preface

Ever since paper and ink were invented many hundreds of years ago, people have been recording their well wishes and thoughts of admiration to others in the form of a letter. Show me someone who says they don't have a hero or heroine, someone they don't truly admire, and I'll show you someone who's being less than candid.

What you are holding in your hands is a book that allows you to continue the hundreds-of-years-old tradition of communicating with someone you admire, someone you'd like to just send thanks to, or maybe someone you'd like to ask a question. It can be used for these and many other purposes. If you're a fundraiser looking for a contribution to your silent auction, this book is a must-have. If you're a student doing research and need information from a mover and shaker in a particular field, this book is for you. And if you're just a plain old-fashioned fan who'd like to write to your favorite celebrity and ask for an autograph, this book is invaluable.

On these pages are addresses of the richest, most powerful and famous people of our time. You read about them in newspapers and magazines, you see them on TV and in movies. Maybe you've always wanted to write your favorite singer, but didn't think it was possible. I'm here to tell you that it is possible! It's not only possible to write them at an address where your letter will reach them, it's possible – and proven – to even get a personal response from many of them! In fact, the author has obtained hundreds of autographed photos, notes and thoughtful letters from celebrities whose addresses are listed on these pages.

While I encourage you to use these addresses to correspond with a celebrity, I cannot state strongly enough that I vehemently discourage you from paying a visit in person. This is not only an intrusion, it is unwelcome and could have very negative consequences. Respect the space and privacy of these great people. A kind letter or note will convey your feelings without being unwelcome. And, when writing, be patient. A fan's letter to supermodel Christie Brinkley once took two years to elicit a response. But respond she did, enclosing a lovely, signed 8x10 photo of herself.

Finally, once you begin the wonderful odyssey of writing to many of these national treasures, you will find yourself literally waiting by your window to see what the mailman has in store for you. It's an exciting, rewarding pursuit, and one that I hope you'll thoroughly enjoy.

Bill Miller & Darrell Talbert
Publishers
Autograph Collector Magazine

About the Author

Cynthia Mattison is a nationally recognized journalist and has reported on collectibles since 1996. After graduating from high school, Cynthia continued her education, earning a paralegal degree while simultaneously pursuing her interest in writing. Her subjects range from racing collectibles and autographs to conducting celebrity interviews.

Now 24, Cynthia serves as a contributing editor for *Autograph Collector.* Her work also has been published in other high-profile magazines, including *Inside NASCAR, Beckett Sports Collectibles & Autographs* and Tuff Stuff's *RPM Racing* and *Die Cast Digest*. In addition to her print journalism work, Mattison is the resident collectibles expert for America Online (keyword: ADNASCAR). She is also a nominated member of NAFE (National Association for Female Executives). Cynthia authored two books in 2000. *Addresses of the Rich and Famous* is her third book.

For more information on Cynthia Mattison, please visit her official Web site at http://www.CynthiaMattison.com

Table of Contents

Introduction

For me, autograph collecting is more than a hobby – it's a very special collection of memories from years gone by. I began collecting autographs through the mail at a very young age. Now, 16 years after receiving my first autograph, I love it just as much as I did years ago. What is it that makes this hobby so loved by so many? Perhaps it's because it gives collectors a sense of closeness to their favorite celebrities. Or maybe because it's a terrific pastime for families to enjoy together as they share a common interest. In my opinion, it is both of these – and so much more.

Collectors have several options when it comes to acquiring autographs – through the mail, in person or by purchasing from a dealer. For reasons of both time and expense, mailed requests are quickly becoming the popular choice among collectors. This book is designed to help introduce new collectors to an exciting hobby, as well as to further educate veteran autograph seekers.

With *Addresses of the Rich and Famous*, I have made every effort to include as much information as possible. I not only have included the occupation of each individual celebrity, but also noted the response time and details for each verified address.

As a longtime through-the-mail collector, I realize that the success of this hobby depends on the addresses we use when sending our requests. Of course, you cannot be successful if the information you possess isn't accurate. This book is designed to give collectors a list of accurate, up-to-date mailing addresses for thousands of celebrities. Through my own research and maintaining detailed records, I have put together an extensive list of both verified and non-verified addresses.

Please be aware that the response times in this book, where noted, are not guarantees that you will receive a reply from a given celebrity. These estimates are based on my own personal experience, research and files. Please also understand that, from time to time, celebrities may change addresses. As a result, it is impossible to guarantee a response or ensure that any signature received is authentic.

I hope you will find this book to be a valuable resource for starting, or adding to, your autograph collection. After using this guide, please feel free to contact me with any address changes, requests or submissions that you would like me to include in a future edition. If you have access to the Internet and would like to send mail electronically, please contact me at CDMattison@aol.com. If you prefer to use regular mail, please write to: Cynthia Mattison, c/o Odyssey Publications, 510-A South Corona Mall, Corona, CA 92879-1420.

Getting Started
A How-To Guide For Beginners

Welcome to the wonderful world of autograph collecting! It's fun, and if approached correctly, it can also be free! Did you know that celebrities really do appreciate receiving fan mail and that many of them will respond with an autograph? All it takes is a nicely written letter and an accurate address.

Before your mailbox is full of autographs, however, there are several things to consider before sending your first request. The first is to decide whether to ask for a signed photo or send your own item to be signed. If you send your own item, what should it be? When making this decision, it is important to consider the celebrity's signing habits, if known. For those who are generally good through-the-mail signers (which I have noted in this book wherever possible), it may be a good idea to send your own item to be signed. On the other hand, if there is no information available on the signing habits of a given celebrity, it's probably better to start off by asking for a signed photo or sending a blank index card and requesting a signature. If you request a signed photo, please do not request multiples. However, if you have photos and/or index cards to be signed, a limit of two is almost always considered a reasonable request.

If a celebrity usually sends an inscribed photo (i.e. To Cynthia), this is a good indication that they may also be willing to sign items you provide. These may include index cards, special photos, memorabilia, or other items. If a photo is inscribed, it means that the celebrity was actually there to sign it especially for you. It also indicates that the celebrity may stop by his/her office to answer their mail, which is a good thing for collectors who choose to send their own items to be signed.

At times, collectors may receive a signed photo that is not inscribed. This could mean one of two things – either the celebrity does not inscribe or he/she pre-signs photos for their fans as time permits. This doesn't mean that the celebrity won't sign items sent to them, however collectors may want to try sending index cards to test the signing habits before sending a more special item. If you receive a photo with a non-authentic signature (i.e. preprint, autopen, etc.), it may be a good idea to send an index card and ask the celebrity to sign it. I have found this to be very helpful when dealing with celebrities who send non-authentic signed photos. Many notables will only sign if an item is provided, and otherwise may send preprinted photos.

One example is Charles Bronson who, upon my first request, sent a lovely 8x10 photo with a preprinted signature. So I followed up with one blank index card and a letter kindly asking him to sign it for me. Bronson signed and returned the card within a month. This is just one example of how sending your own item can sometimes result in an authentic response. But remember – before sending any of your special items to be signed, it is always best to test the celebrity's signing habits with an index card first.

What types of collectibles are best for autographs? Photos and index cards are always nice, but we all enjoy collecting rare memorabilia – that's what makes your collection unique. A collection should, in some way, reflect the owner's personality. If you are like most collectors, you are looking for ways to make your collection a "star." Consider purchasing a box of special occasion cards (i.e. Birthday, Anniversary, Christmas, New Years, etc.). These are wonderful for requesting autographs. A politely written letter asking the celebrity to sign your special occasion card often will result in your receiving a very unique signed collectible. During Christmas 1999, I received 80 signed cards by using this method. Some are even dated and have personalized notes written on them. Any type of special occasion cards will work nicely.

If you're still looking for the perfect item to send, try the newsstands. Is there a magazine that features an article or photo about your favorite celebrity? If so, pick up a copy and ask them to autograph it for you! What about books? How many celebrities have published biographies or written books? These make wonderful items for autographing and can be mailed affordably using book rate postage, which is considerably less expensive than First Class mail. The following items are ideal for obtaining autographs:

- CD Inserts
- Drumsticks
- Guitar picks
- Sheet music
- Golf balls
- Hockey pucks
- Books
- Boxing gloves
- Movie posters
- Footballs
- Baseballs
- Basketballs
- Baseball caps
- Tennis balls
- T-shirts
- Special occasion cards

All of these items are generally easy to find. For example, movie posters can be purchased at almost any movie theater or video store. Most are in the $2-$10 range. However, it's a good idea to call ahead and reserve the poster that you want because they are extremely popular among collectors. Sheet music, drumsticks, guitar picks and other music collectibles can be purchased at most music stores.

Now that you have an idea of what type of items to send, let's get ready to mail the perfect autograph request.

If you are not already familiar with collecting, here's what you'll need:

- One tablet of ruled 6x9 writing paper
- One package of 3x5 unruled index cards
- Several new writing utensils
- One box of 9x12 envelopes
- One box of #10 business-size envelopes
- One box of standard size envelopes
- One book of 76-cent stamps
- One book of 34-cent stamps

Now that we have our shopping list out of the way, it's time to write your first letter.

First, always remember to be polite and complimentary. A fan letter should never be demanding or make the celebrity feel as if he/she is being taken advantage of. So please – do not request more than one signed photo. It is also important to acknowledge some aspect of the celebrity's career. For example, if you are writing to an actor, you may want to mention a recent movie that he starred in. If you are writing to a musician, mention the song of his/hers that you enjoy the most. While you should make sure your words are genuine, do not exceed one page in length. It is possible that longer letters, which take more time to read, may be set aside for later consideration, but don't bet on it. I've included some sample request letters on the following pages to give you an idea of what to say.

Now that you have decided what to ask for and composed the perfect letter, it's time to prepare your envelope or package for mailing.

Keep in mind that you should never send anything you cannot afford to lose. There is always the possibility that your item(s) may be lost or damaged in the mail, either en route to the celebrity or on the way back to you. It is also possible that your item(s) may be misplaced in the celebrity's office due to the large amount of mail he/she receives. Also remember that a celebrity can stop signing at any time. Due to work schedules, illness or simply a change of heart, celebrities have been known to refuse autograph requests in the mail. If this happens, there is no guarantee that your item(s) will be returned.

Perhaps the most important guideline to remember is to always include a SASE (Self-Addressed Stamped Envelope). For photo requests, the most economical way of doing this is to address a business-size #10 envelope to the celebrity, with your return address in the upper left-hand corner. Take a 9x12 clasp envelope, address it to yourself, and put a 76-cent stamp on it. This larger envelope will act as your SASE and will be more than sufficient to hold an 8x10 photo from the celebrity. Always remember to write "Photo – Do Not Bend" on the front and back of your SASE. Fold the 9x12 envelope three ways so it will fit inside the #10 envelope along with your letter. The #10 envelope should require one 34-cent stamp. If you are sending smaller items like index and/or trading cards to be signed, a regular size SASE with a 34-cent stamp should be sufficient.

What is the most affordable way to mail a larger item? If you decide to send a basketball, baseball, football or other large item, you'll need a box. Buy one that will be large enough for the item to fit into. Place the item inside the box, but do not seal it. Take the package to the Post Office and have it weighed. Once you are quoted a mailing price for the box (let's say it's $2.50), you will need to purchase $5 worth of stamps. Return home with your package and place $2.50 worth of stamps along with a self-adhesive mailing label addressed to you inside with your letter and item. Ask the celebrity to return the item in your box and advise them that you are sending the required postage and an address label for them to affix on the outside. Now you are ready to seal the box. Address it to the celebrity and place the other $2.50 worth of stamps on the outside. That's it – your package is ready to go. When the celebrity opens your package, all he/she needs to do is sign the item, place the stamps on the outside of your box and attach the address label. It's that simple.

Before you put your request in the mail, don't forget to keep a record. It's a good idea to keep a detailed log of all the autograph requests you send out, including the date you sent the request, the address you used, what type of autograph you requested, and so on. This will be very beneficial when you receive a response and can note the date and what you received. Why is this information so important? If you ever decide to write to the celebrity again, you will know which address to use and how to estimate the response time. You can keep excellent records in one of two ways – a computer database program or a ruled notebook. Either method is a great way to keep track of your mailed autograph requests. If you choose to keep records on a computer, be sure to make a backup copy of your file!

Here's a good example of an autograph request log entry:

October 10, 2000
Jack Wagner (Photo) – 1134 Alto Loma #115, W. Hollywood, CA 90069
Received: 8x10 Signed Photo – October 30, 2000

Now that your requests are mailed, it all comes down to a waiting game. As collectors, we must be patient if we are to have success in autograph collecting. If you send out requests and expect to receive replies from everyone in a month or less, you may become frustrated and lose interest in what otherwise would have been a terrific pastime for you to enjoy. Patience is the key when collecting autographs through the mail. It's true that some celebrities will respond in as little as a week, but others take much longer. To date, my longest response time was eight years and, while this is by no means a "norm" in the collecting industry, it is a possibility. If you write to a very popular star at the height of his/her career, be ready for a wait! The autograph that took me eight years to receive – a Sylvester Stallone color 8x10 photo that I provided – is my most prized through-the-mail autograph. To me, it was definitely worth the wait. Whether it takes one week, one month or one year, please be patient and keep writing! If one celebrity doesn't respond, there's always one who will.

Once you begin to receive autographs, it is very important to keep them protected from damage. After all this effort, you wouldn't want to see your photo have something spilled on it or have sunlight damage. It's a good idea to keep your photos in plastic, top-loading storage sheets. They can be purchased at most department stores and can be found in the paper aisle. These sheets are binder-ready, meaning they are already pre-punched and can be inserted into a sturdy binder for added protection. With different sizes available, these sheets are also ideal for index and trading card storage.

One final note. Please understand that the addresses in this book are to be used for fan mail purposes only. Do not under any circumstances attempt to visit a celebrity's home or send unsolicited gifts, as everyone is entitled to his/her privacy.

Sample Letters

Dear John Travolta:

Hello – I am a very big fan of yours. I love movies and really enjoyed your work in *Grease*. It is one of my all time favorite films and I really admire your talent and dedication.

Will you please send me an autographed photo? I would really appreciate it – I'm also enclosing a SASE. Thank you very much for your time. Continued best wishes!

Sincerely,
Cynthia Mattison

Dear Elle MacPherson:

Hello – I am a very big fan of yours. I really admire the talent and dedication that you contribute to the world of modeling.

Will you please autograph my index cards? I would really appreciate it – I'm also enclosing a SASE. Thank you very much for your time. Continued best wishes!

Sincerely,
Cynthia Mattison

Dear Barbara Streisand:

Hello – I am a very big fan of yours. I love music and I really admire your talent and dedication. I find your songs to be extremely beautiful and have also enjoyed your work as an actress.

Will you please autograph my book and send it back to me? I would really appreciate it – I'm also enclosing a SASE. Thank you very much for your time. Continued best wishes!

Sincerely,
Cynthia Mattison

Frequently Asked Questions

Q: I am new to autograph collecting and would like to know if it is best to handwrite or type my letter to a celebrity?

A: If possible, try and print your letter in legible handwriting. If you feel that your handwriting may be illegible for some reason, it is also acceptable to type your letter. Please keep in mind that, whenever possible, it is best to handwrite all letters of request to avoid giving them a "form-letter" appearance.

Q: When writing a letter, should I keep it short and to the point, or send a long letter of praise?

A: It is very important to keep an autograph request brief and to the point. That said, it is also important to mention some aspect of the celebrity's career. Like everyone else, celebrities enjoy a compliment. If you take the time to write to a celebrity, you obviously enjoy his/her work. So while your letter should not exceed one page in length, it is very important to be polite and complimentary in your request.

Q: Is it necessary to include a Self-Addressed Stamped Envelope?

A: Perhaps the most important thing to remember when requesting autographs through the mail is to always include a SASE. Due to the overwhelming amounts of fan mail that some celebrities receive, sending no SASE often means no reply.

Q: Do celebrities *really* read their fan mail?

A: Absolutely! Fan mail is very important to a celebrity and provides a special way for them to connect with their fans. Due to hectic work schedules, some celebrities may have an assistant who handles much of his/her incoming mail. Most celebrities are reported to actually read some, if not all, of their fan mail.

Q: After I mail an autograph request, how long will it take to receive a reply?

A: Celebrities are extremely busy people. While they do appreciate their fan mail, it can take some time to respond to every request. Many celebrities receive hundreds of autograph requests each week. It is important to recognize this, and have patience. After mailing an autograph request, it can take anywhere from several weeks to a year or more. (Note: The author's longest wait time for a mailed autograph request – to Sylvester Stallone – was eight years!)

Q: I have just received an autograph in the mail. How do I know if it's authentic?

A: Since you did not actually see the celebrity sign the autograph, it is nearly impossible to guarantee that it is authentic. This is one of the risks you take when collecting autographs through the mail. The signature may be authentic, signed by a secretary, a preprint, or even an autopen.

Q: What is the difference between a secretarial, preprint and autopen signature?

A: A secretarial signature, as its name implies, is one signed by a celebrity's assistant or secretary. This type of signature may be difficult to identify because, in many cases, the secretary's signature may be very similar to that of the celebrity.

A preprinted signature is one that is part of the photo production process. For example, think of a celebrity signing one photo and that photo is copied. The copies, which are known as preprints, are produced in volume and sent out to fans requesting an autograph. A preprint is perhaps the most easily to spot because it does not appear to have been made on top of the photo. A genuine autograph, on the other hand, will give the appearance of the ink being above the photo.

An autopen signature is not as easily identified. The only way to know for sure is to compare it to known autopen examples. If the signature matches exactly, it may be an autopen because no person can sign exactly the same way twice. One final identifying characteristic of autopen signatures is that each stroke of ink is consistent. Unlike a human signature, in which the pen strokes vary in speed and pressure, an autopen machine creates a signature at the same speed and pressure.

Q: Why do some celebrities have multiple addresses?
A: You will notice that some celebrities in this book have multiple addresses. That's because they may have agents, publicists, managers and/or fan clubs. It is also possible to write to a celebrity in care of a television show that he/she is currently cast in. With all of these options, it is a good idea to try several different addresses when requesting an autograph.

Q: If a celebrity charges money for an autograph, should I send cash, check or money order?
A: When making a mail order purchase, it is usually in your best interest to pay with a credit card or personal check. Either of these methods will serve as your receipt and show that you paid for the item, which is helpful in the event a problem arises with the purchase.

Abbreviations

BH - Beverly Hills
IC – Index Card
LA - Los Angeles
NY - New York
SASE – Self-Addressed Stamped Envelope
SIC – Signed Index Card
SP – Signed Photo
STC – Signed Trading Card
TLS – Typed Letter Signed

This book contains verified addresses with response times, along with non-verified entries. If a signed photo was received using a particular address, a 9x12 SASE was sent with the autograph request. If a signed index card was received, a blank index card and standard size SASE was sent with the request.

4 Guys, The
P.O. Box 0865
Murfreesboro, TN 37133-0865
Music Group
Response Time: 25 Days
Received: Signed Photo

Aadland, Beverly
P.O. Box 1115
Canyon Country, CA 91350
Actress
Response Time: N/A
Received: N/A

Aaron, Hank
P.O. Box 4064
Atlanta, GA 30302
Baseball Legend
Response Time: 18 Days
Received: Signed Photo

Abbott, Gregory
P.O. Box 68
Bergenfield, NJ 07621
Singer
Response Time: N/A
Received: N/A

Abercrombie, Neil
U.S. House of Representatives
Washington, DC 20515
Politician
Response Time: N/A
Received: N/A

Abernathy, Donzaleigh
5555 Melrose Ave.
Hollywood, CA 90038-3197
Actress
Response Time: N/A
Received: N/A

Acevedo-Vila, Anibal
U.S. House of Representatives
Washington, DC 20515
Politician
Response Time: N/A
Received: N/A

Ackerman, Gary L.
U.S. House of Representatives
Washington, DC 20515
Politician
Response Time: N/A
Received: N/A

Adams, Don
2160 Century Park East #110
LA, CA 90067
Actor
Response Time: 112 Days
Received: Signed Photo

Adams, Hunter Patch
6877 Washington St.
Arlington, VA 22143
Doctor
Response Time: N/A
Received: N/A

Adams, Julie
5915 Corbin Ave.
Tarzana, CA 91356
Actress
Response Time: N/A
Received: N/A

Adams, Rhonda
9242 Beverly Blvd.
BH, CA 90210
Playboy Playmate
Response Time: N/A
Received: N/A

Adams, Stephanie
9242 Beverly Blvd.
BH, CA 90210
Playboy Playmate
Response Time: N/A
Received: N/A

Adamson, James C.
2101 NASA Rd. 1
Houston, TX 77058
Astronaut
Response Time: N/A
Received: N/A

Addabbo, Anthony
51 W. 52 St.
NY, NY 10019
Actor
Response Time: N/A
Received: N/A

Adell, Traci
9242 Beverly Blvd.
BH, CA 90210
Playboy Playmate
Response Time: N/A
Received: N/A

Aderholt, Robert B.
U.S. House of Representatives
Washington, DC 20515
Politician
Response Time: N/A
Received: N/A

Adkins, Trace
P.O. Box 121889
Nashville, TN 37212
Singer
Response Time: N/A
Received: N/A

Adler, Lou
3969 Villa Costera
Malibu, CA 90265
Actor
Response Time: N/A
Received: N/A

Affleck, Ben
9830 Wilshire Blvd.
BH, CA 90212
Actor
Response Time: N/A
Received: N/A

Agar, John
639 N. Hollywood Way
Burbank, CA 91505
Actor
Response Time: N/A
Received: N/A

Agassi, Andre
8921 Andre Dr.
Las Vegas, NV 89113
Tennis Player
Response Time: 150 Days
Received: Signed Photo

Agena, Keiko
4000 Warner Blvd.
Burbank, CA 91522
Actress
Response Time: N/A
Received: N/A

Aiello, Danny
30 Chestnut Ridge Rd.
Saddle River, NJ 07458-3302
Actor
Response Time: N/A
Received: N/A

Aiken, Kimberly
Two Ocean Way, Ste. 1000
Atlantic City, NJ 08401
Miss America 1994
Response Time: N/A
Received: N/A

Aikman, Troy
1 Cowboy Parkway
Irving, TX 75063
Football Player
Response Time: 24 Days
Received: Signed Photo

Akaka, Daniel
720 Hart Senate Office Bldg.
Washington, DC 20510
Senator
Response Time: N/A
Received: N/A

Akers, Thomas D.
2101 NASA Rd. 1
Houston, TX 77058
Astronaut
Response Time: N/A
Received: N/A

Akin, Susan
Two Ocean Way, Ste. 1000
Atlantic City, NJ 08401
Miss America 1986
Response Time: N/A
Received: N/A

Akin, W. Todd
U.S. House of Representatives
Washington, DC 20515
Politician
Response Time: N/A
Received: N/A

Akins, Rhett
P.O. Box 120279
Nashville, TN 37212
Singer
Response Time: N/A
Received: N/A

Alabama
P.O. Box 680529
Fort Payne, AL 35968
Music Group
Response Time: 11 Days
Received: Signed Photo

Skantz, Alan
c/o Home Shopping Network
St. Petersburg, FL 33701
Home Shopping Network Host
Response Time: N/A
Received: N/A

Albright, Madeleine
1318 34th St. N.W.
Washington, DC 20007
Politician
Response Time: 18 Days
Received: Signed Photo

Albright, Madeleine
Department of State
Washington, DC 20520
Politician
Response Time: 14 Days
Received: Signed Photo

Alda, Alan
641 Lexington Ave. #1400
NY, NY 10022
Actor
Response Time: N/A
Received: N/A

Alderson, Kristen
56 West 66th St.
NY, NY 10023
Actress
Response Time: N/A
Received: N/A

Aldrich, Sarah
4151 Prospect Ave.
LA, CA 90027
Actress
Response Time: N/A
Received: N/A

Aldrin, Buzz
2101 NASA Rd. 1
Houston, TX 77058
Astronaut
Response Time: N/A
Received: N/A

Aleksander, Grant
51 W. 52 St.
NY, NY 10019
Actor
Response Time: N/A
Received: N/A

Alexander, Blaise
1801 West Int'l. Spdwy. Blvd.
Daytona Beach, FL 32114
Auto Racing Personality
Response Time: 248 Days
Received: Signed Photo

Alexis, Kim
345 N. Maple Dr. #185
BH, CA 90210-3827
Model
Response Time: 32 Days
Received: Signed Photo

Alfonso, Kristian
3000 W. Alameda Ave.
Burbank, CA 91523
Actress
Response Time: N/A
Received: N/A

Alfonso, Kristian
P.O. Box 557
Brockton, MA 02403
Actress
Response Time: 10 Days
Received: Signed Photo

Ali, Muhammad
P.O. Box 160
Berrien Springs, MI 49103
Boxer
Response Time: 19 Days
Received: Signed Photo

Ali, Muhammad
P.O. Box 187
Berrien Springs, MI 49103
Boxer
Response Time: 44 Days
Received: Signed Photo

Ali, Tatyana
4924 Balboa Blvd. #377
Encino, CA 91316-3402
Actress, Singer
Response Time: 18 Days
Received: Signed Photo

Allan, Jennifer
9242 Beverly Blvd.
BH, CA 90210
Playboy Playmate
Response Time: N/A
Received: N/A

Allard, Wayne
513 Hart Senate Office Bldg.
Washington, DC 20510
Senator
Response Time: N/A
Received: N/A

Allen, Andrew M.
2101 NASA Rd. 1
Houston, TX 77058
Astronaut
Response Time: N/A
Received: N/A

Allen, Ashley
9242 Beverly Blvd.
BH, CA 90210
Playboy Playmate
Response Time: N/A
Received: N/A

Allen, Deborah
P.O. Box 120849
Nashville, TN 37212
Singer
Response Time: N/A
Received: N/A

Allen, George
United States Senate
Washington, DC 20510
Senator
Response Time: N/A
Received: N/A

Allen, Glenn
P.O. Box 2247
Cornelius, NC 28031
Auto Racing Personality
Response Time: N/A
Received: N/A

Allen, Glenn
1801 West Int'l. Spdwy. Blvd.
Daytona Beach, FL 32114
Auto Racing Personality
Response Time: 157 Days
Received: Signed Photo

Allen, Joseph P.
2101 NASA Rd. 1
Houston, TX 77058
Astronaut
Response Time: N/A
Received: N/A

Allen, Krista
c/o Baywatch Productions
510-18th Ave., Honolulu, HI 96816
Actress
Response Time: N/A
Received: N/A

Allen, Laura
320 West 66th St.
NY, NY 10023
Actress
Response Time: N/A
Received: N/A

Allen, Thomas H.
U.S. House of Representatives
Washington, DC 20515
Politician
Response Time: N/A
Received: N/A

Allen, Woody
930 Fifth Ave.
NY, NY 10018
Actor, Director
Response Time: 28 Days
Received: Signed Photo

Allison, Bobby
140 Church St.
Heuytown, AL 35023
Auto Racing Personality
Response Time: 36 Days
Received: Signed Photo

Allison, Bobby
1801 West Int'l. Spdwy. Blvd.
Daytona Beach, FL 32114
Auto Racing Personality
Response Time: 262 Days
Received: Signed Photo

Almond, Lincoln
State House
Providence, RI 02903
Governor
Response Time: N/A
Received: N/A

Alonso, Maria Conchita
P.O. Box 537
BH, CA 90213
Actress
Response Time: N/A
Received: N/A

Alseep At The Wheel
P.O. Box 463
Austin, TX 78767
Music Group
Response Time: 19 Days
Received: Signed Photo - $5

Altman, Scott D.
2101 NASA Rd. 1
Houston, TX 77058
Astronaut
Response Time: N/A
Received: N/A

Ames, Rachel
4151 Prospect Ave.
LA, CA 90027
Actress
Response Time: N/A
Received: N/A

Amick, Lyndon
1801 West Int'l. Spdwy. Blvd.
Daytona Beach, FL 32114
Auto Racing Personality
Response Time: 100 Days
Received: Signed Photo

Anders, William A.
2101 NASA Rd. 1
Houston, TX 77058
Astronaut
Response Time: N/A
Received: N/A

Anderson, Bill
P.O. Box 888
Hermitage, TN 37076
Singer
Response Time: 12 Days
Received: Signed Photo & TLS

Anderson, Clayton C.
2101 NASA Rd. 1
Houston, TX 77058
Astronaut
Response Time: N/A
Received: N/A

Anderson, Loni
20652 Lassen #98
Chatsworth, CA 91311
Actress
Response Time: N/A
Received: N/A

Anderson, Lynn
P.O. Box 90454
Charleston, SC 29410
Singer
Response Time: N/A
Received: N/A

Anderson, Michael P.
2101 NASA Rd. 1
Houston, TX 77058
Astronaut
Response Time: N/A
Received: N/A

Anderson, Pamela
c/o Baywatch Productions
510-18th Ave., Honolulu, HI 96816
Actress, Playboy Playmate
Response Time: N/A
Received: N/A

Anderson, Pamela
9242 Beverly Blvd.
BH, CA 90210
Actress, Playboy Playmate
Response Time: N/A
Received: N/A

Anderson, Sparky
P.O. Box 6415
Thousand Oaks, CA 91359
Baseball Player
Response Time: 16 Days
Received: Signed Photo

Andes, Keith
26231 Larkhaven Place
Santa Clarita, CA 91321
Actor
Response Time: 18 Days
Received: Signed Photo

Andrada, Marilece
c/o Baywatch Productions
510-18th Ave., Honolulu, HI 96816
Actress
Response Time: N/A
Received: N/A

Andrada, Marilece
9242 Beverly Blvd.
BH, CA 90210
Playboy Playmate
Response Time: N/A
Received: N/A

Andretti, John
1801 West Int'l. Spdwy. Blvd.
Daytona Beach, FL 32114
Auto Racing Personality
Response Time: 214 Days
Received: Signed Photo

Andretti, John
311 Branson Mill Rd.
Randleman, NC 28317
Auto Racing Personality
Response Time: 30 Days
Received: Signed Photo

Andretti, Mario
53 Victory Lane
Nazareth, PA 18064
Auto Racing Personality
Response Time: N/A
Received: N/A

Andretti, Michael
457 Rose Inn Ave.
Nazareth, PA 18064
Auto Racing Personality
Response Time: N/A
Received: N/A

Andrews, Jessica
P.O. Box 121411
Nashville, TN 37212
Singer
Response Time: 24 Days
Received: Signed Photo

Andrews, Real
4151 Prospect Ave.
LA, CA 90027
Actor
Response Time: N/A
Received: N/A

Andrews, Robert E.
U.S. House of Representatives
Washington, DC 20515
Politician
Response Time: N/A
Received: N/A

Angarano, Michael
1230 Ave. of Americas
NY, NY 10020
Actor
Response Time: N/A
Received: N/A

Anholt, Christien
5555 Melrose Ave.
Hollywood, CA 90038-3197
Actor
Response Time: N/A
Received: N/A

Aniston, Jennifer
4000 Warner Blvd.
Burbank, CA 91522
Actress
Response Time: N/A
Received: N/A

Aniston, John
3000 W. Alameda Ave.
Burbank, CA 91523
Actor
Response Time: N/A
Received: N/A

Anka, Paul
10573 W. Pico Blvd. #159
LA, CA 90064
Singer
Response Time: N/A
Received: N/A

Anka, Paul
433 N. Camden Dr., Ste. 960
BH, CA 90210
Singer
Response Time: 13 Days
Received: Signed Photo

Anselmo, Tony
500 S. Buena Vista St.
Burbank, CA 91521
Voice Actor - Donald Duck
Response Time: 8 Days
Received: Signed Photo

Appleby, Shiri
4000 Warner Blvd.
Burbank, CA 91522
Actress
Response Time: 30 Days
Received: Signed Photo

Appleby, Stuart
1360 East 9th St., Ste. 100
Cleveland, OH 44114-1782
Golfer
Response Time: N/A
Received: N/A

Applegate, Christina
20411 Chapter Dr.
Woodland Hills, CA 91364-5612
Actress
Response Time: N/A
Received: N/A

April Sokolova, Natalia
9242 Beverly Blvd.
BH, CA 90210
Playboy Playmate
Response Time: N/A
Received: N/A

Apt, Jerome
2101 NASA Rd. 1
Houston, TX 77058
Astronaut
Response Time: N/A
Received: N/A

Archambault, Lee J.
2101 NASA Rd. 1
Houston, TX 77058
Astronaut
Response Time: N/A
Received: N/A

Arkin, Adam
2372 Veteran Ave.
LA, CA 90069
Actor
Response Time: N/A
Received: N/A

Arkin, Alan
1325 Ave. of the Americas
NY, NY 10019
Actor
Response Time: N/A
Received: N/A

Armey, Richard K.
U.S. House of Representatives
Washington, DC 20515
Politician
Response Time: N/A
Received: N/A

Armstrong, Neil A.
2101 NASA Rd. 1
Houston, TX 77058
Astronaut
Response Time: N/A
Received: N/A

Arnaz Jr., Desi
P.O. Box 60684
Boulder City, NV 89006
Actor
Response Time: 56 Days
Received: Signed Photo

Arquette, David
409 N. Camden Dr. #202
BH, CA 90210
Actor
Response Time: N/A
Received: N/A

Arquette, David
8942 Wilshire Blvd.
BH, CA 90211
Actor
Response Time: 119 Days
Received: Signed Photo

Arthur, Beatrice
2000 Old Ranch Rd.
LA, CA 90049
Actress
Response Time: 61 Days
Received: Signed Photo

Arthur, Stacy Leigh
9242 Beverly Blvd.
BH, CA 90210
Playboy Playmate
Response Time: N/A
Received: N/A

Ash, Mary Kay
8787 N. Stemmons Freeway
Dallas, TX 75247
Mary Kay Cosmetics Founder
Response Time: N/A
Received: N/A

Ashby, Jeffrey S.
2101 NASA Rd. 1
Houston, TX 77058
Astronaut
Response Time: N/A
Received: N/A

Asner, Ed
3556 Mound View Ave.
Studio City, CA 91604
Actor
Response Time: N/A
Received: N/A

Asner, Ed
P.O. Box 7407
Studio City, CA 91604
Actor
Response Time: N/A
Received: N/A

Assante, Armand
Rd. 1 Box 561
Cambell Hall, NY 10915
Actor
Response Time: N/A
Received: N/A

Astin, Sean
151 El Camino Dr.
BH, CA 90212
Actor
Response Time: N/A
Received: N/A

Atkins, Chet
3716 Timberlake Rd.
Knoxville, TN 37920
Singer
Response Time: N/A
Received: N/A

Attenborough, Richard
Old Farms, Beaver Lodge
Surrey TW9 JNQ, United Kingdom
Actor
Response Time: N/A
Received: N/A

Atwood, Casey
P.O. Box 37, 321 W. Reservoir
Central City, KY 42330
Auto Racing Personality
Response Time: N/A
Received: N/A

Atwood, Casey
1801 West Int'l. Spdwy. Blvd.
Daytona Beach, FL 32114
Auto Racing Personality
Response Time: 179 Days
Received: Signed Photo

August Altice, Summer
9242 Beverly Blvd.
BH, CA 90210
Playboy Playmate
Response Time: N/A
Received: N/A

Austin, Sherrie
P.O. Box 121254
Nashville, TN 37212
Singer
Response Time: N/A
Received: N/A

Autry, Alan
P.O. Box 989
Clovis, CA 93613
Actor
Response Time: 42 Days
Received: Signed Photo

Axelrod, Amy
c/o Home Shopping Network
St. Petersburg, FL 33701
Home Shopping Network Host
Response Time: N/A
Received: N/A

Axum, Donna
Two Ocean Way, Ste. 1000
Atlantic City, NJ 08401
Miss America 1964
Response Time: N/A
Received: N/A

Ay, Evelyn
Two Ocean Way, Ste. 1000
Atlantic City, NJ 08401
Miss America 1954
Response Time: N/A
Received: N/A

Aykroyd, Dan
1180 South Beverly Dr. #618
LA, CA 90035
Actor
Response Time: 138 Days
Received: SIC

Aykroyd, Dan
9830 Wilshire Blvd.
BH, CA 90212
Actor
Response Time: N/A
Received: N/A

Azinger, Paul
7847 Chick Evans Pl.
Sarasota, FL 34240-8752
Golfer
Response Time: N/A
Received: N/A

Azinger, Paul
390 N. Orange Ave. #2600
Orlando, FL 32801-1642
Golfer
Response Time: 72 Days
Received: Signed Photo

Baca, Joe
U.S. House of Representatives
Washington, DC 20515
Politician
Response Time: N/A
Received: N/A

Bacall, Lauren
1 W. 72nd St. #43
NY, NY 10023
Actress
Response Time: 44 Days
Received: Signed Photo

Bacall, Lauren
151 El Camino Dr.
BH, CA 90212
Actress
Response Time: N/A
Received: N/A

Bachus, Spencer
U.S. House of Representatives
Washington, DC 20515
Politician
Response Time: N/A
Received: N/A

Badalucco, Michael
10201 West Pico Blvd.
LA, CA 90035
Actor
Response Time: 29 Days
Received: SIC

Bader, Diedrich
4000 Warner Blvd.
Burbank, CA 91522
Actor
Response Time: N/A
Received: N/A

Badham, Mary
3344 Clarendon Rd.
BH, CA 90210
Actress
Response Time: N/A
Received: N/A

Baez, Joan
P.O. Box 1026
Mento Park, CA 94025
Singer
Response Time: 26 Days
Received: Signed Photo

Bagian, James P.
2101 NASA Rd. 1
Houston, TX 77058
Astronaut
Response Time: N/A
Received: N/A

Bagwell, Buff
P.O. Box 7
Bloomingdale, GA 31302
Wrestler
Response Time: N/A
Received: N/A

Bailey, F. Lee
1400 Centre Park Blvd. #909
W. Palm Beach, FL 33401
Defense Attorney for O.J. Simpson
Response Time: 20 Days
Received: Signed Photo

Baio, Scott
4333 Forman Ave.
Toluca Lake, CA 91602
Actor
Response Time: 71 Days
Received: Signed Photo

Baird, Brian
U.S. House of Representatives
Washington, DC 20515
Politician
Response Time: N/A
Received: N/A

Baiul, Oksana
P.O. Box 577
Simsbury, CT 06070
Figure Skater
Response Time: N/A
Received: N/A

Bakay, Nick
5555 Melrose Ave.
Hollywood, CA 90038-3197
Actor
Response Time: N/A
Received: N/A

Baker, Ellen S.
2101 NASA Rd. 1
Houston, TX 77058
Astronaut
Response Time: N/A
Received: N/A

Baker, Kenny
P.O. Box 111000
Aurora, CO 80042
Actor
Response Time: 40 Days
Received: Signed Photo

Baker, Michael A.
2101 NASA Rd. 1
Houston, TX 77058
Astronaut
Response Time: N/A
Received: N/A

Baker, Richard H.
U.S. House of Representatives
Washington, DC 20515
Politician
Response Time: N/A
Received: N/A

Baldacci, John Elias
U.S. House of Representatives
Washington, DC 20515
Politician
Response Time: N/A
Received: N/A

Baldwin, Alec
4833 Don Juan Pl.
Woodland Hills, CA 91367
Actor
Response Time: N/A
Received: N/A

Baldwin, Tammy
U.S. House of Representatives
Washington, DC 20515
Politician
Response Time: N/A
Received: N/A

Ball, David
Box 120546
Nashville, TN 31212
Singer
Response Time: 7 Days
Received: Signed Photo

Ballard, Robert
55 Coogan Blvd.
Mystic, CT 06335
Historian - Found the Titanic
Response Time: N/A
Received: N/A

Ballard, Robert
Woods Hole Oceanographic
Water St., Woods Hole, MA 02543
Historian - Found the Titanic
Response Time: 11 Days
Received: Signed Photo

Ballenger, Cass
U.S. House of Representatives
Washington, DC 20515
Politician
Response Time: N/A
Received: N/A

Bambard, Tom
1801 West Int'l. Spdwy. Blvd.
Daytona Beach, FL 32114
Auto Racing Personality
Response Time: 95 Days
Received: Signed Photo

Bancroft, Anne
2301 La Mesa Dr.
Santa Monica, CA 90405
Actress
Response Time: N/A
Received: N/A

Banderas, Antonio
3110 Main St. #205
Santa Monica, CA 90405-5353
Actor
Response Time: N/A
Received: N/A

Banks, Ernie
P.O. Box 590
Cooperstown, NY 13326
Baseball Player
Response Time: N/A
Received: N/A

Banks, Tyra
9830 Wilshire Blvd.
BH, CA 90212
Actress, Model
Response Time: N/A
Received: N/A

Baraquio, Angela Perez
Two Ocean Way, Ste. 1000
Atlantic City, NJ 08401
Miss America 2001
Response Time: N/A
Received: N/A

Barbeau, Adrienne
9255 Sunset Blvd. #515
LA, CA 90069
Actress
Response Time: N/A
Received: N/A

Barbeau, Adrienne
P.O. Box 1839
Studio City, CA 91614
Actress
Response Time: 60 Days
Received: Signed Photo

Barbera, Joseph
15303 Ventura Blvd. #1400
Sherman Oaks, CA 91403
Co-Owner, Hanna Barbera
Response Time: 14 Days
Received: Signed Photo

Barcia, James A.
U.S. House of Representatives
Washington, DC 20515
Politician
Response Time: N/A
Received: N/A

Bardot, Brigitte
La Madrague
F-83990 St. Tropez, France
Actress
Response Time: N/A
Received: N/A

Barfield, Ron
1801 West Int'l. Spdwy. Blvd.
Daytona Beach, FL 32114
Auto Racing Personality
Response Time: 212 Days
Received: Signed Photo

Barker, Bob
5730 Wilshire Blvd., Ste. 475
LA, CA 90036
Television Personality
Response Time: N/A
Received: N/A

Barker, Bob
7800 Beverly Blvd.
LA, CA 90036
Television Personality
Response Time: 31 Days
Received: Signed Photo

Barker, Bob
5757 Wilshire Blvd. #206
LA, CA 90036
Television Personality
Response Time: 31 Days
Received: Signed Photo

Barker, Clive
P.O. Box 691885
LA, CA 90069
Author
Response Time: 200 Days
Received: Signed Photo

Barker, Kylene
Two Ocean Way, Ste. 1000
Atlantic City, NJ 08401
Miss America 1979
Response Time: N/A
Received: N/A

Barnes, Debra
Two Ocean Way, Ste. 1000
Atlantic City, NJ 08401
Miss America 1968
Response Time: N/A
Received: N/A

Barnes, Roy
203 State Capitol
Atlanta, GA 30334
Governor
Response Time: N/A
Received: N/A

Barney
2435 N. Central Expressway
Richardson, TX 75680
Cartoon Character
Response Time: N/A
Received: N/A

Barr, Bob
U.S. House of Representatives
Washington, DC 20515
Politician
Response Time: N/A
Received: N/A

Barr, Julia
320 West 66th St.
NY, NY 10023
Actress
Response Time: N/A
Received: N/A

Barrett, Thomas M.
U.S. House of Representatives
Washington, DC 20515
Politician
Response Time: N/A
Received: N/A

Barrowman, John
5700 Wilshire, Ste. 575
LA, CA 90036
Actor
Response Time: N/A
Received: N/A

Barry, Daniel T.
2101 NASA Rd. 1
Houston, TX 77058
Astronaut
Response Time: N/A
Received: N/A

Bartel, Jean
Two Ocean Way, Ste. 1000
Atlantic City, NJ 08401
Miss America 1943
Response Time: N/A
Received: N/A

Bartlett, Roscoe G.
U.S. House of Representatives
Washington, DC 20515
Politician
Response Time: N/A
Received: N/A

Barton, Joe
U.S. House of Representatives
Washington, DC 20515
Politician
Response Time: N/A
Received: N/A

Bashioum, Ashley
7800 Beverly Blvd.
LA, CA 90036
Actress
Response Time: N/A
Received: N/A

Basinger, Kim
11288 Ventura Blvd. #414
Studio City, CA 91604-3149
Actress
Response Time: N/A
Received: N/A

Basinger, Kim
4833 Don Juan Pl.
Woodland Hills, CA 91364-4705
Actress
Response Time: 65 Days
Received: Signed Photo

Bass, Charles F.
U.S. House of Representatives
Washington, DC 20515
Politician
Response Time: N/A
Received: N/A

Bass, Sam
6104 Performance Dr. S.W.
Concord, NC 28027
Auto Racing Artist
Response Time: N/A
Received: N/A

Bassey, Jennifer
320 West 66th St.
NY, NY 10023
Actress
Response Time: N/A
Received: N/A

Bates, Kathy
121 N. San Vicente Blvd.
BH, CA 90211
Actress
Response Time: 90 Days
Received: Signed Photo

Baucus, Max
511 Hart Senate Office Bldg.
Washington, DC 20510
Senator
Response Time: N/A
Received: N/A

Bauer, Jill
c/o QVC, 1200 Wilson Dr.
West Chester, PA 19380
QVC Host
Response Time: N/A
Received: N/A

Bauer, Kristin
5555 Melrose Ave.
Hollywood, CA 90038-3197
Actress
Response Time: N/A
Received: N/A

Baxter, Arlene
9242 Beverly Blvd.
BH, CA 90210
Playboy Playmate
Response Time: N/A
Received: N/A

Bayh, Evan
717 Hart Senate Office Bldg.
Washington, DC 20510
Senator
Response Time: N/A
Received: N/A

Beach Boys, The
P.O. Box 130579
Carlsbad, CA 92013
Music Group
Response Time: N/A
Received: N/A

Beach Boys, The
252 Convention Center Dr.
Las Vegas, NV 89109
Music Group
Response Time: N/A
Received: N/A

Beach, Michael
4000 Warner Blvd.
Burbank, CA 91522
Actor
Response Time: N/A
Received: N/A

Bean, Alan L.
2101 NASA Rd. 1
Houston, TX 77058
Astronaut
Response Time: N/A
Received: N/A

Beauvais, Garcelle
4000 Warner Blvd.
Burbank, CA 91522
Actress
Response Time: N/A
Received: N/A

Becerra, Xavier
U.S. House of Representatives
Washington, DC 20515
Politician
Response Time: N/A
Received: N/A

Beckham, Brice
2242 E. Adams Ave.
Orange, CA 92867-6104
Actor
Response Time: N/A
Received: N/A

Bee Gees, The
1801 Bay Rd.
Miami Beach, FL 33139
Music Group
Response Time: N/A
Received: N/A

Beecroft, David
320 West 66th St.
NY, NY 10023
Actor
Response Time: N/A
Received: N/A

Behr, Jason
4000 Warner Blvd.
Burbank, CA 91522
Actor
Response Time: N/A
Received: N/A

Belafonte, Harry
300 West End Ave. #5A
NY, NY 10023
Singer
Response Time: N/A
Received: N/A

Bell, Catherine
5555 Melrose Ave.
Hollywood, CA 90038-3197
Actress
Response Time: N/A
Received: N/A

Bell, Coby
4000 Warner Blvd.
Burbank, CA 91522
Actor
Response Time: N/A
Received: N/A

Bell, Lauralee
7800 Beverly Blvd.
LA, CA 90036
Actress
Response Time: N/A
Received: N/A

Bell, Michelle
100 International Golf Dr.
Daytona Beach, FL 32124
Actress
Response Time: N/A
Received: N/A

Bellamy Brothers, The
Box 801
San Antonio, FL 33576
Music Group
Response Time: 80 Days
Received: Signed Photo

Belushi, James
8033 Sunset Blvd. #88
LA, CA 90046
Actor
Response Time: 31 Days
Received: Signed Photo

Belzer, Richard
1230 Ave. of Americas
NY, NY 10020
Actor
Response Time: N/A
Received: N/A

Benard, Maurice
4151 Prospect Ave.
LA, CA 90027
Actor
Response Time: N/A
Received: N/A

Benbrook, Liz
c/o Home Shopping Network
St. Petersburg, FL 33701
Home Shopping Network Host
Response Time: N/A
Received: N/A

Benedict, Marina
4000 Warner Blvd.
Burbank, CA 91522
Actress
Response Time: N/A
Received: N/A

Benedicto, Lourdes
5700 Wilshire, Ste. 575
LA, CA 90036
Actress
Response Time: N/A
Received: N/A

Benham, Dorothy
Two Ocean Way, Ste. 1000
Atlantic City, NJ 08401
Miss America 1977
Response Time: N/A
Received: N/A

Bennett, Brad
1801 West Int'l. Spdwy. Blvd.
Daytona Beach, FL 32114
Auto Racing Personality
Response Time: 90 Days
Received: Signed Photo

Bennett, Robert
431 Dirksen Senate Office Bldg.
Washington, DC 20510
Senator
Response Time: N/A
Received: N/A

Bennett, Tony
130 W. 57th St. #9-D
NY, NY 10019-3311
Singer
Response Time: N/A
Received: N/A

Benson, Johnny
1801 West Int'l. Spdwy. Blvd.
Daytona Beach, FL 32114
Auto Racing Personality
Response Time: 189 Days
Received: Signed Photo

Bently, Lamont
5555 Melrose Ave.
Hollywood, CA 90038-3197
Actor
Response Time: N/A
Received: N/A

Bentsen, Ken
U.S. House of Representatives
Washington, DC 20515
Politician
Response Time: N/A
Received: N/A

Bereuter, Doug
U.S. House of Representatives
Washington, DC 20515
Politician
Response Time: N/A
Received: N/A

Bergeron, Marian
Two Ocean Way, Ste. 1000
Atlantic City, NJ 08401
Miss America 1933
Response Time: N/A
Received: N/A

Bergin, Michael
c/o Baywatch Productions
510-18th Ave., Honolulu, HI 96816
Actor
Response Time: N/A
Received: N/A

Bergman, Alan
714 N. Maple Dr.
BH, CA 90210
Actor
Response Time: N/A
Received: N/A

Bergman, Jaime
9242 Beverly Blvd.
BH, CA 90210
Playboy Playmate
Response Time: N/A
Received: N/A

Bergman, Marilyn
714 N. Maple Dr.
BH, CA 90210
Actress
Response Time: N/A
Received: N/A

Bergman, Peter
7800 Beverly Blvd.
LA, CA 90036
Actor
Response Time: N/A
Received: N/A

Berkley, Shelley
U.S. House of Representatives
Washington, DC 20515
Politician
Response Time: N/A
Received: N/A

Berman, Howard L.
U.S. House of Representatives
Washington, DC 20515
Politician
Response Time: N/A
Received: N/A

Bernaola, Carol
9242 Beverly Blvd.
BH, CA 90210
Playboy Playmate
Response Time: N/A
Received: N/A

Berra, Yogi
19 Highland Ave.
Monclair, NJ 07042
Baseball Player
Response Time: 10 Days
Received: SIC

Berrier, Ed
1801 West Int'l. Spdwy. Blvd.
Daytona Beach, FL 32114
Auto Racing Personality
Response Time: 140 Days
Received: Signed Photo

Berry, Brooke
9242 Beverly Blvd.
BH, CA 90210
Playboy Playmate
Response Time: N/A
Received: N/A

Berry, John
P.O. Box 121162
Nashville, TN 37212
Singer
Response Time: N/A
Received: N/A

Berry, Marion
U.S. House of Representatives
Washington, DC 20515
Politician
Response Time: N/A
Received: N/A

Berry, Tina
c/o Home Shopping Network
St. Petersburg, FL 33701
Home Shopping Network Host
Response Time: N/A
Received: N/A

Bertinelli, Valerie
9255 W. Sunset Blvd., PMB #1010
W. Hollywood, CA 90069-3309
Actress
Response Time: N/A
Received: N/A

Bessey, Joe
1801 West Int'l. Spdwy. Blvd.
Daytona Beach, FL 32114
Auto Racing Personality
Response Time: 138 Days
Received: Signed Photo

Betbeze, Yolande
Two Ocean Way, Ste. 1000
Atlantic City, NJ 08401
Miss America 1951
Response Time: N/A
Received: N/A

Beyer, Tanya
9242 Beverly Blvd.
BH, CA 90210
Playboy Playmate
Response Time: N/A
Received: N/A

Bialik, Mayim
1529 N. Cahuenga Blvd. #19
LA, CA 90028
Actress
Response Time: N/A
Received: N/A

Bibb, Leslie
4000 Warner Blvd.
Burbank, CA 91522
Actress
Response Time: N/A
Received: N/A

Bickle, Rich
1801 West Int'l. Spdwy. Blvd.
Daytona Beach, FL 32114
Auto Racing Personality
Response Time: 237 Days
Received: Signed Photo

Biden Jr., Joseph
221 Russell Senate Office Bldg.
Washington, DC 20510
Senator
Response Time: N/A
Received: N/A

Biel, Jessica
c/o The WB Network, 3701 Oak St.
Bldg. 34R, Burbank, CA 91505
Actress
Response Time: N/A
Received: N/A

Biffle, Greg
1801 West Int'l. Spdwy. Blvd.
Daytona Beach, FL 32114
Auto Racing Personality
Response Time: 106 Days
Received: Signed Photo

Biggert, Judy
U.S. House of Representatives
Washington, DC 20515
Politician
Response Time: N/A
Received: N/A

Biggs, Richard
5555 Melrose Ave.
Hollywood, CA 90038-3197
Actor
Response Time: N/A
Received: N/A

Bilirakis, Michael
U.S. House of Representatives
Washington, DC 20515
Politician
Response Time: N/A
Received: N/A

Bingaman, Jeff
703 Hart Senate Office Bldg.
Washington, DC 20510
Senator
Response Time: N/A
Received: N/A

Bingham, Traci
c/o Baywatch Productions
510-18th Ave., Honolulu, HI 96816
Actress
Response Time: N/A
Received: N/A

Biondi, Matt
1404 Rimer Dr.
Moraga, CA 94556
Olympian
Response Time: N/A
Received: N/A

Bird, Larry
RR#1 Box 77-A
West Baden Springs, IN 47469
Basketball Legend
Response Time: 364 Days
Received: Signed Photo

Birkelund, Olivia
320 West 66th St.
NY, NY 10023
Actress
Response Time: N/A
Received: N/A

Bishop Jr., Sanford D.
U.S. House of Representatives
Washington, DC 20515
Politician
Response Time: N/A
Received: N/A

Bishop, Joey
534 Via Lido Nord
Newport Beach, CA 92660
Entertainer, Actor
Response Time: 10 Days
Received: Signed Photo

Bishop, Kelly
4000 Warner Blvd.
Burbank, CA 91522
Actress
Response Time: N/A
Received: N/A

Bissett, Jacqueline
118 S. Beverly Dr.
BH, CA 90212
Actress
Response Time: N/A
Received: N/A

Bissett, Jacqueline
1815 Benedict Canyon
BH, CA 90210-2006
Actress
Response Time: 13 Days
Received: Signed Photo

Bjorlin, Nadia
3000 W. Alameda Ave.
Burbank, CA 91523
Actress
Response Time: N/A
Received: N/A

Black, Clint
8489 W. Third St., 2nd Fl.
LA, CA 90048
Singer
Response Time: 14 Days
Received: Unsigned Photo

Black, Lisa Hartman
8489 W. Third St., 2nd Fl.
LA, CA 90048
Actress, Singer
Response Time: 12 Days
Received: Signed Photo

Black, Lucas
7652 Highway 36
Danville, AL 35619
Actor
Response Time: N/A
Received: N/A

Blackhawk
Box 121804
Nashville, TN 37212
Music Group
Response Time: 14 Days
Received: Unsigned Photo

Blackmon, Edafe
4000 Warner Blvd.
Burbank, CA 91522
Actor
Response Time: N/A
Received: N/A

Blades, Ruben
500 S. Buena Vista St.
Burbank, CA 91521
Actor
Response Time: N/A
Received: N/A

Blagojevich, Rod R.
U.S. House of Representatives
Washington, DC 20515
Politician
Response Time: N/A
Received: N/A

Blaha, John E.
2101 NASA Rd. 1
Houston, TX 77058
Astronaut
Response Time: N/A
Received: N/A

Blanchard, Rachel
5555 Melrose Ave.
Hollywood, CA 90038-3197
Actress
Response Time: N/A
Received: N/A

Blanchard, Tully
P.O. Box 2724
Matthews, NC 28106-2724
Wrestler
Response Time: N/A
Received: N/A

Blanda, George
2121 George Halas Dr. N.W.
Canton, OH 44708
Football Player
Response Time: N/A
Received: N/A

Blaney, Dave
1801 West Int'l. Spdwy. Blvd.
Daytona Beach, FL 32114
Auto Racing Personality
Response Time: 215 Days
Received: Signed Photo

Bledel, Alexis
4000 Warner Blvd.
Burbank, CA 91522
Actress
Response Time: N/A
Received: N/A

Bleeth, Yasmine
104-60 Queens Blvd. #10C
Forest Hills, NY 11375
Actress
Response Time: 196 Days
Received: Signed Photo

Bleeth, Yasmine
c/o Baywatch Productions
510-18th Ave., Honolulu, HI 96816
Actress
Response Time: N/A
Received: N/A

Bleeth, Yasmine
5700 Wilshire, Ste. 575
LA, CA 90036
Actress
Response Time: N/A
Received: N/A

Bliss, Mike
1801 West Int'l. Spdwy. Blvd.
Daytona Beach, FL 32114
Auto Racing Personality
Response Time: 231 Days
Received: Signed Photo

Block, Hunt
1268 East 14th St.
Brooklyn, NY 11230
Actor
Response Time: N/A
Received: N/A

Bloom, Brian
11 Croydon Court
Dix Hills, NY 11746
Actor
Response Time: 23 Days
Received: SIC

Bloomfield, Michael J.
2101 NASA Rd. 1
Houston, TX 77058
Astronaut
Response Time: N/A
Received: N/A

Blucas, Marc
4000 Warner Blvd.
Burbank, CA 91522
Actor
Response Time: N/A
Received: N/A

Bluford Jr., Guion S.
2101 NASA Rd. 1
Houston, TX 77058
Astronaut
Response Time: N/A
Received: N/A

Blumenauer, Earl
U.S. House of Representatives
Washington, DC 20515
Politician
Response Time: N/A
Received: N/A

Blunt, Roy
U.S. House of Representatives
Washington, DC 20515
Politician
Response Time: N/A
Received: N/A

Boatman, Michael
100 Universal City Plaza
Universal City, CA 91608
Actor
Response Time: N/A
Received: N/A

Bobko, Karol J.
2101 NASA Rd. 1
Houston, TX 77058
Astronaut
Response Time: N/A
Received: N/A

Bockrath, Tina
9242 Beverly Blvd.
BH, CA 90210
Playboy Playmate
Response Time: N/A
Received: N/A

Bodine, Brett
1801 West Int'l. Spdwy. Blvd.
Daytona Beach, FL 32114
Auto Racing Personality
Response Time: 214 Days
Received: Signed Photo

Bodine, Geoffrey
1801 West Int'l. Spdwy. Blvd.
Daytona Beach, FL 32114
Auto Racing Personality
Response Time: 212 Days
Received: Signed Photo

Bodine, Todd
1801 West Int'l. Spdwy. Blvd.
Daytona Beach, FL 32114
Auto Racing Personality
Response Time: 179 Days
Received: Signed Photo

Boehlert, Sherwood L.
U.S. House of Representatives
Washington, DC 20515
Politician
Response Time: N/A
Received: N/A

Boehner, John A.
U.S. House of Representatives
Washington, DC 20515
Politician
Response Time: N/A
Received: N/A

Boggs, Wade
6006 Windham Place
Tampa, FL 33647
Baseball Player
Response Time: 44 Days
Received: Signed Photo

Bogush, Elizabeth
5700 Wilshire, Ste. 575
LA, CA 90036
Actress
Response Time: N/A
Received: N/A

Bolden Jr., Charles F.
2101 NASA Rd. 1
Houston, TX 77058
Astronaut
Response Time: N/A
Received: N/A

Bolger, John
56 West 66th St.
NY, NY 10023
Actor
Response Time: N/A
Received: N/A

Bonaduce, Danny
2651 La Cuesta Dr.
LA, CA 90046
Actor
Response Time: N/A
Received: N/A

Bond, Christopher
274 Russell Senate Office Bldg.
Washington, DC 20510
Senator
Response Time: N/A
Received: N/A

Bonet, Lisa
22764 Chamera Ln.
Topanga, CA 90290
Actress
Response Time: 32 Days
Received: Signed Photo

Bonifield, Phil
1801 West Int'l. Spdwy. Blvd.
Daytona Beach, FL 32114
Auto Racing Personality
Response Time: 154 Days
Received: Signed Photo

Bonilla, Henry
U.S. House of Representatives
Washington, DC 20515
Politician
Response Time: N/A
Received: N/A

Bonior, David E.
U.S. House of Representatives
Washington, DC 20515
Politician
Response Time: N/A
Received: N/A

Bonner, Gillian
9242 Beverly Blvd.
BH, CA 90210
Playboy Playmate
Response Time: N/A
Received: N/A

Bono, Mary
U.S. House of Representatives
Washington, DC 20515
Politician
Response Time: 56 Days
Received: Signed Photo

Boone, Lesley
5555 Melrose Ave.
Hollywood, CA 90038-3197
Actress
Response Time: N/A
Received: N/A

Booth, Lindy
5555 Melrose Ave.
Hollywood, CA 90038-3197
Actress
Response Time: N/A
Received: N/A

Boreanaz, David
4000 Warner Blvd.
Burbank, CA 91522
Actor
Response Time: N/A
Received: N/A

Borgnine, Ernest
3055 Lake Glen Dr.
BH, CA 90210
Actor
Response Time: 35 Days
Received: Signed Photo

Borgnine, Tova
c/o QVC, 1200 Wilson Dr.
West Chester, PA 19380
Fragrance Creator
Response Time: N/A
Received: N/A

Boris, Angel
9242 Beverly Blvd.
BH, CA 90210
Playboy Playmate
Response Time: N/A
Received: N/A

Borman, Frank
2101 NASA Rd. 1
Houston, TX 77058
Astronaut
Response Time: N/A
Received: N/A

Borski, Robert A.
U.S. House of Representatives
Washington, DC 20515
Politician
Response Time: N/A
Received: N/A

Bostwick, Barry
100 Universal City Plaza
Universal City, CA 91608
Actor
Response Time: N/A
Received: N/A

Boswell, Leonard L.
U.S. House of Representatives
Washington, DC 20515
Politician
Response Time: N/A
Received: N/A

Boucher, Rick
U.S. House of Representatives
Washington, DC 20515
Politician
Response Time: N/A
Received: N/A

Boudreau, Michelle
c/o Home Shopping Network
St. Petersburg, FL 33701
Home Shopping Network Host
Response Time: N/A
Received: N/A

Bowden, Bobby
Box 2195
Tallahassee, FL 32316
Football Coach
Response Time: 12 Days
Received: Signed Photo

Bowen, Julie
5555 Melrose Ave.
Hollywood, CA 90038-3197
Actress
Response Time: N/A
Received: N/A

Bowersox, Bob
c/o QVC, 1200 Wilson Dr.
West Chester, PA 19380
QVC Host
Response Time: N/A
Received: N/A

Bowersox, Kenneth D.
2101 NASA Rd. 1
Houston, TX 77058
Astronaut
Response Time: N/A
Received: N/A

Boxer, Barbara
112 Hart Senate Office Bldg.
Washington, DC 20510
Senator
Response Time: N/A
Received: N/A

Boyd, Allen
U.S. House of Representatives
Washington, DC 20515
Politician
Response Time: N/A
Received: N/A

Boyd, Stan
1801 West Int'l. Spdwy. Blvd.
Daytona Beach, FL 32114
Auto Racing Personality
Response Time: 110 Days
Received: Signed Photo

Boyd, Tanya
3000 W. Alameda Ave.
Burbank, CA 91523
Actress
Response Time: N/A
Received: N/A

Boyle, Lara Flynn
10201 West Pico Blvd.
LA, CA 90035
Actress
Response Time: N/A
Received: N/A

BR5-49
P.O. Box 23288
Nashville, TN 37202
Music Group
Response Time: 27 Days
Received: Signed Photo

Bracco, Lorraine
18 E. 53rd St., #400
NY, NY 10022
Actress
Response Time: N/A
Received: N/A

Bradberry, Gary
1801 West Int'l. Spdwy. Blvd.
Daytona Beach, FL 32114
Auto Racing Personality
Response Time: 129 Days
Received: Signed Photo

Bradley, Bill
395 Pleasant Valley Way
West Orange, NJ 07052
Politician
Response Time: N/A
Received: N/A

Bradley, Kathleen
5757 Wilshire Blvd. #206
LA, CA 90036
Television Personality
Response Time: N/A
Received: N/A

Bradshaw, Terry
8911 Shady Lane Dr.
Shreveport, LA 71118-1227
Football Player
Response Time: 14 Days
Received: Signed Photo

Bradshaw, Terry
2121 George Halas Dr. N.W.
Canton, OH 44708
Football Player
Response Time: N/A
Received: N/A

Brady Jr., Charles E.
2101 NASA Rd. 1
Houston, TX 77058
Astronaut
Response Time: N/A
Received: N/A

Brady, Kevin
U.S. House of Representatives
Washington, DC 20515
Politician
Response Time: N/A
Received: N/A

Brady, Robert A.
U.S. House of Representatives
Washington, DC 20515
Politician
Response Time: N/A
Received: N/A

Brady, Wayne
10201 West Pico Blvd.
LA, CA 90035
Actor
Response Time: N/A
Received: N/A

Braeden, Eric
7800 Beverly Blvd.
LA, CA 90036
Actor
Response Time: N/A
Received: N/A

Brand, Vance D.
2101 NASA Rd. 1
Houston, TX 77058
Astronaut
Response Time: N/A
Received: N/A

Brandenstein, Daniel C.
2101 NASA Rd. 1
Houston, TX 77058
Astronaut
Response Time: N/A
Received: N/A

Brandis, Jonathan
11684 Ventura Blvd., Ste. 966
Studio City, CA 91604
Actor
Response Time: 151 Days
Received: Signed Photo

Brandy
5555 Melrose Ave.
Hollywood, CA 90038-3197
Actress, Singer
Response Time: N/A
Received: N/A

Brannon, Chad
4151 Prospect Ave.
LA, CA 90027
Actor
Response Time: N/A
Received: N/A

Braugher, Andre
500 S. Buena Vista St.
Burbank, CA 91521
Actor
Response Time: N/A
Received: N/A

Breaux, John
503 Hart Senate Office Bldg.
Washington, DC 20510
Senator
Response Time: N/A
Received: N/A

Brendon, Nicholas
4000 Warner Blvd.
Burbank, CA 91522
Actor
Response Time: N/A
Received: N/A

Brewster, Paget
5555 Melrose Ave.
Hollywood, CA 90038-3197
Actress
Response Time: N/A
Received: N/A

Breyer, Stephen
Supreme Court of the United States
Washington, DC 20543
Supreme Court Justice
Response Time: 26 Days
Received: Signed Photo

Bridges Jr., Roy D.
2101 NASA Rd. 1
Houston, TX 77058
Astronaut
Response Time: N/A
Received: N/A

Bridges, Angelica
c/o Baywatch Productions
510-18th Ave., Honolulu, HI 96816
Actress
Response Time: N/A
Received: N/A

Bridges, Beau
5525 N. Jed Smith Rd.
Hidden Hills, CA 91302
Actor
Response Time: N/A
Received: N/A

Bridges, Elisa
9242 Beverly Blvd.
BH, CA 90210
Playboy Playmate
Response Time: N/A
Received: N/A

Bridges, Jeff
985 Hot Springs Rd.
Montecito, CA 93108
Actor
Response Time: 90 Days
Received: Signed Photo

Briggs, Randy
1801 West Int'l. Spdwy. Blvd.
Daytona Beach, FL 32114
Auto Racing Personality
Response Time: 104 Days
Received: Signed Photo

Brochtrup, Bill
10201 West Pico Blvd.
LA, CA 90035
Actor
Response Time: N/A
Received: N/A

Broderick, Beth
5555 Melrose Ave.
Hollywood, CA 90038-3197
Actress
Response Time: N/A
Received: N/A

Broderick, Matthew
P.O. Box 69646
LA, CA 90069
Actor
Response Time: 16 Days
Received: Signed Photo

Brockovich, Erin
5707 Corsa Ave., 2nd Fl.
Westlake Village, CA 91362
Lawyer
Response Time: 51 Days
Received: SIC

Bronson, Charles
P.O. Box 2644
Malibu, CA 90265
Actor
Response Time: 86 Days
Received: Signed Photo

Brooks & Dunn
P.O. Box 120669
Nashville, TN 37212-0669
Music Group
Response Time: 7 Days
Received: Signed Photo

Brooks, Deanna
9242 Beverly Blvd.
BH, CA 90210
Playboy Playmate
Response Time: N/A
Received: N/A

Brooks, Golden
5555 Melrose Ave.
Hollywood, CA 90038-3197
Actress
Response Time: N/A
Received: N/A

Brooks, Jason
c/o Baywatch Productions
510-18th Ave., Honolulu, HI 96816
Actor
Response Time: N/A
Received: N/A

Brooks, Jim
2257 Mandeville Canyon Rd.
LA, CA 90049
World War II Veteran
Response Time: 57 Days
Received: SIC

Brosnan, Pierce
23715 W. Malibu Rd.
Malibu, CA 90265
Actor
Response Time: N/A
Received: N/A

Brosnan, Pierce
9830 Wilshire Blvd.
BH, CA 90212
Actor
Response Time: N/A
Received: N/A

Brothers, Joyce
1530 Palisades Ave.
Ft. Lee, NJ 07024
Doctor
Response Time: N/A
Received: N/A

Brown Jr., Curtis L.
2101 NASA Rd. 1
Houston, TX 77058
Astronaut
Response Time: N/A
Received: N/A

Brown Jr., Henry E.
U.S. House of Representatives
Washington, DC 20515
Politician
Response Time: N/A
Received: N/A

Brown, Corrine
U.S. House of Representatives
Washington, DC 20515
Politician
Response Time: N/A
Received: N/A

Brown, Cynthia Gwyn
9242 Beverly Blvd.
BH, CA 90210
Playboy Playmate
Response Time: N/A
Received: N/A

Brown, David M.
2101 NASA Rd. 1
Houston, TX 77058
Astronaut
Response Time: N/A
Received: N/A

Brown, Jayne
c/o QVC, 1200 Wilson Dr.
West Chester, PA 19380
QVC Host
Response Time: N/A
Received: N/A

Brown, Mark N.
2101 NASA Rd. 1
Houston, TX 77058
Astronaut
Response Time: N/A
Received: N/A

Brown, Ryan
51 W. 52 St.
NY, NY 10019
Actor
Response Time: N/A
Received: N/A

Brown, Sarah
4151 Prospect Ave.
LA, CA 90027
Actress
Response Time: N/A
Received: N/A

Brown, Sherrod
U.S. House of Representatives
Washington, DC 20515
Politician
Response Time: N/A
Received: N/A

Brown, Susan
4151 Prospect Ave.
LA, CA 90027
Actress
Response Time: N/A
Received: N/A

Brown, T. Graham
P.O. Box 1547
Goodlettsville, TN 37072
Singer
Response Time: N/A
Received: N/A

Brownback, Sam
303 Hart Senate Office Bldg.
Washington, DC 20510
Senator
Response Time: N/A
Received: N/A

Browne, Kale
56 West 66th St.
NY, NY 10023
Actor
Response Time: N/A
Received: N/A

Brumbly, Charlie
c/o Baywatch Productions
510-18th Ave., Honolulu, HI 96816
Actor
Response Time: N/A
Received: N/A

Bryant, Deborah
Two Ocean Way, Ste. 1000
Atlantic City, NJ 08401
Miss America 1966
Response Time: N/A
Received: N/A

Bryant, Ed
U.S. House of Representatives
Washington, DC 20515
Politician
Response Time: N/A
Received: N/A

Bryant, Steve
c/o QVC, 1200 Wilson Dr.
West Chester, PA 19380
QVC Host
Response Time: N/A
Received: N/A

Bryggman, Larry
1268 East 14th St.
Brooklyn, NY 11230
Actor
Response Time: N/A
Received: N/A

Buchanan, Pat
6862 Elm St. #210
McLean, VA 22101
Politician
Response Time: N/A
Received: N/A

Buchanan, Pat
P.O. Box 1919
Merrifield, VA 22116-1919
Politician
Response Time: 71 Days
Received: Signed Photo

Buchli, James F.
2101 NASA Rd. 1
Houston, TX 77058
Astronaut
Response Time: N/A
Received: N/A

Budig, Rebecca
320 West 66th St.
NY, NY 10023
Actress
Response Time: N/A
Received: N/A

Buferd, Marilyn
Two Ocean Way, Ste. 1000
Atlantic City, NJ 08401
Miss America 1946
Response Time: N/A
Received: N/A

Buffett, Jimmy
550-B Duval St.
Key West, FL 33040
Singer
Response Time: N/A
Received: N/A

Bull, John S.
2101 NASA Rd. 1
Houston, TX 77058
Astronaut
Response Time: N/A
Received: N/A

Bulloch, Jeremy
10 Birchwood Rd.
London SW17 9BQ, England
Actor
Response Time: 34 Days
Received: Signed Photo

Bulloch, Jeremy
47 West Square
London SE11 4SP, England
Actor
Response Time: N/A
Received: N/A

Bunning, Jim
818 Hart Senate Office Bldg.
Washington, DC 20510
Senator
Response Time: N/A
Received: N/A

Burbank, Daniel C.
2101 NASA Rd. 1
Houston, TX 77058
Astronaut
Response Time: N/A
Received: N/A

Burgi, Richard
5555 Melrose Ave.
Hollywood, CA 90038-3197
Actor
Response Time: N/A
Received: N/A

Burke, Delta
1012 Royal St.
New Orleans, LA 70116
Actress, Fashion Designer
Response Time: 217 Days
Received: Signed Photo

Burke, Delta
1407 Broadway, Ste. 1920
NY, NY 10018
Actress, Fashion Designer
Response Time: 92 Days
Received: Signed Photo

Burke, Delta
c/o QVC, 1200 Wilson Dr.
West Chester, PA 19380
Actress, Fashion Designer
Response Time: N/A
Received: N/A

Burke, Frances
Two Ocean Way, Ste. 1000
Atlantic City, NJ 08401
Miss America 1940
Response Time: N/A
Received: N/A

Burnett, Carol
5750 Wilshire Blvd. #590
LA, CA 90036
Actress, Comedian
Response Time: N/A
Received: N/A

Burnett, Carol
7800 Beverly Blvd.
LA, CA 90036-2165
Actress, Comedian
Response Time: N/A
Received: N/A

Burnett, Carol
8383 Wilshire Blvd. #1034
BH, CA 90211
Actress, Comedian
Response Time: 58 Days
Received: Signed Photo

Burns, Brooke
c/o Baywatch Productions
510-18th Ave., Honolulu, HI 96816
Actress
Response Time: N/A
Received: N/A

Burns, Conrad
187 Dirksen Senate Office Bldg.
Washington, DC 20510
Senator
Response Time: N/A
Received: N/A

Burr, Richard
U.S. House of Representatives
Washington, DC 20515
Politician
Response Time: N/A
Received: N/A

Bursch, Daniel W.
2101 NASA Rd. 1
Houston, TX 77058
Astronaut
Response Time: N/A
Received: N/A

Burstyn, Ellen
5555 Melrose Ave.
Hollywood, CA 90038-3197
Actress
Response Time: N/A
Received: N/A

Burstyn, Ellen
P.O. Box 217
Palisades, NY 10964
Actress
Response Time: 39 Days
Received: Signed Photo

Burton, Dan
U.S. House of Representatives
Washington, DC 20515
Politician
Response Time: N/A
Received: N/A

Burton, Jeff
1801 West Int'l. Spdwy. Blvd.
Daytona Beach, FL 32114
Auto Racing Personality
Response Time: 250 Days
Received: Signed Photo

Burton, Lance
3770 S. Las Vegas Blvd.
Las Vegas, NV 89109
Magician
Response Time: 13 Days
Received: Signed Photo & TLS

Burton, Steve
4151 Prospect Ave.
LA, CA 90027
Actor
Response Time: N/A
Received: N/A

Burton, Ward
1801 West Int'l. Spdwy. Blvd.
Daytona Beach, FL 32114
Auto Racing Personality
Response Time: 231 Days
Received: Signed Photo

Busch, Kurt
1801 West Int'l. Spdwy. Blvd.
Daytona Beach, FL 32114
Auto Racing Personality
Response Time: 194 Days
Received: Signed Photo

Busey, Gary
18424 Coastline Dr.
Malibu, CA 90265
Actor
Response Time: N/A
Received: N/A

Bush, Barbara
10000 Memorial Dr., Ste. 900
Houston, TX 77024
Former First Lady
Response Time: N/A
Received: N/A

Bush, George
10000 Memorial Dr., Ste. 900
Houston, TX 77024
Politician
Response Time: N/A
Received: N/A

Bush, George W.
1600 Pennsylvania Ave. N.W.
Washington, DC 20500
U.S. President
Response Time: N/A
Received: N/A

Bush, Laura
1600 Pennsylvania Ave. N.W.
Washington, DC 20500
First Lady - Wife of George W. Bush
Response Time: N/A
Received: N/A

Bush, Jeb
Office Of The Govenor
Tallahassee, FL 32399-0001
Politician
Response Time: 18 Days
Received: Signed Photo

Butler, Brandon
1801 West Int'l. Spdwy. Blvd.
Daytona Beach, FL 32114
Auto Racing Personality
Response Time: 122 Days
Received: Signed Photo

Buttons, Red
778 Tortuoso Way
LA, CA 90077
Comedian
Response Time: 18 Days
Received: Signed Photo

Buxton, Sarah
7800 Beverly Blvd.
LA, CA 90036
Actress
Response Time: 27 Days
Received: Signed Photo

Buyer, Steve
U.S. House of Representatives
Washington, DC 20515
Politician
Response Time: N/A
Received: N/A

Buzzi, Ruth
2309 Malaga Rd.
LA, CA 90068
Comedian
Response Time: 16 Days
Received: Signed Sketch

Byrd, Dan
5555 Melrose Ave.
Hollywood, CA 90038-3197
Actor
Response Time: N/A
Received: N/A

Byrd, Robert
311 Hart Senate Office Bldg.
Washington, DC 20510
Politician
Response Time: 20 Days
Received: Signed Photo

Byrne, Gabriel
34-12 36th St.
Astoria, NY 11106
Actor
Response Time: N/A
Received: N/A

Byrne, Martha
1268 East 14th St.
Brooklyn, NY 11230
Actress
Response Time: N/A
Received: N/A

Cabana, Robert D.
2101 NASA Rd. 1
Houston, TX 77058
Astronaut
Response Time: N/A
Received: N/A

Cafagna, Ashley
7800 Beverly Blvd.
LA, CA 90036
Actress
Response Time: N/A
Received: N/A

Cagle, Yvonne D.
2101 NASA Rd. 1
Houston, TX 77058
Astronaut
Response Time: N/A
Received: N/A

Cain, Dean
11718 Darrington Ct. #513
LA, CA 90049
Actor
Response Time: N/A
Received: N/A

Cain, Dean
1050 Techwood Dr. N.W.
Atlanta, GA 30318
Actor
Response Time: 85 Days
Received: Signed Photo

Cain, Mick
7800 Beverly Blvd.
LA, CA 90036
Actor
Response Time: N/A
Received: N/A

Caldeiro, Fernando "Frank"
2101 NASA Rd. 1
Houston, TX 77058
Astronaut
Response Time: N/A
Received: N/A

Calderon, Sila M.
La Fortaleza
San Juan, PR 00901
Governor
Response Time: N/A
Received: N/A

Caldwell, Tracy E.
2101 NASA Rd. 1
Houston, TX 77058
Astronaut
Response Time: N/A
Received: N/A

Caliendo, Frank
4000 Warner Blvd.
Burbank, CA 91522
Actor
Response Time: N/A
Received: N/A

Callahan, John
320 West 66th St.
NY, NY 10023
Actor
Response Time: N/A
Received: N/A

Callahan, Sonny
U.S. House of Representatives
Washington, DC 20515
Politician
Response Time: N/A
Received: N/A

Calvert, Ken
U.S. House of Representatives
Washington, DC 20515
Politician
Response Time: N/A
Received: N/A

Camarda, Charles J.
2101 NASA Rd. 1
Houston, TX 77058
Astronaut
Response Time: N/A
Received: N/A

Cameron, James
919 Santa Monica Blvd.
Santa Monica, CA 90401
Director
Response Time: N/A
Received: N/A

Cameron, Kenneth D.
2101 NASA Rd. 1
Houston, TX 77058
Astronaut
Response Time: N/A
Received: N/A

Cameron, Kirk
P.O. Box 8665
Calabasas, CA 91372-8665
Actor
Response Time: 36 Days
Received: Signed Photo

Cameron-Bure, Candace
8369 Sausalito Ave., Ste. A
West Hills, CA 91304
Actress
Response Time: N/A
Received: N/A

Camp, Dave
U.S. House of Representatives
Washington, DC 20515
Politician
Response Time: N/A
Received: N/A

Campbell, Ben Nighthorse
380 Russell Senate Office Bldg.
Washington, DC 20510
Senator
Response Time: N/A
Received: N/A

Campbell, Billy
8660 Hayden Place
Culver City, CA 90232
Actor
Response Time: N/A
Received: N/A

Campbell, Glen
10351 Santa Monica Blvd. #300
LA, CA 90025
Singer
Response Time: 33 Days
Received: Signed Photo

Campbell, Larry Joe
5555 Melrose Ave.
Hollywood, CA 90038-3197
Actor
Response Time: N/A
Received: N/A

Campbell, Naomi
40-42 Parker St.
London WC2B 6PQ, England
Model
Response Time: N/A
Received: N/A

Cannavale, Bobby
4000 Warner Blvd.
Burbank, CA 91522
Actor
Response Time: N/A
Received: N/A

Cannon, Chris
U.S. House of Representatives
Washington, DC 20515
Politician
Response Time: N/A
Received: N/A

Cantor, Eric
U.S. House of Representatives
Washington, DC 20515
Politician
Response Time: N/A
Received: N/A

Cantrell, Cady
9242 Beverly Blvd.
BH, CA 90210
Playboy Playmate
Response Time: N/A
Received: N/A

Cantwell, Maria
United States Senate
Washington, DC 20510
Senator
Response Time: N/A
Received: N/A

Capito, Shelley Moore
U.S. House of Representatives
Washington, DC 20515
Politician
Response Time: N/A
Received: N/A

Capps, Lois
U.S. House of Representatives
Washington, DC 20515
Politician
Response Time: N/A
Received: N/A

Capriati, Jennifer
5435 Blue Heron Lane
Wesley Chapel, FL 33543
Tennis Player
Response Time: 37 Days
Received: Signed Photo

Capriati, Jennifer
1730 Walton Rd. #300
Blue Bell, PA 19422
Tennis Player
Response Time: N/A
Received: N/A

Capuano, Michael E.
U.S. House of Representatives
Washington, DC 20515
Politician
Response Time: N/A
Received: N/A

Cardin, Benjamin L.
U.S. House of Representatives
Washington, DC 20515
Politician
Response Time: N/A
Received: N/A

Cardwell, Lena
4024 Radford Ave.
Studio City, CA 91604
Actress
Response Time: N/A
Received: N/A

Carelli, Rick
1801 West Int'l. Spdwy. Blvd.
Daytona Beach, FL 32114
Auto Racing Personality
Response Time: 217 Days
Received: Signed Photo

Carey, Drew
4000 Warner Blvd.
Burbank, CA 91522
Actor
Response Time: N/A
Received: N/A

Carey, Drew
10201 West Pico Blvd.
LA, CA 90035
Actor
Response Time: N/A
Received: N/A

Carey, Duane G.
2101 NASA Rd. 1
Houston, TX 77058
Astronaut
Response Time: N/A
Received: N/A

Carey, Phil
56 West 66th St.
NY, NY 10023
Actor
Response Time: N/A
Received: N/A

Carlson, Gretchen
Two Ocean Way, Ste. 1000
Atlantic City, NJ 08401
Miss America 1989
Response Time: N/A
Received: N/A

Carmack, Kona
9242 Beverly Blvd.
BH, CA 90210
Playboy Playmate
Response Time: N/A
Received: N/A

Carnahan, Jean
United States Senate
Washington, DC 20510
Senator
Response Time: N/A
Received: N/A

Carney, Art
143 Kingfisher Ln.
Westbrook, CT 06498
Actor
Response Time: 8 Days
Received: Signed Photo

Carney, Art
RR #20 Box 911
Westbrook, CT 06498
Actor
Response Time: 8 Days
Received: Signed Photo

Carpenter, Charisma
4000 Warner Blvd.
Burbank, CA 91522
Actress
Response Time: N/A
Received: N/A

Carpenter, John
8532 Hollywood Blvd.
LA, CA 90069-1414
Director
Response Time: 27 Days
Received: Signed Photo

Carpenter, M. Scott
2101 NASA Rd. 1
Houston, TX 77058
Astronaut
Response Time: N/A
Received: N/A

Carpenter, Richard
P.O. Box 1084
Downey, CA 90240
Singer
Response Time: 15 Days
Received: Signed Photo

Carper, Thomas
United States Senate
Washington, DC 20510
Senator
Response Time: N/A
Received: N/A

Carr, Gerald P.
2101 NASA Rd. 1
Houston, TX 77058
Astronaut
Response Time: N/A
Received: N/A

Carrere, Tia
8228 Sunset Blvd. #300
LA, CA 90046
Actress
Response Time: 84 Days
Received: Signed Photo

Carrere, Tia
5555 Melrose Ave.
Hollywood, CA 90038-3197
Actress
Response Time: N/A
Received: N/A

Carrey, Jim
P.O. Box 57593
Sherman Oaks, CA 91403
Actor
Response Time: 61 Days
Received: Signed Photo

Carson, Brad
U.S. House of Representatives
Washington, DC 20515
Politician
Response Time: N/A
Received: N/A

Carson, Julia
U.S. House of Representatives
Washington, DC 20515
Politician
Response Time: N/A
Received: N/A

Carter, Bobbi Ray
c/o Home Shopping Network
St. Petersburg, FL 33701
Home Shopping Network Host
Response Time: N/A
Received: N/A

Carter, Deana
P.O. Box 559
Hermitage, TN 37076
Singer
Response Time: N/A
Received: N/A

Carter, Elan
9242 Beverly Blvd.
BH, CA 90210
Playboy Playmate
Response Time: N/A
Received: N/A

Carter, Jimmy
1 Woodland Dr.
Plains, GA 31780
Politician; Former U.S. President
Response Time: 15 Days
Received: Signed Book I Sent

Carter, Nell
8484 Wilshire Blvd. #500
BH, CA 90211-3220
Actress
Response Time: N/A
Received: N/A

Carter, Rosalynn
1 Woodland Dr.
Plains, GA 31780
Former First Lady
Response Time: 4 Days
Received: Signed Book I Sent

Cartwright, Lionel
P.O. Box 50835
Nashville, TN 37205
Singer
Response Time: 30 Days
Received: Signed Photo

Cartwright, Nancy
P.O. Box 900
BH, CA 90213
Voice Actor
Response Time: 34 Days
Received: Signed Photo

Carvey, Dana
775 E. Blythdale Ave.
Mill Valley, CA 94941
Actor
Response Time: N/A
Received: N/A

Case, Sharon
7800 Beverly Blvd.
LA, CA 90036
Actress
Response Time: N/A
Received: N/A

Cash, Kellye
Two Ocean Way, Ste. 1000
Atlantic City, NJ 08401
Miss America 1987
Response Time: N/A
Received: N/A

Cash, Rosanne
326 Carlton Ave. #3
Brooklyn, NY 11205
Singer
Response Time: N/A
Received: N/A

Casper, John H.
2101 NASA Rd. 1
Houston, TX 77058
Astronaut
Response Time: N/A
Received: N/A

Cassidy, David
3700 West Flamingo Rd.
Las Vegas, NV 89103
Actor, Singer
Response Time: N/A
Received: N/A

Cassidy, Joanna
133 N. Irving Blvd.
LA, CA 90004-3804
Actress
Response Time: N/A
Received: N/A

Cast, Tricia
7800 Beverly Blvd.
LA, CA 90036
Actress
Response Time: N/A
Received: N/A

Castellaneta, Dan
P.O. Box 900
BH, CA 90213
Voice of "Homer Simpson"
Response Time: 45 Days
Received: Signed Photo

Castellanos, John
7800 Beverly Blvd.
LA, CA 90036
Actor
Response Time: N/A
Received: N/A

Castle, Michael N.
U.S. House of Representatives
Washington, DC 20515
Politician
Response Time: N/A
Received: N/A

Cattrall, Kim
151 El Camino Dr.
BH, CA 90212
Actress
Response Time: 11 Days
Received: Signed Photo

Caulfield, Emme
4000 Warner Blvd.
Burbank, CA 91522
Actress
Response Time: N/A
Received: N/A

Cavanagh, Thomas
5555 Melrose Ave.
Hollywood, CA 90038-3197
Actor
Response Time: N/A
Received: N/A

Cayetano, Benjamin J.
State Capitol
Honolulu, HI 96813
Governor
Response Time: N/A
Received: N/A

Cedeno, Matt
3000 W. Alameda Ave.
Burbank, CA 91523
Actor
Response Time: N/A
Received: N/A

Cedric "The Entertainer"
4000 Warner Blvd.
Burbank, CA 91522
Actor
Response Time: N/A
Received: N/A

Cellucci, Argeo Paul
State House, Room 360
Boston, MA 02133
Governor
Response Time: N/A
Received: N/A

Cerf, Vint
22001 Loudon County Pkwy.
Bldg. F2, Ashburn, VA 20147
Creator of the Internet
Response Time: 8 Days
Received: Signed Photo

Cernan, Eugene A.
2101 NASA Rd. 1
Houston, TX 77058
Astronaut
Response Time: N/A
Received: N/A

Cerny, Jobe
259 Hazel Ave.
Highland Park, IL 60035-3359
Voice of the Pillsbury Doughboy
Response Time: 19 Days
Received: Signed Photo

Chabert, Lacey
8942 Wilshire Blvd.
BH, CA 90211
Actress
Response Time: N/A
Received: N/A

Chabot, Steve
U.S. House of Representatives
Washington, DC 20515
Politician
Response Time: N/A
Received: N/A

Chafee, Lincoln
505 Dirksen Senate Office Bldg.
Washington, DC 20510
Senator
Response Time: N/A
Received: N/A

Chamberlin, Beth
51 W. 52 St.
NY, NY 10019
Actress
Response Time: N/A
Received: N/A

Chambliss, Saxby
U.S. House of Representatives
Washington, DC 20515
Politician
Response Time: N/A
Received: N/A

Chamitoff, Gregory E.
2101 NASA Rd. 1
Houston, TX 77058
Astronaut
Response Time: N/A
Received: N/A

Chamorro, Charissa
56 West 66th St.
NY, NY 10023
Actress
Response Time: N/A
Received: N/A

Chan, Jackie
Waterloo Rd. #145
Kowloon, Hong Kong
Actor
Response Time: 26 Days
Received: Signed Photo

Chan, Michael Paul
4000 Warner Blvd.
Burbank, CA 91522
Actor
Response Time: N/A
Received: N/A

Chang-Dìaz, Franklin R.
2101 NASA Rd. 1
Houston, TX 77058
Astronaut
Response Time: N/A
Received: N/A

Channing, Carol
1 Osprey Ct.
Ocean Ridge, FL 33435
Actress
Response Time: 21 Days
Received: Signed Photo

Channing, Stockard
4000 Warner Blvd.
Burbank, CA 91522
Actress
Response Time: N/A
Received: N/A

Chanz, Nadine
9242 Beverly Blvd.
BH, CA 90210
Playboy Playmate
Response Time: N/A
Received: N/A

Chapman, Philip K.
2101 NASA Rd. 1
Houston, TX 77058
Astronaut
Response Time: N/A
Received: N/A

Chappell, Crystal
51 W. 52 St.
NY, NY 10019
Actress
Response Time: N/A
Received: N/A

Charles, Ray
2107 W. Washington Blvd., Ste. 200
LA, CA 90018-1597
Singer
Response Time: N/A
Received: N/A

Charles, Suzette
Two Ocean Way, Ste. 1000
Atlantic City, NJ 08401
Miss America 1984
Response Time: N/A
Received: N/A

Charleson, Leslie
4151 Prospect Ave.
LA, CA 90027
Actress
Response Time: N/A
Received: N/A

Charvet, David
c/o Baywatch Productions
510-18th Ave., Honolulu, HI 96816
Actor
Response Time: N/A
Received: N/A

Chase, Chevy
9830 Wilshire Blvd.
BH, CA 90212
Actor
Response Time: 42 Days
Received: SIC

Chase, Chevy
P.O. Box 257
Bedford, NY 10506-2057
Actor
Response Time: N/A
Received: N/A

Chavez, Nick
c/o QVC, 1200 Wilson Dr.
West Chester, PA 19380
Celebrity Hairstylist
Response Time: N/A
Received: N/A

Chawla, Kalpana
2101 NASA Rd. 1
Houston, TX 77058
Astronaut
Response Time: N/A
Received: N/A

Checa, Maria
9242 Beverly Blvd.
BH, CA 90210
Playboy Playmate
Response Time: N/A
Received: N/A

Cheli, Maurizio
2101 NASA Rd. 1
Houston, TX 77058
Astronaut
Response Time: N/A
Received: N/A

Cheney, Dick
1600 Pennsylvania Ave. N.W.
Washington, DC 20500
U.S. Vice President
Response Time: N/A
Received: N/A

Cheney, Lynn
1600 Pennsylvania Ave. N.W.
Washington, DC 20500
Wife of U.S. Vice President
Response Time: N/A
Received: N/A

Cher
P.O. Box 2425
Milford, CT 06460
Singer
Response Time: 20 Days
Received: Signed Photo

Chesney, Kenny
P.O. Box 128558
Nashville, TN 37212
Singer
Response Time: 120 Days
Received: Signed Photo

Chestnutt, Mark
P.O. Box 128031
Nashville, TN 37212
Singer
Response Time: N/A
Received: N/A

Chiao, Leroy
2101 NASA Rd. 1
Houston, TX 77058
Astronaut
Response Time: N/A
Received: N/A

Child, Julia
103 Irving St.
Cambridge, MA 02138
Chef
Response Time: 28 Days
Received: Signed Photo

Childress, Richard
1675 Coddle Creek Hwy.
Mooresville, NC 28115
NASCAR Team Owner
Response Time: 34 Days
Received: Signed STC

Chilton, Kevin P.
2101 NASA Rd. 1
Houston, TX 77058
Astronaut
Response Time: N/A
Received: N/A

Cho, Margaret
1815 Butler Ave. #120
LA, CA 90025
Actress
Response Time: N/A
Received: N/A

Chong, Tommy
1625 Casale Rd.
Pacific Palisades, CA 90272-2717
Actor
Response Time: 15 Days
Received: Signed Photo

Chretien, Jean-Loup
2101 NASA Rd. 1
Houston, TX 77058
Astronaut
Response Time: N/A
Received: N/A

Christensen, Donna M.
U.S. House of Representatives
Washington, DC 20515
Politician
Response Time: N/A
Received: N/A

Christensen, Tonja
9242 Beverly Blvd.
BH, CA 90210
Playboy Playmate
Response Time: N/A
Received: N/A

Christopher, Robin
56 West 66th St.
NY, NY 10023
Actress
Response Time: N/A
Received: N/A

Christopher, William
P.O. Box 50698
Pasadena, CA 91115-0698
Actor
Response Time: N/A
Received: N/A

Christopher, William
P.O. Box 50700
Pasadena, CA 91115-0700
Actor
Response Time: N/A
Received: N/A

Cialini, Julie Lynn
9242 Beverly Blvd.
BH, CA 90210
Playboy Playmate
Response Time: N/A
Received: N/A

Cibrian, Eddie
4000 Warner Blvd.
Burbank, CA 91522
Actor
Response Time: N/A
Received: N/A

Clapp, Gordon
10201 West Pico Blvd.
LA, CA 90035
Actor
Response Time: N/A
Received: N/A

Clapton, Eric
18 Harley Ave., Regents Park
London NW1, England
Singer
Response Time: 77 Days
Received: Signed Photo

Clapton, Eric
9830 Wilshire Blvd.
BH, CA 90212
Singer
Response Time: 186 Days
Received: Signed Photo

Clark, Dick
3003 W. Olive Ave.
Burbank, CA 91505
Television Personality
Response Time: 230 Days
Received: Signed Photo

Clark, Laurel B.
2101 NASA Rd. 1
Houston, TX 77058
Astronaut
Response Time: N/A
Received: N/A

Clark, Marcia
151 El Camino Blvd.
BH, CA 90212
Former O.J. Simpson Prosecutor
Response Time: 30 Days
Received: Signed Photo

Clark, Roy
1800 Forrest Blvd.
Tulsa, OK 74114
Singer
Response Time: 26 Days
Received: Signed Photo

Clark, Terri
P.O. Box 1079
Gallatin, TN 37066
Singer
Response Time: 13 Days
Received: Signed Photo

Clarke, Bobby
1930 Glenwood Dr.
Ocean City, NJ 08226-2611
Hockey Player
Response Time: N/A
Received: N/A

Clarke, John
3000 W. Alameda Ave.
Burbank, CA 91523
Actor
Response Time: N/A
Received: N/A

Clarke, Jordan
51 W. 52 St.
NY, NY 10019
Actor
Response Time: N/A
Received: N/A

Clarke, Julie Anne
9242 Beverly Blvd.
BH, CA 90210
Playboy Playmate
Response Time: N/A
Received: N/A

Clary, Robert
10001 Sun Dial Ln.
BH, CA 90210
Actor
Response Time: 10 Days
Received: Signed Photo

Clatterbuck, Tamara
4151 Prospect Ave.
LA, CA 90027
Actress
Response Time: N/A
Received: N/A

Clay, Wm. Lacy
U.S. House of Representatives
Washington, DC 20515
Politician
Response Time: N/A
Received: N/A

Clayton, Eva M.
U.S. House of Representatives
Washington, DC 20515
Politician
Response Time: N/A
Received: N/A

Cleave, Mary L.
2101 NASA Rd. 1
Houston, TX 77058
Astronaut
Response Time: N/A
Received: N/A

Cleland, Max
461 Dirksen Senate Office Bldg.
Washington, DC 20510
Senator
Response Time: N/A
Received: N/A

Clement, Bob
U.S. House of Representatives
Washington, DC 20515
Politician
Response Time: N/A
Received: N/A

Clennon, David
8660 Hayden Place
Culver City, CA 90232
Actor
Response Time: N/A
Received: N/A

Clervoy, Jean-Francois
2101 NASA Rd. 1
Houston, TX 77058
Astronaut
Response Time: N/A
Received: N/A

Cleveland, Alice
c/o Home Shopping Network
St. Petersburg, FL 33701
Home Shopping Network Host
Response Time: N/A
Received: N/A

Clifford, Michael R.
2101 NASA Rd. 1
Houston, TX 77058
Astronaut
Response Time: N/A
Received: N/A

Cline, Kristi
9242 Beverly Blvd.
BH, CA 90210
Playboy Playmate
Response Time: N/A
Received: N/A

Clinton, Hillary
United States Senate
Washington, DC 20510
Senator, Former First Lady
Response Time: N/A
Received: N/A

Clyburn, James E.
U.S. House of Representatives
Washington, DC 20515
Politician
Response Time: N/A
Received: N/A

Coats, Michael L.
2101 NASA Rd. 1
Houston, TX 77058
Astronaut
Response Time: N/A
Received: N/A

Coble, Howard
U.S. House of Representatives
Washington, DC 20515
Politician
Response Time: N/A
Received: N/A

Cochran, Anita
P.O. Box 128317
Nashville, TN 37212
Singer
Response Time: N/A
Received: N/A

Cochran, Thad
326 Russell Senate Office Bldg.
Washington, DC 20510
Senator
Response Time: N/A
Received: N/A

Cockrell, Kenneth D.
2101 NASA Rd. 1
Houston, TX 77058
Astronaut
Response Time: N/A
Received: N/A

Coe, David Allen
P.O. Box 270188
Nashville, TN 37227-0188
Singer
Response Time: 14 Days
Received: Signed Photo

Cohen, Scott
12400 Ventura Blvd., Box 363
Studio City, CA 91604
Actor
Response Time: N/A
Received: N/A

Cole, Bradley
51 W. 52 St.
NY, NY 10019
Actor
Response Time: N/A
Received: N/A

Coleman, Catherine G.
2101 NASA Rd. 1
Houston, TX 77058
Astronaut
Response Time: N/A
Received: N/A

Coles, Kim
500 S. Buena Vista St.
Burbank, CA 91521
Actress
Response Time: N/A
Received: N/A

Colin, Margaret
41 Bradford Ave.
Mont Clair, NJ 07043-1024
Actress
Response Time: 29 Days
Received: Signed Photo

Collins, Eileen M.
2101 NASA Rd. 1
Houston, TX 77058
Astronaut
Response Time: N/A
Received: N/A

Collins, Mac
U.S. House of Representatives
Washington, DC 20515
Politician
Response Time: N/A
Received: N/A

Collins, Michael
2101 NASA Rd. 1
Houston, TX 77058
Astronaut
Response Time: N/A
Received: N/A

Collins, Phil
30 Ives St.
London SW3 2ND, England
Singer
Response Time: 10 Days
Received: Signed Photo

Collins, Stephen
c/o The WB Network, 3701 Oak St.
Bldg. 34R, Burbank, CA 91505
Actor
Response Time: 150 Days
Received: Signed Photo

Collins, Stephen
1207 4th St., 4th Fl.
Santa Monica, CA 90401
Actor
Response Time: N/A
Received: N/A

Collins, Susan
172 Russell Senate Office Bldg.
Washington, DC 20510
Senator
Response Time: N/A
Received: N/A

Collinsworth, Kimm
c/o Baywatch Productions
510-18th Ave., Honolulu, HI 96816
Actress
Response Time: N/A
Received: N/A

Comaneci, Nadia
3214 Bart Conner Dr.
Norman, OK 73072
Gymnast
Response Time: N/A
Received: N/A

Comaneci, Nadia
4421 Hidden Hills Rd.
Norman, OK 73072-2899
Gymnast
Response Time: 31 Days
Received: Signed Photo

Combest, Larry
U.S. House of Representatives
Washington, DC 20515
Politician
Response Time: N/A
Received: N/A

Combs, Holly Marie
5555 Melrose Ave.
Hollywood, CA 90038-3197
Actress
Response Time: N/A
Received: N/A

Como, Perry
40 Cuttermill Rd., Ste. 305
Great Neck, NY 11021-3213
Singer
Response Time: N/A
Received: N/A

Compton, Stacy
1801 West Int'l. Spdwy. Blvd.
Daytona Beach, FL 32114
Auto Racing Personality
Response Time: 213 Days
Received: Signed Photo

Condit, Gary A.
U.S. House of Representatives
Washington, DC 20515
Politician
Response Time: N/A
Received: N/A

Confederate Railroad
P.O. Box 128185
Nashville, TN 37212
Music Group
Response Time: 19 Days
Received: Signed Photo - $4

Conlee, John
38 Music Square East, Ste. 117
Nashville, TN 37203
Singer
Response Time: 11 Days
Received: Signed Photo

Conley, Darlene
7800 Beverly Blvd.
LA, CA 90036
Actress
Response Time: N/A
Received: N/A

Conn, Terri
1268 East 14th St.
Brooklyn, NY 11230
Actress
Response Time: N/A
Received: N/A

Connelly, Jennifer
8942 Wilshire Blvd.
BH, CA 90211
Actress
Response Time: 37 Days
Received: Signed Photo

Connery, Sean
9830 Wilshire Blvd.
BH, CA 90212
Actor
Response Time: N/A
Received: N/A

Conrad, Kent
530 Hart Senate Office Bldg.
Washington, DC 20510
Senator
Response Time: N/A
Received: N/A

Consuelos, Mark
320 West 66th St.
NY, NY 10023
Actor
Response Time: N/A
Received: N/A

Conti, Bill
117 Fremont Pl.
LA, CA 90005
Composer - "Rocky"
Response Time: 131 Days
Received: SIC

Contreras, Carlos
1801 West Int'l. Spdwy. Blvd.
Daytona Beach, FL 32114
Auto Racing Personality
Response Time: 159 Days
Received: Signed Photo

Conway, Tim
P.O. Box 17047
Encino, CA 91416-7047
Actor, Comedian
Response Time: 33 Days
Received: Signed Photo

Conwell, Carolyn
7800 Beverly Blvd.
LA, CA 90036
Actress
Response Time: N/A
Received: N/A

Conyers Jr., John
U.S. House of Representatives
Washington, DC 20515
Politician
Response Time: N/A
Received: N/A

Cook, Jason
3000 W. Alameda Ave.
Burbank, CA 91523
Actor
Response Time: N/A
Received: N/A

Cook, Rachael Leigh
4570 Van Nuys Blvd. #71
Sherman Oaks, CA 91403
Actress
Response Time: N/A
Received: N/A

Cook, Terry
1801 West Int'l. Spdwy. Blvd.
Daytona Beach, FL 32114
Auto Racing Personality
Response Time: 163 Days
Received: Signed Photo

Cooksey, John
U.S. House of Representatives
Washington, DC 20515
Politician
Response Time: N/A
Received: N/A

Cooley, Dr. Denton
3014 Del Monte Dr.
Houston, TX 77019-3214
Famous Heart Surgeon
Response Time: 10 Days
Received: SIC

Cooper Jr., L. Gordon
2101 NASA Rd. 1
Houston, TX 77058
Astronaut
Response Time: N/A
Received: N/A

Cooper, Bette
Two Ocean Way, Ste. 1000
Atlantic City, NJ 08401
Miss America 1937
Response Time: N/A
Received: N/A

Cooper, Jackie
9612 Hazen Dr.
BH, CA 90210
Actor
Response Time: N/A
Received: N/A

Cooper, Jeanne
7800 Beverly Blvd.
LA, CA 90036
Actress
Response Time: N/A
Received: N/A

Copperfield, David
11777 San Vicente Blvd. #601
LA, CA 90048
Magician
Response Time: 57 Days
Received: Signed Photo

Cornett, Leanza
Two Ocean Way, Ste. 1000
Atlantic City, NJ 08401
Miss America 1993
Response Time: N/A
Received: N/A

Corporal Cajun
P.O. Box 2002
Anniston, AL 36202
Wrestler
Response Time: 31 Days
Received: Signed Photo

Corwin, Morena
9242 Beverly Blvd.
BH, CA 90210
Playboy Playmate
Response Time: N/A
Received: N/A

Corzine, Jon
United States Senate
Washington, DC 20510
Senator
Response Time: N/A
Received: N/A

Cosby, Bill
c/o Cosby Show, ABC-TV
77 West 66th St., NY, NY 10023
Actor, Comedian
Response Time: N/A
Received: N/A

Cosby, Bill
P.O. Box 4049
Santa Monica, CA 90411
Actor, Comedian
Response Time: 21 Days
Received: Signed Photo

Cosby, Bill
P.O. Box 808
Greenfield, MA 01301
Actor, Comedian
Response Time: 26 Days
Received: Signed Photo

Costa, Mary
3340 Kingston Pike, Unit 1
Knoxville, TN 37919
Voice of Sleeping Beauty
Response Time: 12 Days
Received: Signed Photo

Costello, Jerry F.
U.S. House of Representatives
Washington, DC 20515
Politician
Response Time: N/A
Received: N/A

Costner, Kevin
4000 Warner Blvd.
Burbank, CA 91522
Actor
Response Time: 30 Days
Received: Signed Photo

Cothran, Shirley
Two Ocean Way, Ste. 1000
Atlantic City, NJ 08401
Miss America 1975
Response Time: N/A
Received: N/A

Couch, Rich
2906 Rivercove Ct.
Ft. Worth, TX 76116
Test Pilot
Response Time: 7 Days
Received: SIC

Couric, Katie
1100 Park Ave. #15A
NY, NY 10128-1202
Television Personality
Response Time: N/A
Received: N/A

Couric, Katie
30 Rockefeller Plaza
NY, NY 10112
Television Personality
Response Time: N/A
Received: N/A

Cousino, Tishara Lee
9242 Beverly Blvd.
BH, CA 90210
Playboy Playmate
Response Time: N/A
Received: N/A

Cover, Laura
9242 Beverly Blvd.
BH, CA 90210
Playboy Playmate
Response Time: N/A
Received: N/A

Covey, Richard O.
2101 NASA Rd. 1
Houston, TX 77058
Astronaut
Response Time: N/A
Received: N/A

Cox, Archibald
Glesen Lane
Wayland, MA 01778
Politician
Response Time: 17 Days
Received: SIC

Cox, Christopher
U.S. House of Representatives
Washington, DC 20515
Politician
Response Time: N/A
Received: N/A

Cox, Jennifer Elise
4000 Warner Blvd.
Burbank, CA 91522
Actress
Response Time: N/A
Received: N/A

Cox, Nikki
4000 Warner Blvd.
Burbank, CA 91522
Actress
Response Time: N/A
Received: N/A

Cox, Ronny
13948 Magnolia Blvd.
Sherman Oaks, CA 91423
Actor, Singer
Response Time: N/A
Received: N/A

Cox-Arquette, Courtney
4000 Warner Blvd.
Burbank, CA 91522
Actress
Response Time: N/A
Received: N/A

Coyne, William J.
U.S. House of Representatives
Washington, DC 20515
Politician
Response Time: N/A
Received: N/A

Craig, Connie
c/o Home Shopping Network
St. Petersburg, FL 33701
Home Shopping Network Host
Response Time: N/A
Received: N/A

Craig, Jenny
445 Marine View Dr. #300
Del Mar, CA 92014
Weight-Loss Expert
Response Time: 42 Days
Received: Signed Photo

Craig, Larry
520 Hart Senate Office Bldg.
Washington, DC 20510
Senator
Response Time: N/A
Received: N/A

Craig, Yvonne
P.O. Box 827
Pacific Palisades, CA 90272-0827
Actress
Response Time: N/A
Received: N/A

Cramer Jr., Robert E. "Bud"
U.S. House of Representatives
Washington, DC 20515
Politician
Response Time: N/A
Received: N/A

Crane, Philip M.
U.S. House of Representatives
Washington, DC 20515
Politician
Response Time: N/A
Received: N/A

Crapo, Mike
111 Russell Senate Office Bldg.
Washington, DC 20510
Senator
Response Time: N/A
Received: N/A

Craven, Ricky
1801 West Int'l. Spdwy. Blvd.
Daytona Beach, FL 32114
Auto Racing Personality
Response Time: 50 Days
Received: Signed Photo

Craven, Wes
2419 Solar Dr.
LA, CA 90068
Director
Response Time: 20 Days
Received: Signed Photo

Craven, Wes
11846 Ventura Blvd., Ste. 208
Studio City, CA 91604
Director
Response Time: N/A
Received: N/A

Crawford, Cindy
132 S. Rodeo Dr., Ste. 300
BH, CA 90212
Model
Response Time: N/A
Received: N/A

Crawford, Gavin
4000 Warner Blvd.
Burbank, CA 91522
Actor
Response Time: N/A
Received: N/A

Crawford, Rick
1801 West Int'l. Spdwy. Blvd.
Daytona Beach, FL 32114
Auto Racing Personality
Response Time: 93 Days
Received: Signed Photo

Creamer, Timothy J.
2101 NASA Rd. 1
Houston, TX 77058
Astronaut
Response Time: N/A
Received: N/A

Creech, Cassandra
1268 East 14th St.
Brooklyn, NY 11230
Actress
Response Time: N/A
Received: N/A

Creighton, John O.
2101 NASA Rd. 1
Houston, TX 77058
Astronaut
Response Time: N/A
Received: N/A

Cremeans, John
c/o Home Shopping Network
St. Petersburg, FL 33701
Home Shopping Network Host
Response Time: N/A
Received: N/A

Crenna, Richard
3884 Sherwood Place
Sherman Oaks, CA 91423
Actor
Response Time: N/A
Received: N/A

Crenshaw, Ander
U.S. House of Representatives
Washington, DC 20515
Politician
Response Time: N/A
Received: N/A

Crichton, Michael
2118 Wilshire Blvd. #433
Santa Monica, CA 90403
Writer
Response Time: 77 Days
Received: Signed Photo

Crichton, Michael
433 N. Camden Dr. #500
BH, CA 90210
Writer
Response Time: N/A
Received: N/A

Crippen, Robert L.
2101 NASA Rd. 1
Houston, TX 77058
Astronaut
Response Time: N/A
Received: N/A

Cromwell, James
1801 Ave. of the Stars, Ste. 902
LA, CA 90067
Actor
Response Time: N/A
Received: N/A

Cronkite, Walter
51 W. 52nd St. #1934
NY, NY 10019-6188
News Anchor
Response Time: 14 Days
Received: Signed Photo

Cross, Joseph
1268 East 14th St.
Brooklyn, NY 11230
Actor
Response Time: N/A
Received: N/A

Crowell, Judy
c/o QVC, 1200 Wilson Dr.
West Chester, PA 19380
QVC Host
Response Time: N/A
Received: N/A

Crowley, Joseph
U.S. House of Representatives
Washington, DC 20515
Politician
Response Time: N/A
Received: N/A

Crowley, Pat
4151 Prospect Ave.
LA, CA 90027
Actress
Response Time: N/A
Received: N/A

Cruise, Tom
9830 Wilshire Blvd.
BH, CA 90212
Actor
Response Time: 62 Days
Received: Signed Photo

Cryer, Jon
5555 Melrose Ave.
Hollywood, CA 90038-3197
Actor
Response Time: N/A
Received: N/A

Cryer, Suzanne
10201 West Pico Blvd.
LA, CA 90035
Actress
Response Time: N/A
Received: N/A

Crystal, Jennifer
8660 Hayden Place
Culver City, CA 90232
Actress
Response Time: N/A
Received: N/A

Cubin, Barbara
U.S. House of Representatives
Washington, DC 20515
Politician
Response Time: N/A
Received: N/A

Culberson, John Abney
U.S. House of Representatives
Washington, DC 20515
Politician
Response Time: N/A
Received: N/A

Culbertson Jr., Frank L.
2101 NASA Rd. 1
Houston, TX 77058
Astronaut
Response Time: N/A
Received: N/A

Cummings, Elijah E.
U.S. House of Representatives
Washington, DC 20515
Politician
Response Time: N/A
Received: N/A

Cunningham, Randy "Duke"
U.S. House of Representatives
Washington, DC 20515
Politician
Response Time: N/A
Received: N/A

Cunningham, Walter
2101 NASA Rd. 1
Houston, TX 77058
Astronaut
Response Time: N/A
Received: N/A

Curbeam Jr., Robert L.
2101 NASA Rd. 1
Houston, TX 77058
Astronaut
Response Time: N/A
Received: N/A

Currie, Nancy J.
2101 NASA Rd. 1
Houston, TX 77058
Astronaut
Response Time: N/A
Received: N/A

Curtis, Jamie Lee
955 S. Carrillo Dr. #200
LA, CA 90048
Actress
Response Time: 48 Days
Received: Signed Photo

Curtis, Tony
11831 Folkstone Ln.
LA, CA 90077
Actor
Response Time: 41 Days
Received: Signed Photo

Cusack, Ann
5555 Melrose Ave.
Hollywood, CA 90038-3197
Actress
Response Time: N/A
Received: N/A

Cusack, John
151 El Camino Dr.
Bevery Hills, CA 90212
Actor
Response Time: N/A
Received: N/A

Cyrus, Billy Ray
P.O. Box 1206
Franklin, TN 37065
Singer
Response Time: 15 Days
Received: Signed Photo

Dafoe, Willem
33 Wooster St. #200
NY, NY 10013
Actor
Response Time: 361 Days
Received: Signed Photo

Dahm, Erica
9242 Beverly Blvd.
BH, CA 90210
Playboy Playmate
Response Time: N/A
Received: N/A

Daley, John Francis
500 S. Buena Vista St.
Burbank, CA 91521
Actor
Response Time: N/A
Received: N/A

Dallenbach, Wally
1801 West Int'l. Spdwy. Blvd.
Daytona Beach, FL 32114
Auto Racing Personality
Response Time: 201 Days
Received: Signed Photo

Dalton, Timothy
21 Golden Square #200
London W1R 3PA, England
Actor
Response Time: N/A
Received: N/A

Dalton, Timothy
Oxford House, 76 Oxford St.
London W1N 0AX, England
Actor
Response Time: N/A
Received: N/A

Daly, Tyne
5555 Melrose Ave.
Hollywood, CA 90038
Actress
Response Time: 34 Days
Received: Signed Photo

Damon, Matt
9830 Wilshire Blvd.
BH, CA 90212
Actor
Response Time: N/A
Received: N/A

Damon, Stuart
4151 Prospect Ave.
LA, CA 90027
Actor
Response Time: N/A
Received: N/A

Dane, Eric
500 S. Buena Vista St.
Burbank, CA 91521
Actor
Response Time: N/A
Received: N/A

Danes, Claire
P.O. Box 1837
Santa Monica, CA 90406-1837
Actress
Response Time: 452 Days
Received: Signed Photo

Dangerfield, Rodney
10580 Wilshire Blvd. #21 N.E.
LA, CA 90024
Actor, Comedian
Response Time: 20 Days
Received: Signed Photo

Daniels, Charlie
17060 Central Pike
Lebanon, TN 37090
Singer
Response Time: N/A
Received: N/A

Dano, Linda
1010 Nautilus Ln.
Mamaroneck, NY 15043
Actress
Response Time: 30 Days
Received: Signed Photo

Dano, Linda
320 West 66th St.
NY, NY 10023
Actress
Response Time: N/A
Received: N/A

Dano, Linda
4151 Prospect Ave.
LA, CA 90027
Actress
Response Time: N/A
Received: N/A

Dano, Linda
56 West 66th St.
NY, NY 10023
Actress
Response Time: N/A
Received: N/A

Danson, Ted
955 S. Carrillo Dr., 3rd Fl.
LA, CA 90048
Actor
Response Time: 64 Days
Received: Signed Photo

Danson, Ted
5555 Melrose Ave.
Hollywood, CA 90038-3197
Actor
Response Time: N/A
Received: N/A

Danza, Tony
10202 W. Washington Blvd.
Culver City, CA 90232
Actor
Response Time: 13 Days
Received: Signed Photo

D'Arbanville, Patti
51 W. 52 St.
NY, NY 10019
Actress
Response Time: N/A
Received: N/A

Darbo, Patrika
3000 W. Alameda Ave.
Burbank, CA 91523
Actress
Response Time: N/A
Received: N/A

Daschle, Thomas
509 Hart Senate Office Bldg.
Washington, DC 20510
Senator
Response Time: N/A
Received: N/A

Dash, Stacey
5555 Melrose Ave.
Hollywood, CA 90038-3197
Actress
Response Time: N/A
Received: N/A

Dattilo, Bryan
3000 W. Alameda Ave.
Burbank, CA 91523
Actor
Response Time: N/A
Received: N/A

Davenport, Lindsay
22 East 71st St.
NY, NY 10021-4911
Tennis Player
Response Time: 71 Days
Received: Signed Photo

Davidson, Doug
7800 Beverly Blvd.
LA, CA 90036
Actor
Response Time: N/A
Received: N/A

Davidson, Eileen
7800 Beverly Blvd.
LA, CA 90036
Actress
Response Time: N/A
Received: N/A

Davis Jr., Billy
2639 Lavery Court #5
Newbury Park, CA 91320
Singer
Response Time: N/A
Received: N/A

Davis, Neriah
9242 Beverly Blvd.
BH, CA 90210
Playboy Playmate
Response Time: N/A
Received: N/A

Davis, Ann B.
23315 Eagle Gap Dr.
San Antonio, TX 78255
Actress
Response Time: 55 Days
Received: Signed Photo

Davis, Danny K.
U.S. House of Representatives
Washington, DC 20515
Politician
Response Time: N/A
Received: N/A

Davis, Geena
9830 Wilshire Blvd.
BH, CA 90212
Actress
Response Time: N/A
Received: N/A

Davis, Geena
500 S. Buena Vista St.
Burbank, CA 91521
Actress
Response Time: N/A
Received: N/A

Davis, Gray
State Capitol
Sacramento, CA 95814
Governor
Response Time: N/A
Received: N/A

Davis, Jim
3300 Chadham Ln.
Muncie, IN 47302
Creator of Garfield
Response Time: 28 Days
Received: Signed Photo

Davis, Jim
U.S. House of Representatives
Washington, DC 20515
Politician
Response Time: N/A
Received: N/A

Davis, Jo Ann
U.S. House of Representatives
Washington, DC 20515
Politician
Response Time: N/A
Received: N/A

Davis, Josie
5700 Wilshire, Ste. 575
LA, CA 90036
Actress
Response Time: N/A
Received: N/A

Davis, Kristin
c/o Sex and the City
1100 6th Ave., NY, NY 10036
Actress
Response Time: N/A
Received: N/A

Davis, N. Jan
2101 NASA Rd. 1
Houston, TX 77058
Astronaut
Response Time: N/A
Received: N/A

Davis, Susan A.
U.S. House of Representatives
Washington, DC 20515
Politician
Response Time: N/A
Received: N/A

Davis, Thomas M.
U.S. House of Representatives
Washington, DC 20515
Politician
Response Time: N/A
Received: N/A

Davis, Warwick
63 St. Martin's Rd.
Walmer, CT 14 9N, England
Actor
Response Time: N/A
Received: N/A

Davison, Bruce
P.O. Box 57593
Sherman Oaks, CA 91403
Actor
Response Time: N/A
Received: N/A

Dawber, Pam
2236A Encitas Blvd.
Encitas, CA 92024-4553
Actress
Response Time: 31 Days
Received: Signed Photo

Day, Doris
P.O. Box 223163
Carmel, CA 93922
Actress
Response Time: 43 Days
Received: Signed Photo

Dayton, Mark
United States Senate
Washington, DC 20510
Senator
Response Time: N/A
Received: N/A

de los Reyes, Kamar
56 West 66th St.
NY, NY 10023
Actor
Response Time: N/A
Received: N/A

de Ravin, Emilie
4000 Warner Blvd.
Burbank, CA 91522
Actress
Response Time: N/A
Received: N/A

Deal, Nathan
U.S. House of Representatives
Washington, DC 20515
Politician
Response Time: N/A
Received: N/A

Dean, Billy
P.O. Box 23617
Nashville, TN 37202
Singer
Response Time: 10 Days
Received: Signed Photo

Dean, Howard
Vermont Pavilion Office Bldg.
Montpelier, VT 05609
Governor
Response Time: N/A
Received: N/A

Dean, Jimmy
8000 Centerview Pkwy., Ste. 400
Cordova, TN 38018-7927
Actor
Response Time: 36 Days
Received: Signed Photo

Deane, Meredith
8660 Hayden Place
Culver City, CA 90232
Actress
Response Time: N/A
Received: N/A

Deas, Justin
51 W. 52 St.
NY, NY 10019
Actor
Response Time: N/A
Received: N/A

Deasy, Paul
c/o QVC, 1200 Wilson Dr.
West Chester, PA 19380
QVC Host
Response Time: N/A
Received: N/A

DeBakey, Michael
1200 Moursund Ave.
Houston, TX 77030
World-Famous Heart Surgeon
Response Time: 30 Days
Received: SIC

DeCamp, Rosemary
317 Camino de las Colinas
Redondo Beach, CA 90277
Actress
Response Time: 10 Days
Received: Signed Photo

DeFazio, Peter A.
U.S. House of Representatives
Washington, DC 20515
Politician
Response Time: N/A
Received: N/A

DeForest, Calvert
84 Kennedy St.
Hackensack, NJ 07675
Actor
Response Time: 24 Days
Received: Signed Photo

DeGette, Diana
U.S. House of Representatives
Washington, DC 20515
Politician
Response Time: N/A
Received: N/A

De La Hoya, Oscar
2401 S. Atlantic Blvd.
Monterey Park, CA 91754
Boxer
Response Time: 211 Days
Received: Signed Photo

De La Hoya, Oscar
633 W. 5th St. #6700
LA, CA 90071
Boxer
Response Time: 120 Days
Received: Signed Photo

Delahunt, William D.
U.S. House of Representatives
Washington, DC 20515
Politician
Response Time: N/A
Received: N/A

Delaney, Kim
10201 West Pico Blvd.
LA, CA 90035
Actress
Response Time: N/A
Received: N/A

Delany, Dana
3435 Ocean Park Blvd. #112-N
Santa Monica, CA 90405
Actress
Response Time: 17 Days
Received: Signed Photo

DeLauro, Rosa L.
U.S. House of Representatives
Washington, DC 20515
Politician
Response Time: N/A
Received: N/A

DeLay, Tom
U.S. House of Representatives
Washington, DC 20515
Politician
Response Time: N/A
Received: N/A

Delfino, Majandra
4000 Warner Blvd.
Burbank, CA 91522
Actress
Response Time: N/A
Received: N/A

DeLorenzo, Michael
5555 Melrose Ave.
Hollywood, CA 90038-3197
Actor
Response Time: N/A
Received: N/A

DelosSantos, Becky
9242 Beverly Blvd.
BH, CA 90210
Playboy Playmate
Response Time: N/A
Received: N/A

DeLuise, Dom
1186 Corsica Dr.
Pacific Palisades, CA 90272
Actor
Response Time: 62 Days
Received: Signed Photo

DeLuise, Michael
1186 Corsica Dr.
Pacific Palisades, CA 90272
Actor
Response Time: 31 Days
Received: Signed Photo

DeMint, Jim
U.S. House of Representatives
Washington, DC 20515
Politician
Response Time: N/A
Received: N/A

Denberg, Lori Beth
4000 Warner Blvd.
Burbank, CA 91522
Actress
Response Time: N/A
Received: N/A

Dench, Dame Judi
46 Albemarle St.
London W1X 4PP, England
Actress
Response Time: N/A
Received: N/A

Dench, Dame Judi
BBC TV Centre, Wood Lane
London W1R 7RJ, England
Actress
Response Time: N/A
Received: N/A

Deneuve, Catherine
76 Rue Bonaparte
75006 Paris, France
Actress
Response Time: 29 Days
Received: Signed Photo

DeNiro, Robert
375 Greenwich St., 7th Fl.
NY, NY 10013-2379
Actor
Response Time: 35 Days
Received: SIC

Denisof, Alexis
4000 Warner Blvd.
Burbank, CA 91522
Actress
Response Time: N/A
Received: N/A

Dennehy, Brian
121 N. San Vicente Blvd.
BH, CA 90211
Actor
Response Time: N/A
Received: N/A

Dennis, Dan
c/o Home Shopping Network
St. Petersburg, FL 33701
Home Shopping Network Host
Response Time: N/A
Received: N/A

Dennison, Jo-Carroll
Two Ocean Way, Ste. 1000
Atlantic City, NJ 08401
Miss America 1942
Response Time: N/A
Received: N/A

Denver, Bob
c/o GFC, Box 269
Princeton, WV 24740
Actor
Response Time: 31 Days
Received: Signed Photo I Sent

DePaiva, James
56 West 66th St.
NY, NY 10023
Actor
Response Time: N/A
Received: N/A

DePaiva, Kassie
56 West 66th St.
NY, NY 10023
Actress
Response Time: N/A
Received: N/A

Depardieu, Gerard
c/o Artmedia, 10 Av. George V.
F-75008 Paris, France
Actor
Response Time: 183 Days
Received: Signed Photo I Sent

Dergan, Lisa
9242 Beverly Blvd.
BH, CA 90210
Playboy Playmate
Response Time: N/A
Received: N/A

Dern, Laura
2401 Main St.
Santa Monica, CA 90405
Actress
Response Time: 161 Days
Received: Signed Photo

D'Errico, Donna
c/o Baywatch Productions
510-18th Ave., Honolulu, HI 96816
Actress, Playboy Playmate
Response Time: N/A
Received: N/A

D'Errico, Donna
9242 Beverly Blvd.
BH, CA 90210
Actress, Playboy Playmate
Response Time: N/A
Received: N/A

Derwin, Mark
56 West 66th St.
NY, NY 10023
Actor
Response Time: N/A
Received: N/A

Desert, Alex
5555 Melrose Ave.
Hollywood, CA 90038-3197
Actor
Response Time: N/A
Received: N/A

Deutsch, Peter
U.S. House of Representatives
Washington, DC 20515
Politician
Response Time: N/A
Received: N/A

Devine, Loretta
4000 Warner Blvd.
Burbank, CA 91522
Actress
Response Time: N/A
Received: N/A

DeVito, Danny
31020 Broad Beach Rd.
Malibu, CA 90265
Actor
Response Time: 78 Days
Received: Signed Photo

DeVito, Danny
P.O. Box 491246
LA, CA 90049
Actor
Response Time: 78 Days
Received: Signed Photo

DeWine, Mike
140 Russell Senate Office Bldg.
Washington, DC 20510
Senator
Response Time: N/A
Received: N/A

Dewitt, Joyce
1250 6th St. #403
Santa Monica, CA 90401
Actress
Response Time: N/A
Received: N/A

Diamond Rio
P.O. Box 506
White House, TN 37188-0506
Music Group
Response Time: 26 Days
Received: Signed Photo

Diamond, Neil
10345 W. Olympic Blvd. #200
LA, CA 90064-2548
Singer
Response Time: 20 Days
Received: Signed Photo

Diamont, Don
7800 Beverly Blvd.
LA, CA 90036
Actor
Response Time: N/A
Received: N/A

Diaz-Balart, Lincoln
U.S. House of Representatives
Washington, DC 20515
Politician
Response Time: N/A
Received: N/A

diCesare, Michael
c/o QVC, 1200 Wilson Dr.
West Chester, PA 19380
Celebrity Hairstylist
Response Time: N/A
Received: N/A

Dickens, Jimmy
5010 W. Concord Rd.
Brentwood, TN 37027-6520
Singer
Response Time: 21 Days
Received: Signed Photo

Dickenson, Angie
1715 Carla Ridge
BH, CA 90210-1911
Actress
Response Time: 152 Days
Received: Signed Photo

Dickenson, Angie
9580 Lime Orchard Rd.
BH, CA 90210
Actress
Response Time: 294 Days
Received: Signed Photo

Dicks, Norman D.
U.S. House of Representatives
Washington, DC 20515
Politician
Response Time: N/A
Received: N/A

Dicopoulos, Frank
51 W. 52 St.
NY, NY 10019
Actor
Response Time: N/A
Received: N/A

Diffie, Joe
50 Music Square West, Ste. 300
Nashville, TN 37203
Singer
Response Time: 42 Days
Received: Signed Photo

Diffie, Joe
P.O. Box 479
Velma, OK 73091
Singer
Response Time: N/A
Received: N/A

Diller, Phyllis
163 S. Rockingham Dr.
Brentwood, CA 90049
Comedian
Response Time: 22 Days
Received: Signed Photo

Dillon, Kevin
5555 Melrose Ave.
Hollywood, CA 90038-3197
Actor
Response Time: N/A
Received: N/A

Dillon, Mike
P.O. Box 30414
Winston-Salem, NC 27130
Actor
Response Time: N/A
Received: N/A

Dillon, Mike
1801 West Int'l. Spdwy. Blvd.
Daytona Beach, FL 32114
Auto Racing Personality
Response Time: 186 Days
Received: Signed Photo

DiMucci, Dion
P.O. Box 1821
Ojai, CA 93024
Singer
Response Time: N/A
Received: N/A

Dingell, John D.
U.S. House of Representatives
Washington, DC 20515
Politician
Response Time: N/A
Received: N/A

Disney, Roy
500 S. Buena Vista St.
Burbank, CA 91521
Nephew of Walt Disney
Response Time: 30 Days
Received: Signed Photo

Ditka, Mike
29 English Turn Dr.
New Orleans, LA 70131
Football Coach
Response Time: N/A
Received: N/A

Dixie Chicks, The
56 Lindsley Ave.
Nashville, TN 37210-2039
Music Group
Response Time: 180 Days
Received: Signed Photo

Dixie Chicks, The
P.O. Box 670444
Dallas, TX 75367
Music Group
Response Time: 90 Days
Received: Signed Photo

D'lyn, Shae
10201 West Pico Blvd.
Trailer 779, LA, CA 90035
Actress
Response Time: N/A
Received: N/A

Dobies, Mark
51 W. 52 St.
NY, NY 10019
Actor
Response Time: N/A
Received: N/A

Dobson, Peter
1230 Ave. of Americas
NY, NY 10020
Actor
Response Time: N/A
Received: N/A

Dodd, Christopher
448 Russell Senate Office Bldg.
Washington, DC 20510
Senator
Response Time: N/A
Received: N/A

Doerr, Bobby
94449 Territorial Rd.
Junction City, OR 97448
Baseball Player
Response Time: 47 Days
Received: Signed Photo

Doggett, Lloyd
U.S. House of Representatives
Washington, DC 20515
Politician
Response Time: N/A
Received: N/A

Doherty, Shannen
5555 Melrose Ave.
Hollywood, CA 90038-3197
Actress
Response Time: N/A
Received: N/A

Doi, Takao
2101 NASA Rd. 1
Houston, TX 77058
Astronaut
Response Time: N/A
Received: N/A

Dolan, Ellen
1268 East 14th St.
Brooklyn, NY 11230
Actress
Response Time: N/A
Received: N/A

Dole, Bob
1035 N. Maple Dr.
Russell, KS 67665
Politician
Response Time: 105 Days
Received: Signed Photo

Dole, Elizabeth
1035 N. Maple Dr.
Russell, KS 67665
Politician
Response Time: 105 Days
Received: Signed Photo

Domeier, Rick
c/o QVC, 1200 Wilson Dr.
West Chester, PA 19380
QVC Host
Response Time: N/A
Received: N/A

Domenici, Pete
328 Hart Senate Office Bldg.
Washington, DC 20510
Senator
Response Time: N/A
Received: N/A

Domino, Fats
5515 Marais St.
New Orleans, LA 70117
Singer
Response Time: 24 Days
Received: SIC

Donley, Kimberly
9242 Beverly Blvd.
BH, CA 90210
Playboy Playmate
Response Time: N/A
Received: N/A

Donnelly, Patricia
Two Ocean Way, Ste. 1000
Atlantic City, NJ 08401
Miss America 1939
Response Time: N/A
Received: N/A

Donovan, Elisa
5555 Melrose Ave.
Hollywood, CA 90038-3197
Actress
Response Time: N/A
Received: N/A

Dooley, Calvin M.
U.S. House of Representatives
Washington, DC 20515
Politician
Response Time: N/A
Received: N/A

Doolittle, John T.
U.S. House of Representatives
Washington, DC 20515
Politician
Response Time: N/A
Received: N/A

Dorgan, Byron
713 Hart Senate Office Bldg.
Washington, DC 20510
Senator
Response Time: N/A
Received: N/A

Dorman, Samantha
9242 Beverly Blvd.
BH, CA 90210
Playboy Playmate
Response Time: N/A
Received: N/A

Dotrice, Roy
34-12 36th St.
Astoria, NY 11106
Actor
Response Time: N/A
Received: N/A

Douglas, Donna
P.O. Box 1511
Huntington Beach, CA 92647-1511
Actress
Response Time: 91 Days
Received: Signed Photo

Douglas, Jerry
7800 Beverly Blvd.
LA, CA 90036
Actor
Response Time: N/A
Received: N/A

Doyle, Michael F.
U.S. House of Representatives
Washington, DC 20515
Politician
Response Time: N/A
Received: N/A

Dreier, David
U.S. House of Representatives
Washington, DC 20515
Politician
Response Time: N/A
Received: N/A

Drescher, Fran
9336 W. Washington Blvd.
Culver City, CA 90232
Actress
Response Time: 60 Days
Received: Signed Photo

Drescher, Fran
232 N. Canon Dr.
BH, CA 90210
Actress
Response Time: 88 Days
Received: Signed Photo

Dreyfuss, Richard
1041 N. Formost #104
W. Hollywood, CA 90046
Actor
Response Time: 87 Days
Received: Signed Photo

Dreyfuss, Richard
2300 W. Victory Blvd. #384
Burbank, CA 91306
Actor
Response Time: N/A
Received: N/A

Driggs, Deborah
9242 Beverly Blvd.
BH, CA 90210
Playboy Playmate
Response Time: N/A
Received: N/A

Drozdova, Inga
9242 Beverly Blvd.
BH, CA 90210
Playboy Playmate
Response Time: N/A
Received: N/A

Dubois, Ja'Net
4000 Warner Blvd.
Burbank, CA 91522
Voice Actor
Response Time: N/A
Received: N/A

Duffy, Brian
2101 NASA Rd. 1
Houston, TX 77058
Astronaut
Response Time: N/A
Received: N/A

Duhamel, Josh
320 West 66th St.
NY, NY 10023
Actor
Response Time: N/A
Received: N/A

Dukakis, Michael
85 Perry St.
Brookline, MA 02146
Politician
Response Time: 67 Days
Received: Signed Photo

Dukakis, Olympia
240 Main St.
Little Falls, NJ 07424
Actress
Response Time: 11 Days
Received: Signed Photo

Duke Jr., Charles M.
2101 NASA Rd. 1
Houston, TX 77058
Astronaut
Response Time: N/A
Received: N/A

Dunaway, Faye
2300 W. Victory Blvd. #384
Burbank, CA 91506-1200
Actress
Response Time: 93 Days
Received: Signed Photo

Dunbar, Bonnie J.
2101 NASA Rd. 1
Houston, TX 77058
Astronaut
Response Time: N/A
Received: N/A

Dunbar, Rockmond
5555 Melrose Ave.
Hollywood, CA 90038-3197
Actor
Response Time: N/A
Received: N/A

Duncan Jr., John J.
U.S. House of Representatives
Washington, DC 20515
Politician
Response Time: N/A
Received: N/A

Duncan, Christopher B.
4000 Warner Blvd.
Burbank, CA 91522
Actor
Response Time: N/A
Received: N/A

Dunn, Jennifer
U.S. House of Representatives
Washington, DC 20515
Politician
Response Time: N/A
Received: N/A

Dunst, Kirsten
151 El Camino Dr.
BH, CA 90212
Actress
Response Time: N/A
Received: N/A

Duplaix, Daphnee Lynn
9242 Beverly Blvd.
BH, CA 90210
Playboy Playmate
Response Time: N/A
Received: N/A

Dupuis, Roy
1230 Ave. of Americas
NY, NY 10020
Actor
Response Time: 203 Days
Received: Signed Photo

Duque, Pedro
2101 NASA Rd. 1
Houston, TX 77058
Astronaut
Response Time: N/A
Received: N/A

Durbin, Richard
364 Russell Senate Office Bldg.
Washington, DC 20510
Senator
Response Time: N/A
Received: N/A

Dusay, Marj
320 West 66th St.
NY, NY 10023
Actress
Response Time: N/A
Received: N/A

Duvall, David
c/o IMG, 1360 E. 9th St.
Cleveland, OH 44114
Golfer
Response Time: 118 Days
Received: Signed Photo

Duvall, Robert
P.O. Box 520
The Plains, VA 22171
Actor
Response Time: 367 Days
Received: Signed Photo

Dylan, Bob
P.O. Box 870, Cooper Station
NY, NY 10276
Singer
Response Time: 38 Days
Received: Signed Photo

Earnhardt Jr., Dale
1675 Coddle Creek Highway
Mooresville, NC 28115
Auto Racing Personality
Response Time: 217 Days
Received: Signed Photo

Earnhardt Jr., Dale
1801 West Int'l. Spdwy. Blvd.
Daytona Beach, FL 32114
Auto Racing Personality
Response Time: 217 Days
Received: Signed Photo

Earnhardt, Kerry
1675 Coddle Creek Hwy.
Mooresville, NC 28115
Auto Racing Personality
Response Time: 27 Days
Received: Signed Photo

Easton, Sheena
c/o QVC, 1200 Wilson Dr.
West Chester, PA 19380
Singer, Doll Designer
Response Time: N/A
Received: N/A

Eastwood, Clint
4000 Warner Blvd. #16
Burbank, CA 91522
Actor, Politician
Response Time: N/A
Received: N/A

Eastwood, Clint
P.O. Box 4366
Carmel, CA 93921-4366
Actor, Politician
Response Time: 64 Days
Received: Signed Photo

Ebert, Roger
630 North McClurg Court
Chicago, IL 60611
Movie Critic
Response Time: 25 Days
Received: Signed Photo

Ebsen, Buddy
P.O. Box 2069
Palos Verdes Peninsula, CA 90274
Actor
Response Time: 31 Days
Received: Signed Photo

Eden, Barbara
P.O. Box 5556
Sherman Oaks, CA 91403
Actress
Response Time: 120 Days
Received: Signed Photo

Edwards Jr., Joe F.
2101 NASA Rd. 1
Houston, TX 77058
Astronaut
Response Time: N/A
Received: N/A

Edwards, Anthony
4000 Warner Blvd.
Burbank, CA 91522
Actor
Response Time: N/A
Received: N/A

Edwards, Chet
U.S. House of Representatives
Washington, DC 20515
Politician
Response Time: N/A
Received: N/A

Edwards, John
225 Dirksen Senate Office Bldg.
Washington, DC 20510
Senator
Response Time: N/A
Received: N/A

Edwards, Tracey
c/o Home Shopping Network
St. Petersburg, FL 33701
Home Shopping Network Host
Response Time: N/A
Received: N/A

Egan, Susan
4000 Warner Blvd.
Burbank, CA 91522
Actress
Response Time: N/A
Received: N/A

Eggert, Nicole
c/o Baywatch Productions
510-18th Ave., Honolulu, HI 96816
Actress
Response Time: N/A
Received: N/A

Ehlers, Beth
51 W. 52 St.
NY, NY 10019
Actress
Response Time: N/A
Received: N/A

Ehlers, Vernon J.
U.S. House of Representatives
Washington, DC 20515
Politician
Response Time: N/A
Received: N/A

Ehrlich Jr., Robert L.
U.S. House of Representatives
Washington, DC 20515
Politician
Response Time: N/A
Received: N/A

Eisner, Michael
500 S. Buena Vista St.
Burbank, CA 91521
Chairman CEO, Walt Disney
Response Time: 65 Days
Received: Signed Photo

Eldred, Pam
Two Ocean Way, Ste. 1000
Atlantic City, NJ 08401
Miss America 1970
Response Time: N/A
Received: N/A

Electra, Carmen
c/o Baywatch Productions
510-18th Ave., Honolulu, HI 96816
Actress
Response Time: N/A
Received: N/A

Eleniak, Erika
c/o Baywatch Productions
510-18th Ave., Honolulu, HI 96816
Actress
Response Time: N/A
Received: N/A

Elfman, Jenna
10201 West Pico Blvd.
Trailer 779, LA, CA 90035
Actress
Response Time: N/A
Received: N/A

Elliott, Alecia
P.O. Box 3075
Muscle Shoals, AL 35661
Singer
Response Time: 9 Days
Received: Signed Photo

Elliott, Bill
1801 West Int'l. Spdwy. Blvd.
Daytona Beach, FL 32114
Auto Racing Personality
Response Time: 155 Days
Received: Signed Photo

Elliott, David James
5555 Melrose Ave.
LA, CA 90038
Actor
Response Time: 31 Days
Received: Signed Photo

Elliott, Patricia
56 West 66th St.
NY, NY 10023
Actress
Response Time: N/A
Received: N/A

Ellsworth, Kiko
4151 Prospect Ave.
LA, CA 90027
Actress
Response Time: N/A
Received: N/A

Elway, John
13655 Broncos Pkwy.
Englewood, CO 80112
Football Player
Response Time: 39 Days
Received: Signed Photo

Emerson, Jo Ann
U.S. House of Representatives
Washington, DC 20515
Politician
Response Time: N/A
Received: N/A

Emery, Ralph
6528 Radcliff Dr.
Nashville, TN 37221
Television Personality
Response Time: 29 Days
Received: Signed Photo

Emme
c/o Sarah Hall Productions
670 Broadway, NY, NY 10012
Model
Response Time: 41 Days
Received: Signed Photo

Engel, Eliot L.
U.S. House of Representatives
Washington, DC 20515
Politician
Response Time: N/A
Received: N/A

England, Anthony W.
2101 NASA Rd. 1
Houston, TX 77058
Astronaut
Response Time: N/A
Received: N/A

Engle, Joe H.
2101 NASA Rd. 1
Houston, TX 77058
Astronaut
Response Time: N/A
Received: N/A

Engler, John
P.O. Box 30013
Lansing, MI 48909
Governor
Response Time: N/A
Received: N/A

English, Ellia
4000 Warner Blvd.
Burbank, CA 91522
Actress
Response Time: N/A
Received: N/A

English, Phil
U.S. House of Representatives
Washington, DC 20515
Politician
Response Time: N/A
Received: N/A

Englund, Robert
1616 Santa Cruz St.
Laguna Beach, CA 92651-3350
Actor
Response Time: 118 Days
Received: Signed Photo I Sent

Engvall, Bill
8380 Melrose Ave. #310
LA, CA 90069
Comedian
Response Time: 55 Days
Received: Signed Photo

Engvall, Bill
P.O. Box 60388
Colorado Springs, CO 80960
Comedian
Response Time: N/A
Received: N/A

Ensign, John
United States Senate
Washington, DC 20510
Senator
Response Time: N/A
Received: N/A

Enzi, Mike
290 Russell Senate Office Bldg.
Washington, DC 20510
Senator
Response Time: N/A
Received: N/A

Eplin, Tom
1268 East 14th St.
Brooklyn, NY 11230
Actor
Response Time: N/A
Received: N/A

Ericsson, Ulrika
9242 Beverly Blvd.
BH, CA 90210
Playboy Playmate
Response Time: N/A
Received: N/A

Eshoo, Anna G.
U.S. House of Representatives
Washington, DC 20515
Politician
Response Time: N/A
Received: N/A

Estabrook, Christine
4000 Warner Blvd.
Burbank, CA 91522
Actress
Response Time: N/A
Received: N/A

Estefan, Gloria
420 Jefferson Ave.
Miami Beach, FL 33139
Singer
Response Time: 17 Days
Received: Signed Photo

Estefan, Gloria
P.O. Box 4447
Miami, FL 33269
Singer
Response Time: 17 Days
Received: Signed Photo

Estes, Bob
1821 Westlake Dr. #138
Austin, TX 78746-3704
Golfer
Response Time: 56 Days
Received: Signed Photo

Etheridge, Bob
U.S. House of Representatives
Washington, DC 20515
Politician
Response Time: N/A
Received: N/A

Etheridge, Melissa
3727 West Magnolia Blvd. #813
Burbank, CA 91510
Singer, Television Personality
Response Time: N/A
Received: N/A

Etheridge, Melissa
P.O. Box 884563
San Francisco, CA 94188
Singer, Television Personality
Response Time: 39 Days
Received: Signed Photo

Evans, Andrea
4024 Radford Ave.
Studio City, CA 91604
Actress
Response Time: N/A
Received: N/A

Evans, Janet
8 Barneburg
Dove Canyon, CA 92679-9759
Swimmer
Response Time: N/A
Received: N/A

Evans, Josh Ryan
4024 Radford Ave.
Studio City, CA 91604
Actor
Response Time: N/A
Received: N/A

Evans, Lane
U.S. House of Representatives
Washington, DC 20515
Politician
Response Time: N/A
Received: N/A

Evans, Linda
6714 Villa Madera Dr.
Tacoma, WA 98499
Actress
Response Time: 29 Days
Received: Signed Photo

Evans, Sarah
P.O. Box 509
Knoxville, TN 37901
Singer
Response Time: N/A
Received: N/A

Everett, Terry
U.S. House of Representatives
Washington, DC 20515
Politician
Response Time: N/A
Received: N/A

Everly Brothers, The
P.O. Box 3933
Seattle, WA 98124-3933
Music Group
Response Time: N/A
Received: N/A

Evernham, Ray
1801 West Int'l. Spdwy. Blvd.
Daytona Beach, FL 32114
Auto Racing Personality
Response Time: 361 Days
Received: Signed Photo

Evert, Chris
500 N. 25th St.
Wilton Manors, FL 33305
Tennis Player
Response Time: 11 Days
Received: Signed Photo

Evert, Chris
194 Bellevue Ave.
Newport, RI 02840
Tennis Player
Response Time: N/A
Received: N/A

Evridge, Melissa
9242 Beverly Blvd.
BH, CA 90210
Playboy Playmate
Response Time: N/A
Received: N/A

Ewing, Patrick
5335 Wisconsin Ave. #850
Washington, DC 20015
Basketball Player
Response Time: 27 Days
Received: Signed Photo

Eyharts, Leopold
2101 NASA Rd. 1
Houston, TX 77058
Astronaut
Response Time: N/A
Received: N/A

Fabares, Shelley
P.O. Box 6010-909
Sherman Oaks, CA 91413
Actress
Response Time: 240 Days
Received: Signed Photo

Fabian, John M.
2101 NASA Rd. 1
Houston, TX 77058
Astronaut
Response Time: N/A
Received: N/A

Fabio
11661 San Vicente Blvd.
Ste. 500, LA, CA 90049
Model
Response Time: 11 Days
Received: Signed Photo

Farr, Sam
U.S. House of Representatives
Washington, DC 20515
Politician
Response Time: N/A
Received: N/A

Faison, Donald Adeosun
5555 Melrose Ave.
Hollywood, CA 90038-3197
Actor
Response Time: N/A
Received: N/A

Farrell, Mike
3000 W. Alameda Ave.
Burbank, CA 91523
Actor
Response Time: 31 Days
Received: Signed Photo

Faleomavaega, Eni F. H.
U.S. House of Representatives
Washington, DC 20515
Politician
Response Time: N/A
Received: N/A

Farrell, Mike
P.O. Box 6010-826
Sherman Oaks, CA 91413-5961
Actor
Response Time: 31 Days
Received: Signed Photo

Falk, Peter
1004 N. Roxbury Dr.
BH, CA 90069
Actor
Response Time: 36 Days
Received: Signed Photo

Farrell, Terry
5555 Melrose Ave.
Hollywood, CA 90038-3197
Actress
Response Time: N/A
Received: N/A

Fargo, Donna
P.O. Box 210877
Nashville, TN 37221
Singer
Response Time: N/A
Received: N/A

Fath, Farah
3000 W. Alameda Ave.
Burbank, CA 91523
Actress
Response Time: N/A
Received: N/A

Fattah, Chaka
U.S. House of Representatives
Washington, DC 20515
Politician
Response Time: N/A
Received: N/A

Faustino, David
11350 Ventura Blvd. #206
Studio City, CA 91604-3140
Actor
Response Time: 219 Days
Received: Signed Photo

Favre, Brett
3071 Gothic Court
Green Bay, WI 53213
Football Player
Response Time: 25 Days
Received: Signed Photo

Fawcett, Farrah
3130 Antelo Rd.
LA, CA 90077
Actress
Response Time: 120 Days
Received: Signed Photo

Fedewa, Tim
1801 West Int'l. Spdwy. Blvd.
Daytona Beach, FL 32114
Auto Racing Personality
Response Time: 194 Days
Received: Signed Photo

Fehr, Brendan
4000 Warner Blvd.
Burbank, CA 91522
Actor
Response Time: 411 Days
Received: Signed Photo

Feingold, Russell
716 Hart Senate Office Bldg.
Washington, DC 20510
Senator
Response Time: N/A
Received: N/A

Feinstein, Dianne
331 Hart Senate Office Bldg.
Washington, DC 20510
Senator
Response Time: N/A
Received: N/A

Fellows, Ron
1801 West Int'l. Spdwy. Blvd.
Daytona Beach, FL 32114
Auto Racing Personality
Response Time: 203 Days
Received: Signed Photo

Ferguson, Christopher J.
2101 NASA Rd. 1
Houston, TX 77058
Astronaut
Response Time: N/A
Received: N/A

Ferguson, Craig
4000 Warner Blvd.
Burbank, CA 91522
Actor
Response Time: N/A
Received: N/A

Ferguson, Matthew
1230 Ave. of Americas
NY, NY 10020
Actor
Response Time: N/A
Received: N/A

Ferguson, Mike
U.S. House of Representatives
Washington, DC 20515
Politician
Response Time: N/A
Received: N/A

Ferrell, Jami
9242 Beverly Blvd.
BH, CA 90210
Playboy Playmate
Response Time: N/A
Received: N/A

Field, Sally
9830 Wilshire Blvd.
BH, CA 90212
Actress
Response Time: 24 Days
Received: Signed Photo

Field, Sally
P.O. Box 492417
LA, CA 90049
Actress
Response Time: 16 Days
Received: Signed Photo

Field, Todd
8660 Hayden Place
Culver City, CA 90232
Actor
Response Time: N/A
Received: N/A

Filippo, Fabrizio
5555 Melrose Ave.
Hollywood, CA 90038-3197
Actor
Response Time: N/A
Received: N/A

Fillion, Nathan
10201 West Pico Blvd.
LA, CA 90035
Actor
Response Time: N/A
Received: N/A

Filner, Bob
U.S. House of Representatives
Washington, DC 20515
Politician
Response Time: N/A
Received: N/A

Fincke, E. Michael
2101 NASA Rd. 1
Houston, TX 77058
Astronaut
Response Time: N/A
Received: N/A

Finnigan, Jennifer
7800 Beverly Blvd.
LA, CA 90036
Actress
Response Time: N/A
Received: N/A

Firth, Peter
5555 Melrose Ave.
Hollywood, CA 90038-3197
Actor
Response Time: N/A
Received: N/A

Fisher, Anna L.
2101 NASA Rd. 1
Houston, TX 77058
Astronaut
Response Time: N/A
Received: N/A

Fisher, Carrie
1700 Coldwater Canyon
BH, CA 90210
Actress
Response Time: 82 Days
Received: Signed Photo

Fisher, William F.
2101 NASA Rd. 1
Houston, TX 77058
Astronaut
Response Time: N/A
Received: N/A

Fitzgerald, Peter
555 Dirksen Senate Office Bldg.
Washington, DC 20510
Senator
Response Time: N/A
Received: N/A

Flagg, Fannie
1569 Miramar Ln.
Santa Barbara, CA 93108
Writer
Response Time: 33 Days
Received: Signed Photo

Flake, Jeff
U.S. House of Representatives
Washington, DC 20515
Politician
Response Time: N/A
Received: N/A

Flannery, Susan
7800 Beverly Blvd.
LA, CA 90036
Actress
Response Time: N/A
Received: N/A

Fleming, Nancy
Two Ocean Way, Ste. 1000
Atlantic City, NJ 08401
Miss America 1961
Response Time: N/A
Received: N/A

Fleming, Rhonda
2129 Century Woods Way
LA, CA 90067
Actress
Response Time: N/A
Received: N/A

Fletcher, Ernie
U.S. House of Representatives
Washington, DC 20515
Politician
Response Time: N/A
Received: N/A

Fletcher, Maria
Two Ocean Way, Ste. 1000
Atlantic City, NJ 08401
Miss America 1962
Response Time: N/A
Received: N/A

Florek, Dann
1230 Ave. of Americas
NY, NY 10020
Actor
Response Time: N/A
Received: N/A

Flynt, Larry
9211 Robin Dr.
LA, CA 90069
Magazine Publisher
Response Time: 32 Days
Received: Signed Photo

Foale, C. Michael
2101 NASA Rd. 1
Houston, TX 77058
Astronaut
Response Time: N/A
Received: N/A

Fogelberg, Dan
P.O. Box 2399
Pagosa Springs, CO 81147
Singer
Response Time: 183 Days
Received: Signed Photo

Fogleman, Jay
1801 West Int'l. Spdwy. Blvd.
Daytona Beach, FL 32114
Auto Racing Personality
Response Time: 119 Days
Received: Signed Photo

Foley, Scott
4000 Warner Blvd.
Burbank, CA 91522
Actor
Response Time: N/A
Received: N/A

Foley, Mark
U.S. House of Representatives
Washington, DC 20515
Politician
Response Time: N/A
Received: N/A

Folta, Danelle Marie
9242 Beverly Blvd.
BH, CA 90210
Playboy Playmate
Response Time: N/A
Received: N/A

Fonda, Jane
1050 Techwood Dr. N.W.
Atlanta, GA 30318
Actress
Response Time: 31 Days
Received: Signed Photo

Fontaine, Joan
P.O. Box 222600
Carmel, CA 93922
Actress
Response Time: 35 Days
Received: Signed Photo

Foray, June
22745 Erwin St.
Woodland Hills, CA 91367
Voice of "Snow White"
Response Time: 9 Days
Received: SIC

Forbes, Steve
c/o Forbes 2000, 209 Madison St.
Ste. 400, Alexandria, VA 22314
Politician, Magazine Owner
Response Time: 45 Days
Received: Signed Photo

Forbes, Steve
P.O. Box 1009
Bedminster, NJ 07921
Politician, Magazine Owner
Response Time: N/A
Received: N/A

Force, John
23253 East LaPalma Ave.
Yorba Linda, CA 92687
Auto Racing Personality
Response Time: 8 Days
Received: Signed Photo

Ford Jr., Harold E.
U.S. House of Representatives
Washington, DC 20515
Politician
Response Time: N/A
Received: N/A

Ford, Betty
40365 Sand Dune Rd.
Rancho Mirage, CA 92270-3551
Former First Lady
Response Time: 41 Days
Received: Signed Photo - $5

Ford, Betty
P.O. Box 927
Rancho Mirage, CA 92270
Former First Lady
Response Time: 29 Days
Received: Signed Photo - $5

Ford, British
c/o Home Shopping Network
St. Petersburg, FL 33701
Home Shopping Network Host
Response Time: N/A
Received: N/A

Ford, Faith
300 Television Plaza, Bldg. 137
Burbank, CA 91505
Actress
Response Time: N/A
Received: N/A

Ford, Gerald
40365 Sand Dune Rd.
Rancho Mirage, CA 92270-3551
Politician; Former U.S. President
Response Time: 15 Days
Received: SIC

Ford, Gerald
P.O. Box 927
Rancho Mirage, CA 92270
Politician; Former U.S. President
Response Time: 29 Days
Received: Signed Photo - $3

Ford, Judith
Two Ocean Way, Ste. 1000
Atlantic City, NJ 08401
Miss America 1969
Response Time: N/A
Received: N/A

Foreman, Amanda
4000 Warner Blvd.
Burbank, CA 91522
Actress
Response Time: N/A
Received: N/A

Foreman, George
P.O. Box 14267
Humble, TX 77347
Boxer
Response Time: 81 Days
Received: Signed Photo

Foreman, Michael J.
2101 NASA Rd. 1
Houston, TX 77058
Astronaut
Response Time: N/A
Received: N/A

Forrester, Patrick G.
2101 NASA Rd. 1
Houston, TX 77058
Astronaut
Response Time: 410 Days
Received: Signed Photo

Forsythe, John
3849 Roblar Ave.
Santa Ynez, CA 93460
Actor
Response Time: 134 Days
Received: Signed Photo

Forsythe, William
16027 Ventura Blvd. #420
Encino, CA 91423
Actor
Response Time: 173 Days
Received: Signed Photo

Fossella, Vito
U.S. House of Representatives
Washington, DC 20515
Politician
Response Time: N/A
Received: N/A

Fossum, Michael E.
2101 NASA Rd. 1
Houston, TX 77058
Astronaut
Response Time: N/A
Received: N/A

Foster, Mike
P.O. Box 94004
Baton Rouge, LA 70804-9004
Governor
Response Time: N/A
Received: N/A

Fox, Bernard
6601 Burnet Ave.
Van Nuys, CA 91405
Actor
Response Time: 21 Days
Received: Signed Photo

Fox, Morgan
9242 Beverly Blvd.
BH, CA 90210
Playboy Playmate
Response Time: N/A
Received: N/A

Foxworthy, Jeff
8380 Melrose Ave. #310
LA, CA 90069
Actor, Comedian
Response Time: 47 Days
Received: Signed Photo

Foxx, Jamie
4000 Warner Blvd.
Burbank, CA 91522
Actor
Response Time: N/A
Received: N/A

Frakes, Jonathan
10100 Santa Monica Blvd. #700
LA, CA 90067
Actor
Response Time: N/A
Received: N/A

Francis, Genie
4151 Prospect Ave.
LA, CA 90027
Actress
Response Time: N/A
Received: N/A

Francks, Don
1230 Ave. of Americas
NY, NY 10020
Actor
Response Time: N/A
Received: N/A

Frank, Barney
U.S. House of Representatives
Washington, DC 20515
Politician
Response Time: N/A
Received: N/A

Franken, Al
9830 Wilshire Blvd.
BH, CA 90212
Comedian
Response Time: N/A
Received: N/A

Franklin, Don
5555 Melrose Ave.
Hollywood, CA 90038-3197
Actor
Response Time: N/A
Received: N/A

Frantz, Adrienne
7800 Beverly Blvd.
LA, CA 90036
Actress
Response Time: N/A
Received: N/A

Franz, Dennis
10201 West Pico Blvd.
LA, CA 90035
Actor
Response Time: N/A
Received: N/A

Fraser, Brendan
2118 Wilshire Blvd., PMB 513
Santa Monica, CA 90403-5784
Actor
Response Time: N/A
Received: N/A

Fraser, Brendan
9830 Wilshire Blvd.
BH, CA 90212
Actor
Response Time: 135 Days
Received: Signed Photo

Freeman, Morgan
1325 Ave. of the Americas
NY, NY 10019
Actress
Response Time: N/A
Received: N/A

Frelinghuysen, Rodney P.
U.S. House of Representatives
Washington, DC 20515
Politician
Response Time: N/A
Received: N/A

French, Heather
Two Ocean Way, Ste. 1000
Atlantic City, NJ 08401
Miss America 2000
Response Time: N/A
Received: N/A

Frick, Stephen N.
2101 NASA Rd. 1
Houston, TX 77058
Astronaut
Response Time: N/A
Received: N/A

Friedman, Olivia
5555 Melrose Ave.
Hollywood, CA 90038-3197
Actress
Response Time: N/A
Received: N/A

Frist, William
416 Russell Senate Office Bldg.
Washington, DC 20510
Senator
Response Time: N/A
Received: N/A

Frost, Martin
U.S. House of Representatives
Washington, DC 20515
Politician
Response Time: N/A
Received: N/A

Frye, Soleil Moon
5555 Melrose Ave.
Hollywood, CA 90038-3197
Actress
Response Time: N/A
Received: N/A

Fuglesang, Christer
2101 NASA Rd. 1
Houston, TX 77058
Astronaut
Response Time: N/A
Received: N/A

Fuller, Jeff
1801 West Int'l. Spdwy. Blvd.
Daytona Beach, FL 32114
Auto Racing Personality
Response Time: 123 Days
Received: Signed Photo

Fuller, Victoria Alynette
9242 Beverly Blvd.
BH, CA 90210
Playboy Playmate
Response Time: N/A
Received: N/A

Fullerton, Charles G.
2101 NASA Rd. 1
Houston, TX 77058
Astronaut
Response Time: N/A
Received: N/A

Fulton, Eileen
1268 East 14th St.
Brooklyn, NY 11230
Actress
Response Time: N/A
Received: N/A

Fumero, David
56 West 66th St.
NY, NY 10023
Actor
Response Time: N/A
Received: N/A

Funicello, Annette
16102 Sandy Ln.
Encino, CA 91316
Actress
Response Time: 10 Days
Received: Signed Photo

Fuson, Stacy Marie
9242 Beverly Blvd.
BH, CA 90210
Playboy Playmate
Response Time: N/A
Received: N/A

Gabor, Zsa Zsa
1001 Bel Air Rd.
LA, CA 90077
Actress
Response Time: 381 Days
Received: Signed Photo

Gaither, Daniele
4000 Warner Blvd.
Burbank, CA 91522
Actress
Response Time: N/A
Received: N/A

Gallagher, David
c/o The WB Network, 3701 Oak St.
Bldg. 34R, Burbank, CA 91505
Actor
Response Time: N/A
Received: N/A

Gammon, James
5555 Melrose Ave.
Hollywood, CA 90038-3197
Actor
Response Time: N/A
Received: N/A

Gallagher, Kelly
9242 Beverly Blvd.
BH, CA 90210
Playboy Playmate
Response Time: N/A
Received: N/A

Ganske, Greg
U.S. House of Representatives
Washington, DC 20515
Politician
Response Time: N/A
Received: N/A

Gallagher, Peter
270 N. Canon Dr., Ste. 1064
BH, CA 90210
Actor
Response Time: 23 Days
Received: Signed Photo

Garces, Paula
51 W. 52 St.
NY, NY 10019
Actress
Response Time: N/A
Received: N/A

Gallagher
14984 Roan St.
W. Palm Beach, FL 33414
Comedian
Response Time: 12 Days
Received: Signed Photo

Gardner, Dale A.
2101 NASA Rd. 1
Houston, TX 77058
Astronaut
Response Time: N/A
Received: N/A

Gallegly, Elton
U.S. House of Representatives
Washington, DC 20515
Politician
Response Time: N/A
Received: N/A

Gardner, Guy S.
2101 NASA Rd. 1
Houston, TX 77058
Astronaut
Response Time: N/A
Received: N/A

Garfunkel, Art
9 E. 79th St.
NY, NY 10021
Singer
Response Time: 307 Days
Received: Signed Photo

Garlits, Don
13700 S.W. 16th Ave.
Ocala, FL 32676
NHRA Driver
Response Time: 8 Days
Received: Signed Photo

Garn, Jake
2000 Eagle Gate Tower
Salt Lake City, UT 84111
Astronaut, Politician
Response Time: 30 Days
Received: Signed Photo

Garneau, Marc
2101 NASA Rd. 1
Houston, TX 77058
Astronaut
Response Time: N/A
Received: N/A

Garner, James
33 Oakmont Ln.
LA, CA 90049
Actor
Response Time: 24 Days
Received: Signed Photo

Garr, Teri
9150 Wilshire Blvd. #350
BH, CA 90212
Actress
Response Time: 42 Days
Received: Signed Photo

Garrett, Maureen
51 W. 52 St.
NY, NY 10019
Actress
Response Time: N/A
Received: N/A

Garriott, Owen K.
2101 NASA Rd. 1
Houston, TX 77058
Astronaut
Response Time: N/A
Received: N/A

Gates, Bill
1 Microsoft Way
Redmond, WA 98052-8300
Founder of Microsoft
Response Time: 109 Days
Received: Signed Photo

Gaughan, Brendan
1801 West Int'l. Spdwy. Blvd.
Daytona Beach, FL 32114
Auto Racing Personality
Response Time: 93 Days
Received: Signed Photo

Gayheart, Rebecca
853 7th Ave. #9A
NY, NY 10019
Actress
Response Time: 246 Days
Received: Signed Photo

Gayle, Crystal
51 Music Sq. East
Nashville, TN 37203
Singer
Response Time: 11 Days
Received: Signed Photo

Gaynor, Gloria
P.O. Box 374
Fairview, NJ 07010
Singer
Response Time: 19 Days
Received: Signed Photo

Gaynor, Mitzi
6310 San Vincente Blvd., Ste. 330
LA, CA 90048
Actress, Model
Response Time: 379 Days
Received: Signed Photo I Sent

sentatives
15

le

Gemar, Charles D.
2101 NASA Rd. 1
Houston, TX 77058
Astronaut
Response Time: N/A
Received: N/A

Genet, Sabryn
7800 Beverly Blvd.
LA, CA 90036
Actress
Response Time: N/A
Received: N/A

George, Jason
5700 Wilshire, Ste. 575
LA, CA 90036
Actor
Response Time: N/A
Received: N/A

George, Phyllis
Two Ocean Way, Ste. 1000
Atlantic City, NJ 08401
Miss America 1971
Response Time: N/A
Received: N/A

Gephardt, Richard A.
U.S. House of Representatives
Washington, DC 20515
Politician
Response Time: N/A
Received: N/A

Gere, Richard
15030 Ventura Blvd.
Sherman Oaks, CA 91403
Actor
Response Time: 93 Days
Received: Signed Photo

Gere, Richard
9696 Culver Blvd., Ste. 203
Culver City, CA 90232
Actor
Response Time: 148 Days
Received: Signed Photo

Gering, Galen
4024 Radford Ave.
Studio City, CA 91604
Actor
Response Time: N/A
Received: N/A

Geringer, Jim
State Capitol Bldg., Room 124
Cheyenne, WY 82002
Governor
Response Time: N/A
Received: N/A

Gernhardt, Michael L.
2101 NASA Rd. 1
Houston, TX 77058
Astronaut
Response Time: N/A
Received: N/A

Getty, Estelle
10960 Wilshire Blvd. #2050
LA, CA 90024
Actress
Response Time: 9 Days
Received: Signed Photo

Getz, John
5555 Melrose Ave.
Hollywood, CA 90038-3197
Actor
Response Time: N/A
Received: N/A

Gibbons, Jim
U.S. House of Representatives
Washington, DC 20515
Politician
Response Time: N/A
Received: N/A

Gibbons, Peter
1801 West Int'l. Spdwy. Blvd.
Daytona Beach, FL 32114
Auto Racing Personality
Response Time: 81 Days
Received: Signed Photo

Gibbs, Coy
1801 West Int'l. Spdwy. Blvd.
Daytona Beach, FL 32114
Auto Racing Personality
Response Time: 83 Days
Received: Signed Photo

Gibbs, J.D.
1801 West Int'l. Spdwy. Blvd.
Daytona Beach, FL 32114
Auto Racing Personality
Response Time: 93 Days
Received: Signed Photo

Gibbs, Joe
13415 Reese Blvd. W.
Huntersville, NC 28078
Auto Racing Personality
Response Time: 61 Days
Received: Signed Photo

Gibbs, Joe
1801 West Int'l. Spdwy. Blvd.
Daytona Beach, FL 32114
Auto Racing Personality
Response Time: 359 Days
Received: Signed Photo

Gibbs, Tim
56 West 66th St.
NY, NY 10023
Actor
Response Time: N/A
Received: N/A

Gibson, Debbie
666 Fifth Ave. #302
NY, NY 10103
Singer
Response Time: N/A
Received: N/A

Gibson, Edward G.
2101 NASA Rd. 1
Houston, TX 77058
Astronaut
Response Time: N/A
Received: N/A

Gibson, Robert L.
2101 NASA Rd. 1
Houston, TX 77058
Astronaut
Response Time: N/A
Received: N/A

Gibson, Thomas
10201 West Pico Blvd.
Trailer 779, LA, CA 90035
Actor
Response Time: N/A
Received: N/A

Gifford, Kathie Lee
625 Madison Ave. #1200
NY, NY 10022
Television Personality
Response Time: 50 Days
Received: Signed Photo

Gil, Maria Luisa
9242 Beverly Blvd.
BH, CA 90210
Playboy Playmate
Response Time: N/A
Received: N/A

Gilchrest, Wayne T.
U.S. House of Representatives
Washington, DC 20515
Politician
Response Time: N/A
Received: N/A

Gill, Vince
1908 Wedgewood
Nashville, TN 37212
Singer
Response Time: 29 Days
Received: Signed Photo

Gill, Vince
P.O. Box 1407
White House, TN 37188
Singer
Response Time: N/A
Received: N/A

Gilley, Mickey
P.O. Box 1242
Pasadena, TX 77505
Singer
Response Time: 34 Days
Received: Signed Photo

Gillmor, Paul E.
U.S. House of Representatives
Washington, DC 20515
Politician
Response Time: N/A
Received: N/A

Gilman, Benjamin A.
U.S. House of Representatives
Washington, DC 20515
Politician
Response Time: N/A
Received: N/A

Gilmore III, James S.
State Capitol
Richmond, VA 23219
Governor
Response Time: N/A
Received: N/A

Gilpin, Peri
5555 Melrose Ave.
Hollywood, CA 90038-3197
Actor
Response Time: N/A
Received: N/A

Ginsburg, Nadya
4000 Warner Blvd.
Burbank, CA 91522
Actress
Response Time: N/A
Received: N/A

Ginsburg, Ruth Bader
Supreme Court of the United States
Washington, DC 20543
Supreme Court Justice
Response Time: 21 Days
Received: Signed Photo

Glanville, Jerry
1801 West Int'l. Spdwy. Blvd.
Daytona Beach, FL 32114
Auto Racing Personality
Response Time: 75 Days
Received: Signed Photo

Glazer, Eugene Robert
1230 Ave. of Americas
NY, NY 10020
Actor
Response Time: 76 Days
Received: Signed Photo

Gleason, Vanessa
9242 Beverly Blvd.
BH, CA 90210
Playboy Playmate
Response Time: N/A
Received: N/A

Glendening, Parris N.
State House, 100 State Circle
Annapolis, MD 21401
Governor
Response Time: N/A
Received: N/A

Glenn, John
2101 NASA Rd. 1
Houston, TX 77058
Astronaut, Politician
Response Time: N/A
Received: N/A

Glenn, John
1000 Utlin Ave.
Columbus, OH 43212
Astronaut, Politician
Response Time: 284 Days
Received: Signed Photo

Glenn, John
c/o Ohio State University
Columbus, OH 43210
Astronaut, Politician
Response Time: 284 Days
Received: Signed Photo

Glover, Danny
41 Sutter St. #1648
San Francisco, CA 94104-4903
Actor
Response Time: 280 Days
Received: Signed Photo

Goddard, Anna-Marie
9242 Beverly Blvd.
BH, CA 90210
Playboy Playmate
Response Time: N/A
Received: N/A

Godin, Tawny
Two Ocean Way, Ste. 1000
Atlantic City, NJ 08401
Miss America 1976
Response Time: N/A
Received: N/A

Godwin, Linda M.
2101 NASA Rd. 1
Houston, TX 77058
Astronaut
Response Time: N/A
Received: N/A

Gold, Missy
3500 W. Olive Ave. #1400
Burbank, CA 91505
Actress
Response Time: N/A
Received: N/A

Goldberg, Bill
5737 Kanan Rd. #1229
Agoura Hills, CA 91301
Wrestler
Response Time: 38 Days
Received: Signed Photo

Goldberg, Bill
2300 Bethelview Rd.
Ste. 110-405, Cumming, GA 30040
Wrestler
Response Time: 38 Days
Received: Signed Photo

Goldberg, Whoopi
5555 Melrose Ave. #114
LA, CA 90038-3149
Actress
Response Time: 214 Days
Received: Signed Photo

Goldsboro, Bobby
P.O. Box 5250
Ocala, FL 32678
Singer
Response Time: 11 Days
Received: Signed Photo

Gomez, Ian
300 Television Plaza, Bldg. 137
Burbank, CA 91505
Actor
Response Time: N/A
Received: N/A

Gonzalez, Charles A.
U.S. House of Representatives
Washington, DC 20515
Politician
Response Time: N/A
Received: N/A

Gonzalez, Nicholas
5555 Melrose Ave.
Hollywood, CA 90038-3197
Actor
Response Time: N/A
Received: N/A

Goode Jr., Virgil H.
U.S. House of Representatives
Washington, DC 20515
Politician
Response Time: N/A
Received: N/A

Gooding Jr., Cuba
5750 Wilshire Blvd. #580
LA, CA 90036
Actor
Response Time: 61 Days
Received: Signed Photo

Goodlatte, Bob
U.S. House of Representatives
Washington, DC 20515
Politician
Response Time: N/A
Received: N/A

Gordon Jr., Richard F.
2101 NASA Rd. 1
Houston, TX 77058
Astronaut
Response Time: N/A
Received: N/A

Gordon, Bart
U.S. House of Representatives
Washington, DC 20515
Politician
Response Time: N/A
Received: N/A

Gordon, Jeff
1801 West Int'l. Spdwy. Blvd.
Daytona Beach, FL 32114
Auto Racing Personality
Response Time: 412 Days
Received: Signed Photo

Gordon, Jeff
P.O. Box 9
Harrisburg, NC 28075
Auto Racing Personality
Response Time: 365 Days
Received: STC

Gordon, Robby
1801 West Int'l. Spdwy. Blvd.
Daytona Beach, FL 32114
Auto Racing Personality
Response Time: 112 Days
Received: Signed Photo

Gorham, Christopher
4000 Warner Blvd.
Burbank, CA 91522
Actor
Response Time: N/A
Received: N/A

Gorie, Dominic L.
2101 NASA Rd. 1
Houston, TX 77058
Astronaut
Response Time: N/A
Received: N/A

Gosdin, Vern
7904 Stallion Dr.
Nashville, TN 37221
Singer
Response Time: 39 Days
Received: Signed Photo

Goss, Porter J.
U.S. House of Representatives
Washington, DC 20515
Politician
Response Time: N/A
Received: N/A

Goulet, Robert
2700 E. Sunset Rd.
Las Vegas, NV 89120-3040
Singer, Entertainer
Response Time: 10 Days
Received: Signed Photo

Goulet, Robert
3110 Monte Rosa
Las Vegas, NV 89120
Singer, Entertainer
Response Time: 31 Days
Received: Signed Photo

Goutman, Chris
1268 East 14th St.
Brooklyn, NY 11230
Executive Producer
Response Time: N/A
Received: N/A

Grabe, Ronald J.
2101 NASA Rd. 1
Houston, TX 77058
Astronaut
Response Time: N/A
Received: N/A

Graham, Bob
524 Hart Senate Office Bldg.
Washington, DC 20510
Senator
Response Time: N/A
Received: N/A

Graham, Heather
28721 Timberland Ave.
Agoura Hills, CA 91301
Actress
Response Time: N/A
Received: N/A

Graham, Lauren
4000 Warner Blvd.
Burbank, CA 91522
Actress
Response Time: N/A
Received: N/A

Graham, Lindsey O.
U.S. House of Representatives
Washington, DC 20515
Politician
Response Time: N/A
Received: N/A

Grahn, Nancy Lee
4151 Prospect Ave.
LA, CA 90027
Actress
Response Time: N/A
Received: N/A

Gramm, Phil
370 Russell Senate Office Bldg.
Washington, DC 20510
Senator
Response Time: N/A
Received: N/A

Grammer, Kelsey
5555 Melrose Ave.
Hollywood, CA 90038-3197
Actor
Response Time: N/A
Received: N/A

Granger, Kay
U.S. House of Representatives
Washington, DC 20515
Politician
Response Time: N/A
Received: N/A

Grant, Amy
9 Music Sq. S., Ste. 214
Nashville, TN 37203
Singer
Response Time: 14 Days
Received: Signed Photo

Grant, Hugh
9830 Wilshire Blvd.
BH, CA 90212
Actor
Response Time: 31 Days
Received: Signed Photo

Grant, Hugh
c/o ICM, 76 Oxford St.
London W1N 0AX, England
Actor
Response Time: 31 Days
Received: Signed Photo

Grassle, Karen
3717 Edmond Ln.
Louisville, KY 40207
Actress
Response Time: 32 Days
Received: Signed Photo

Grassley, Chuck
135 Hart Senate Office Bldg.
Washington, DC 20510
Senator
Response Time: N/A
Received: N/A

Graveline, Duane E.
2101 NASA Rd. 1
Houston, TX 77058
Astronaut
Response Time: N/A
Received: N/A

Graver, Susan
c/o QVC, 1200 Wilson Dr.
West Chester, PA 19380
Clothing Designer
Response Time: N/A
Received: N/A

Graves, Bill
Capitol Bldg., 2nd Fl.
Topeka, KS 66612-1590
Governor
Response Time: N/A
Received: N/A

Graves, Sam
U.S. House of Representatives
Washington, DC 20515
Politician
Response Time: N/A
Received: N/A

Gray, Billy
19612 Grandview Dr.
Topanga, CA 90290
Actor
Response Time: N/A
Received: N/A

Great Divide, The
P.O. Box 1072
Stillwater, OK 74076
Music Group
Response Time: 109 Days
Received: Signed Photo

Green Day
5337 College Ave., Ste. 555
Oakland, CA 94628
Music Group
Response Time: 14 Days
Received: Signed Photo

Green, Bill
c/o Home Shopping Network
St. Petersburg, FL 33701
Home Shopping Network Host
Response Time: N/A
Received: N/A

Green, David
1801 West Int'l. Spdwy. Blvd.
Daytona Beach, FL 32114
Auto Racing Personality
Response Time: 91 Days
Received: Signed Photo

Green, Gene
U.S. House of Representatives
Washington, DC 20515
Politician
Response Time: N/A
Received: N/A

Green, Jeff
1801 West Int'l. Spdwy. Blvd.
Daytona Beach, FL 32114
Auto Racing Personality
Response Time: 98 Days
Received: Signed Photo

Green, Mark
1801 West Int'l. Spdwy. Blvd.
Daytona Beach, FL 32114
Auto Racing Personality
Response Time: 93 Days
Received: Signed Photo

Green, Mark
U.S. House of Representatives
Washington, DC 20515
Politician
Response Time: N/A
Received: N/A

Green, Seth
4000 Warner Blvd.
Burbank, CA 91522
Actor
Response Time: N/A
Received: N/A

Greenwood, James C.
U.S. House of Representatives
Washington, DC 20515
Politician
Response Time: N/A
Received: N/A

Greenwood, Lee
P.O. Box 6537
Sevierville, TN 37864
Singer
Response Time: N/A
Received: N/A

Gregg, Judd
393 Russell Senate Office Bldg.
Washington, DC 20510
Senator
Response Time: N/A
Received: N/A

Gregory, Frederick D.
2101 NASA Rd. 1
Houston, TX 77058
Astronaut
Response Time: N/A
Received: N/A

Gregory, William G.
2101 NASA Rd. 1
Houston, TX 77058
Astronaut
Response Time: N/A
Received: N/A

Gretzky, Wayne
650 N. Sepulveda
LA, CA 90049
Hockey Player
Response Time: 71 Days
Received: Signed Photo

Grieco, Richard
95 Public Square, Room 304
Watertown, NY 13601
Actor
Response Time: 39 Days
Received: Signed Photo

Griffin, Merv
9876 Wilshire Blvd.
BH, CA 90210
Game Show Host
Response Time: 57 Days
Received: Signed Photo

Griggs, Andy
P.O. Box 120835
Nashville, TN 37212
Singer
Response Time: 24 Days
Received: Signed Photo

Grimes, Camryn
7800 Beverly Blvd.
LA, CA 90036
Actress
Response Time: N/A
Received: N/A

Grissom, Steve
1801 West Int'l. Spdwy. Blvd.
Daytona Beach, FL 32114
Auto Racing Personality
Response Time: 118 Days
Received: Signed Photo

Grossman, Leslie
4000 Warner Blvd.
Burbank, CA 91522
Actress
Response Time: N/A
Received: N/A

Grubb, Kevin
1801 West Int'l. Spdwy. Blvd.
Daytona Beach, FL 32114
Auto Racing Personality
Response Time: 120 Days
Received: Signed Photo

Grubb, Wayne
1801 West Int'l. Spdwy. Blvd.
Daytona Beach, FL 32114
Auto Racing Personality
Response Time: 115 Days
Received: Signed Photo

Grucci Jr., Felix J.
U.S. House of Representatives
Washington, DC 20515
Politician
Response Time: N/A
Received: N/A

Grunberg, Greg
4000 Warner Blvd.
Burbank, CA 91522
Actor
Response Time: N/A
Received: N/A

Grunsfeld, John M.
2101 NASA Rd. 1
Houston, TX 77058
Astronaut
Response Time: N/A
Received: N/A

Guidoni, Umberto
2101 NASA Rd. 1
Houston, TX 77058
Astronaut
Response Time: N/A
Received: N/A

Guinn, Kenny C.
State Capitol
Carson City, NV 89710
Governor
Response Time: N/A
Received: N/A

Gunn, Jannet
1230 Ave. of Americas
NY, NY 10020
Actress
Response Time: N/A
Received: N/A

Gutierrez, Luis V.
U.S. House of Representatives
Washington, DC 20515
Politician
Response Time: N/A
Received: N/A

Gutierrez, Sidney M.
2101 NASA Rd. 1
Houston, TX 77058
Astronaut
Response Time: N/A
Received: N/A

Gutknecht, Gil
U.S. House of Representatives
Washington, DC 20515
Politician
Response Time: N/A
Received: N/A

Guy, Jasmine
21243 Ventura Blvd. #101
Woodland Hills, CA 91362
Actress
Response Time: 150 Days
Received: Signed Photo

G'Vera, Ivan
3000 W. Alameda Ave.
Burbank, CA 91523
Actor
Response Time: N/A
Received: N/A

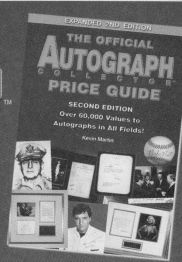
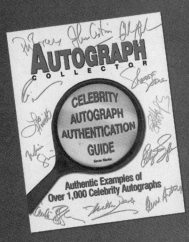

Hackett, Buddy
800 Whittier Dr.
BH, CA 90210
Actor, Comedian
Response Time: 14 Days
Received: Signed Photo

Hackman, Gene
118 S. Beverly Dr. #1201
BH, CA 90212
Actor
Response Time: N/A
Received: N/A

Hadfield, Chris A.
2101 NASA Rd. 1
Houston, TX 77058
Astronaut
Response Time: N/A
Received: N/A

Hagman, Larry
9950 Sulpher Mountain Rd.
Ojai, CA 93023
Actor
Response Time: 24 Days
Received: Signed Photo

Hagel, Charles
346 Russell Senate Office Bldg.
Washington, DC 20510
Senator
Response Time: N/A
Received: N/A

Haig Jr., Alexander
1155 15th St. N.W. #800
Washington, DC 20005
Politician
Response Time: 43 Days
Received: SIC

Haggard, Merle
3009 Easy St.
Sevierville, TN 37862
Singer
Response Time: N/A
Received: N/A

Haise Jr., Fred W.
2101 NASA Rd. 1
Houston, TX 77058
Astronaut
Response Time: N/A
Received: N/A

Haggard, Merle
2054 New Era Rd. #3
Sevierville, TN 37862
Singer
Response Time: 11 Days
Received: Signed Photo

Hale, Ron
4151 Prospect Ave.
LA, CA 90027
Actor
Response Time: N/A
Received: N/A

Haggerty, Dan
5812 Comanche Ave.
Woodland Hills, CA 91367
Actor
Response Time: 110 Days
Received: Signed Photo

Hall, Bruce Michael
4024 Radford Ave.
Studio City, CA 91604
Actor
Response Time: N/A
Received: N/A

Hall, Deidre
3000 W. Alameda Ave.
Burbank, CA 91523
Actress
Response Time: N/A
Received: N/A

Hall, Irma P.
5555 Melrose Ave.
Hollywood, CA 90038-3197
Actress
Response Time: N/A
Received: N/A

Hall, Ralph M.
U.S. House of Representatives
Washington, DC 20515
Politician
Response Time: N/A
Received: N/A

Hall, Tony P.
U.S. House of Representatives
Washington, DC 20515
Politician
Response Time: N/A
Received: N/A

Halliwell, Geri
19-21 Mortimer St.
London W1N 8DX, England
Singer
Response Time: 24 Days
Received: Signed Photo

Halsell Jr., James D.
2101 NASA Rd. 1
Houston, TX 77058
Astronaut
Response Time: N/A
Received: N/A

Ham, Kenneth T.
2101 NASA Rd. 1
Houston, TX 77058
Astronaut
Response Time: N/A
Received: N/A

Hamill, Mark
P.O. Box 124
Malibu, CA 90265
Actor
Response Time: 303 Days
Received: Signed Photo

Hamilton Jr., Bobby
1801 West Int'l. Spdwy. Blvd.
Daytona Beach, FL 32114
Auto Racing Personality
Response Time: 92 Days
Received: Signed Photo

Hamilton, Bobby
1801 West Int'l. Spdwy. Blvd.
Daytona Beach, FL 32114
Auto Racing Personality
Response Time: 103 Days
Received: Signed Photo

Hamilton, George
139 S. Beverly Dr. #330
BH, CA 90212
Actor
Response Time: 18 Days
Received: Signed Photo

Hamilton, Lisa Gay
10201 West Pico Blvd.
LA, CA 90035
Actress
Response Time: N/A
Received: N/A

Hamilton, Marcus
P.O. Box 1997
Monterey, CA 93942
Cartoonist
Response Time: 27 Days
Received: Signed Photo

Hamilton, Wendy
9242 Beverly Blvd.
BH, CA 90210
Playboy Playmate
Response Time: N/A
Received: N/A

Hamm, Mia
1801 S. Prairie Ave.
Chicago, IL 60616
Soccer Player
Response Time: N/A
Received: N/A

Hammond Jr., L. Blaine
2101 NASA Rd. 1
Houston, TX 77058
Astronaut
Response Time: N/A
Received: N/A

Hanks, Colin
4000 Warner Blvd.
Burbank, CA 91522
Actor
Response Time: N/A
Received: N/A

Hanna, Jack
999 Riverside Dr.
Box 400, Powell, OH 43065
Animal Expert
Response Time: 11 Days
Received: Signed Photo

Hanna, William "Bill"
15303 Ventura Blvd. #1400
Sherman Oaks, CA 91403
Co-Owner, Hanna Barbera
Response Time: 17 Days
Received: Signed Photo

Hannigan, Alyson
4000 Warner Blvd.
Burbank, CA 91522
Actress
Response Time: N/A
Received: N/A

Hansen, James V.
U.S. House of Representatives
Washington, DC 20515
Politician
Response Time: N/A
Received: N/A

Hansen, Peter
4151 Prospect Ave.
LA, CA 90027
Actor
Response Time: N/A
Received: N/A

Harbaugh, Gregory J.
2101 NASA Rd. 1
Houston, TX 77058
Astronaut
Response Time: N/A
Received: N/A

Harbour, Vanita
4151 Prospect Ave.
LA, CA 90027
Actress
Response Time: N/A
Received: N/A

Hardin, Melora
1230 Ave. of Americas
NY, NY 10020
Actress
Response Time: N/A
Received: N/A

Hargitay, Mariska
1230 Ave. of Americas
NY, NY 10020
Actress
Response Time: N/A
Received: N/A

Harkin, Tom
731 Hart Senate Office Bldg.
Washington, DC 20510
Senator
Response Time: N/A
Received: N/A

Harlow, Jade
4024 Radford Ave.
Studio City, CA 91604
Actress
Response Time: N/A
Received: N/A

Harman, Jane
U.S. House of Representatives
Washington, DC 20515
Politician
Response Time: N/A
Received: N/A

Harmon, Angie
1230 Ave. of Americas
NY, NY 10020
Actress
Response Time: N/A
Received: N/A

Harmon, Winsor
7800 Beverly Blvd.
LA, CA 90036
Actor
Response Time: N/A
Received: N/A

Harney, Corinna
9242 Beverly Blvd.
BH, CA 90210
Playboy Playmate
Response Time: N/A
Received: N/A

Harris Jr., Bernard A.
2101 NASA Rd. 1
Houston, TX 77058
Astronaut
Response Time: N/A
Received: N/A

Harris, Emmylou
P.O. Box 158568
Nashville, TN 37215
Singer
Response Time: 72 Days
Received: Signed Photo

Harris, Steve
10201 West Pico Blvd.
LA, CA 90035
Actor
Response Time: N/A
Received: N/A

Harrison, Schae
7800 Beverly Blvd.
LA, CA 90036
Actress
Response Time: N/A
Received: N/A

Hart, Holly Joan
9242 Beverly Blvd.
BH, CA 90210
Playboy Playmate
Response Time: N/A
Received: N/A

Hart, Melissa A.
U.S. House of Representatives
Washington, DC 20515
Politician
Response Time: N/A
Received: N/A

Hart, Melissa Joan
5555 Melrose Ave.
Hollywood, CA 90038-3197
Actress
Response Time: N/A
Received: N/A

Hart, Terry J.
2101 NASA Rd. 1
Houston, TX 77058
Astronaut
Response Time: N/A
Received: N/A

Hartsfield Jr., Henry W.
2101 NASA Rd. 1
Houston, TX 77058
Astronaut
Response Time: N/A
Received: N/A

Harvey, Steve
4000 Warner Blvd.
Burbank, CA 91522
Actor
Response Time: N/A
Received: N/A

Harvick, Kevin
1801 West Int'l. Spdwy. Blvd.
Daytona Beach, FL 32114
Auto Racing Personality
Response Time: 156 Days
Received: Signed Photo

Hasselhoff, David
c/o Baywatch Productions
510-18th Ave., Honolulu, HI 96816
Actor
Response Time: N/A
Received: N/A

Hastert, J. Dennis
U.S. House of Representatives
Washington, DC 20515
Politician
Response Time: N/A
Received: N/A

Hastings, Alcee L.
U.S. House of Representatives
Washington, DC 20515
Politician
Response Time: N/A
Received: N/A

Hastings, Doc
U.S. House of Representatives
Washington, DC 20515
Politician
Response Time: N/A
Received: N/A

Hastings, Don
1268 East 14th St.
Brooklyn, NY 11230
Actor
Response Time: N/A
Received: N/A

Hatch, Orrin
131 Dirksen Senate Office Bldg.
Washington, DC 20510
Senator
Response Time: N/A
Received: N/A

Hatch, Rich
21 Annandale Rd.
Newport, RI 02840
Survivor - $1,000,000 Winner
Response Time: N/A
Received: N/A

Hatcher, Teri
151 El Camino Dr.
BH, CA 90212
Actress
Response Time: 365 Days
Received: Signed Photo

Hatcher, Teri
955 S. Carrillo Dr. #300
LA, CA 90048
Actress
Response Time: N/A
Received: N/A

Hauck, Frederick H.
2101 NASA Rd. 1
Houston, TX 77058
Astronaut
Response Time: N/A
Received: N/A

Hauer, Rutger
151 El Camino Dr.
BH, CA 90212
Actor
Response Time: 20 Days
Received: Signed Photo

Hawkins, Sophie B.
1325 Ave. of the Stars
NY, NY 10019
Singer
Response Time: N/A
Received: N/A

Hawley, Steven A.
2101 NASA Rd. 1
Houston, TX 77058
Astronaut
Response Time: N/A
Received: N/A

Hayes, Bill
3000 W. Alameda Ave.
Burbank, CA 91523
Actor
Response Time: N/A
Received: N/A

Hayes, Reggie
5555 Melrose Ave.
Hollywood, CA 90038-3197
Actor
Response Time: N/A
Received: N/A

Hayes, Robin
U.S. House of Representatives
Washington, DC 20515
Politician
Response Time: N/A
Received: N/A

Hayes, Susan
3000 W. Alameda Ave.
Burbank, CA 91523
Actress
Response Time: N/A
Received: N/A

Hays, Kathryn
1268 East 14th St.
Brooklyn, NY 11230
Actress
Response Time: N/A
Received: N/A

Hayworth, J. D.
U.S. House of Representatives
Washington, DC 20515
Politician
Response Time: N/A
Received: N/A

Head, Anthony Stewart
4000 Warner Blvd.
Burbank, CA 91522
Actor
Response Time: N/A
Received: N/A

Heatherly, Eric
P.O. Box 24895
Chattanooga, TN 37422-4895
Singer
Response Time: 12 Days
Received: Signed Photo

Hedeman, Tuff
P.O. Box 224
Morgan Mill, TX 76465
Bullrider
Response Time: 31 Days
Received: Signed Photo

Hedren, Tippi
6867 Soledad Canyon Rd.
Acton, CA 93510
Actress
Response Time: 17 Days
Received: Signed Photo

Hefley, Joel
U.S. House of Representatives
Washington, DC 20515
Politician
Response Time: N/A
Received: N/A

Heft, Robert
4098 Green St.
Saginaw, MI 48603
Designer of current U.S. Flag
Response Time: 10 Days
Received: SIC

Heigl, Katherine
4000 Warner Blvd.
Burbank, CA 91522
Actress
Response Time: N/A
Received: N/A

Helmond, Katherine
2035 Davies Way
LA, CA 90046
Actress
Response Time: 200 Days
Received: Signed Photo

Helms, Jesse
403 Dirksen Senate Office Bldg.
Washington, DC 20510
Senator
Response Time: N/A
Received: N/A

Helms, Susan J.
2101 NASA Rd. 1
Houston, TX 77058
Astronaut
Response Time: N/A
Received: N/A

Hemingway, Mariel
P.O. Box 2249
Ketchum, ID 83340
Actress
Response Time: N/A
Received: N/A

Henderson, Florence
P.O. Box 11295
Marina Del Rey, CA 90295
Actress
Response Time: 16 Days
Received: Signed Photo

Hendrick, Ricky
1801 West Int'l. Spdwy. Blvd.
Daytona Beach, FL 32114
Auto Racing Personality
Response Time: 291 Days
Received: Signed Photo

Hendrickson, Benjamin
1268 East 14th St.
Brooklyn, NY 11230
Actor
Response Time: N/A
Received: N/A

Henricks, Terence T.
2101 NASA Rd. 1
Houston, TX 77058
Astronaut
Response Time: N/A
Received: N/A

Hensel, Karen
7800 Beverly Blvd.
LA, CA 90036
Actress
Response Time: N/A
Received: N/A

Hensley, Jimmy
1801 West Int'l. Spdwy. Blvd.
Daytona Beach, FL 32114
Auto Racing Personality
Response Time: 101 Days
Received: Signed Photo

Hensley, John C.
34-12 36th St.
Astoria, NY 11106
Actor
Response Time: N/A
Received: N/A

Hensley, Jon
1268 East 14th St.
Brooklyn, NY 11230
Actor
Response Time: N/A
Received: N/A

Hensley, Kelley Menighan
1268 East 14th St.
Brooklyn, NY 11230
Actress
Response Time: N/A
Received: N/A

Henson, Darrin Dewitt
5555 Melrose Ave.
Hollywood, CA 90038-3197
Actor
Response Time: N/A
Received: N/A

Hepcat, Harry
53 Old Northport Rd.
Huntington, NY 11743
Singer
Response Time: N/A
Received: N/A

Herbst, Rebecca
4151 Prospect Ave.
LA, CA 90027
Actress
Response Time: N/A
Received: N/A

Herger, Wally
U.S. House of Representatives
Washington, DC 20515
Politician
Response Time: N/A
Received: N/A

Herlie, Eileen
320 West 66th St.
NY, NY 10023
Actress
Response Time: N/A
Received: N/A

Herndon, Ty
P.O. Box 850176
Richardson, TX 75085
Singer
Response Time: N/A
Received: N/A

Herring, Lynn
4151 Prospect Ave.
LA, CA 90027
Actress
Response Time: N/A
Received: N/A

Herrington, John B.
2101 NASA Rd. 1
Houston, TX 77058
Astronaut
Response Time: N/A
Received: N/A

Herrmann, Edward
4000 Warner Blvd.
Burbank, CA 91522
Actor
Response Time: N/A
Received: N/A

Hershey, Erin
4151 Prospect Ave.
LA, CA 90027
Actress
Response Time: N/A
Received: N/A

Heston, Charlton
2859 Coldwater Canyon
BH, CA 90210
Actor
Response Time: 14 Days
Received: Signed Photo

Hickland, Catherine
56 West 66th St.
NY, NY 10023
Actress
Response Time: N/A
Received: N/A

Hicks, Catherine
15422 Brownwood Ln.
LA, CA 90077
Actress
Response Time: 93 Days
Received: Signed Photo

Hicks, Catherine
c/o The WB Network, 3701 Oak St.
Bldg. 34R, Burbank, CA 91505
Actress
Response Time: N/A
Received: N/A

Hieb, Richard J.
2101 NASA Rd. 1
Houston, TX 77058
Astronaut
Response Time: N/A
Received: N/A

Higginbotham, Joan E.
2101 NASA Rd. 1
Houston, TX 77058
Astronaut
Response Time: N/A
Received: N/A

Hilfiger, Tommy
25 W. 39th St.
NY, NY 10018
Designer
Response Time: 22 Days
Received: Signed Photo

Hilfiger, Tommy
485 Fifth Ave.
NY, NY 10017
Designer
Response Time: 22 Days
Received: Signed Photo

Hill, Baron P.
U.S. House of Representatives
Washington, DC 20515
Politician
Response Time: N/A
Received: N/A

Hill, Dule
4000 Warner Blvd.
Burbank, CA 91522
Actor
Response Time: N/A
Received: N/A

Hill, Faith
P.O. Box 24266
Nashville, TN 37202
Singer
Response Time: 22 Days
Received: Signed Photo

Hill, Valerie Parr
c/o QVC, 1200 Wilson Dr.
West Chester, PA 19380
Decorating Expert
Response Time: N/A
Received: N/A

Hilleary, Van
U.S. House of Representatives
Washington, DC 20515
Politician
Response Time: N/A
Received: N/A

Hilliard, Earl F.
U.S. House of Representatives
Washington, DC 20515
Politician
Response Time: N/A
Received: N/A

Hilliard, Patricia C.
2101 NASA Rd. 1
Houston, TX 77058
Astronaut
Response Time: N/A
Received: N/A

Hillin, Bobby
1801 West Int'l. Spdwy. Blvd.
Daytona Beach, FL 32114
Auto Racing Personality
Response Time: 81 Days
Received: Signed Photo

Hilmers, David C.
2101 NASA Rd. 1
Houston, TX 77058
Astronaut
Response Time: N/A
Received: N/A

Hinchey, Maurice D.
U.S. House of Representatives
Washington, DC 20515
Politician
Response Time: N/A
Received: N/A

Hinkle, Marin
8660 Hayden Place
Culver City, CA 90232
Actress
Response Time: N/A
Received: N/A

Hinojosa, Ruben
U.S. House of Representatives
Washington, DC 20515
Politician
Response Time: N/A
Received: N/A

Hire, Kathryn P.
2101 NASA Rd. 1
Houston, TX 77058
Astronaut
Response Time: N/A
Received: N/A

Hirsch, Judd
10345 W. Olympic Blvd.
LA, CA 90064
Actor
Response Time: 17 Days
Received: Signed Photo

Hirschfeld, Al
122 E. 95th St.
NY, NY 10128-1705
Cartoonist
Response Time: 7 Days
Received: SIC

Ho, Don
Box 90039
Honolulu, HI 96035
Singer
Response Time: 61 Days
Received: Signed Photo

Hobaugh, Charles O.
2101 NASA Rd. 1
Houston, TX 77058
Astronaut
Response Time: N/A
Received: N/A

Hobson, David L.
U.S. House of Representatives
Washington, DC 20515
Politician
Response Time: N/A
Received: N/A

Hodge, Kate
5555 Melrose Ave.
Hollywood, CA 90038-3197
Actress
Response Time: N/A
Received: N/A

Hodges, Jim
P.O. Box 11829
Columbia, SC 29211
Governor
Response Time: N/A
Received: N/A

Hoeffel, Joseph M.
U.S. House of Representatives
Washington, DC 20515
Politician
Response Time: N/A
Received: N/A

Hoekstra, Peter
U.S. House of Representatives
Washington, DC 20515
Politician
Response Time: N/A
Received: N/A

Hoeven, John
600 E. Boulevard Ave.
Bismarck, ND 58505-0001
Governor
Response Time: N/A
Received: N/A

Hoffman, Dustin
111 W. 40th St. #20
NY, NY 10018
Actor
Response Time: 42 Days
Received: Signed Photo I Sent

Hoffman, Dustin
1926 Broadway #305
NY, NY 10023-6915
Actor
Response Time: 42 Days
Received: Signed Photo I Sent

Hoffman, Jeffrey A.
2101 NASA Rd. 1
Houston, TX 77058
Astronaut
Response Time: N/A
Received: N/A

Hogan, Hulk
4505 Morella Ave.
Valley Village, CA 91607
Actor, Wrestler
Response Time: 25 Days
Received: Signed Photo

Hogestyn, Drake
3000 W. Alameda Ave.
Burbank, CA 91523
Actor
Response Time: N/A
Received: N/A

Holden, Tim
U.S. House of Representatives
Washington, DC 20515
Politician
Response Time: N/A
Received: N/A

Holland, Sean
5555 Melrose Ave.
Hollywood, CA 90038-3197
Actor
Response Time: N/A
Received: N/A

Holland, Tara Dawn
Two Ocean Way, Ste. 1000
Atlantic City, NJ 08401
Miss America 1997
Response Time: N/A
Received: N/A

Hollenberg, Rich
c/o Home Shopping Network
St. Petersburg, FL 33701
Home Shopping Network Host
Response Time: N/A
Received: N/A

Holliday, Melissa Deanne
9242 Beverly Blvd.
BH, CA 90210
Playboy Playmate
Response Time: N/A
Received: N/A

Hollings, Ernest
125 Russell Senate Office Bldg.
Washington, DC 20510
Senator
Response Time: N/A
Received: N/A

Holmes, Katie
4000 Warner Blvd.
Burbank, CA 91522
Actress
Response Time: N/A
Received: N/A

Holmes, Scott
1268 East 14th St.
Brooklyn, NY 11230
Actor
Response Time: N/A
Received: N/A

Holmquest, Donald L.
2101 NASA Rd. 1
Houston, TX 77058
Astronaut
Response Time: N/A
Received: N/A

Holt, Rush D.
U.S. House of Representatives
Washington, DC 20515
Politician
Response Time: N/A
Received: N/A

Holyfield, Evander
794 Highway #279
Fairburn, GA 30213
Boxer
Response Time: 136 Days
Received: Unsigned Photo

Holyfield, Evander
P.O. Box 1385
Red Oak, GA 30272
Boxer
Response Time: N/A
Received: N/A

Honda, Michael M.
U.S. House of Representatives
Washington, DC 20515
Politician
Response Time: N/A
Received: N/A

Hooley, Darlene
U.S. House of Representatives
Washington, DC 20515
Politician
Response Time: N/A
Received: N/A

Hootie & The Blowfish
P.O. Box 5656
Columbia, SC 29250
Music Group
Response Time: 20 Days
Received: Signed Photo

Hope, Amanda
9242 Beverly Blvd.
BH, CA 90210
Playboy Playmate
Response Time: N/A
Received: N/A

Hope, Bob
10346 Moorpark St.
N. Hollywood, CA 91602
Actor, Comedian
Response Time: 41 Days
Received: Signed Photo

Hope, Bob
3808 W. Riverside Dr., Ste. 100
Burbank, CA 91505
Actor, Comedian
Response Time: N/A
Received: N/A

Hopkins, Anthony
7 High Park Rd., Richmond
Surrey TW9 3BL, United Kingdom
Actor
Response Time: 90 Days
Received: Signed Photo

Horn, Chris
1801 West Int'l. Spdwy. Blvd.
Daytona Beach, FL 32114
Auto Racing Personality
Response Time: 70 Days
Received: Signed Photo

Horn, Stephen
U.S. House of Representatives
Washington, DC 20515
Politician
Response Time: N/A
Received: N/A

Hornaday, Ron
1801 West Int'l. Spdwy. Blvd.
Daytona Beach, FL 32114
Auto Racing Personality
Response Time: 248 Days
Received: Signed Photo

Horne, Lena
23 E. 74th St.
NY, NY 10021
Actress, Singer
Response Time: 10 Days
Received: Signed Photo

Hornsby, Bruce
P.O. Box 3545
Williamsburg, VA 23187
Singer
Response Time: 270 Days
Received: Signed Photo

Hornsby, Russell
500 S. Buena Vista St.
Burbank, CA 91521
Actor
Response Time: N/A
Received: N/A

Horowitz, Scott J.
2101 NASA Rd. 1
Houston, TX 77058
Astronaut
Response Time: N/A
Received: N/A

Horton, Peter
500 S. Buena Vista St.
Burbank, CA 91521
Actor
Response Time: N/A
Received: N/A

Hostetler, Jeff
10400 Little Paxutent Pkwy.
Columbia, MD 21044
Football Player
Response Time: 18 Days
Received: Signed Photo

Hostettler, John N.
U.S. House of Representatives
Washington, DC 20515
Politician
Response Time: N/A
Received: N/A

Houghton, Amo
U.S. House of Representatives
Washington, DC 20515
Politician
Response Time: N/A
Received: N/A

Houston, Andy
1801 West Int'l. Spdwy. Blvd.
Daytona Beach, FL 32114
Auto Racing Personality
Response Time: 197 Days
Received: Signed Photo

Houston, Anjelica
74 Market St.
Venice, CA 90291-3603
Actress
Response Time: 12 Days
Received: Signed Photo

Houston, Marty
1801 West Int'l. Spdwy. Blvd.
Daytona Beach, FL 32114
Auto Racing Personality
Response Time: 72 Days
Received: Signed Photo

Howard, Jan
2804 Opryland Dr.
Nashville, TN 37214
Singer
Response Time: N/A
Received: N/A

Howard, Kyle
4000 Warner Blvd.
Burbank, CA 91522
Actor
Response Time: N/A
Received: N/A

Howard, Shawn Michael
4000 Warner Blvd.
Burbank, CA 91522
Actor
Response Time: N/A
Received: N/A

Howard, Traylor
10201 West Pico Blvd.
LA, CA 90035
Actress
Response Time: N/A
Received: N/A

Howarth, Roger
56 West 66th St.
NY, NY 10023
Actor
Response Time: N/A
Received: N/A

Howe, Gordie
12900 Hall Rd., Ste. 300
Sterling Heights, MI 48313
Hockey Player
Response Time: 74 Days
Received: STC

Hoyer, Steny H.
U.S. House of Representatives
Washington, DC 20515
Politician
Response Time: N/A
Received: N/A

Hubbard, Elizabeth
1268 East 14th St.
Brooklyn, NY 11230
Actress
Response Time: N/A
Received: N/A

Huber, Liza
4024 Radford Ave.
Studio City, CA 91604
Actress
Response Time: N/A
Received: N/A

Hubert, Tom
1801 West Int'l. Spdwy. Blvd.
Daytona Beach, FL 32114
Auto Racing Personality
Response Time: 67 Days
Received: Signed Photo

Huckabee, Mike
250 State Capitol
Little Rock, AR 72201
Governor
Response Time: N/A
Received: N/A

Hugh, Sara
320 West 66th St.
NY, NY 10023
Actress
Response Time: N/A
Received: N/A

Hughes, Dan
c/o QVC, 1200 Wilson Dr.
West Chester, PA 19380
QVC Host
Response Time: N/A
Received: N/A

Hughes, Finola
320 West 66th St.
NY, NY 10023
Actress
Response Time: N/A
Received: N/A

Hull, Jane Dee
State Capitol
Phoenix, AZ 85007
Governor
Response Time: N/A
Received: N/A

Hulshof, Kenny C.
U.S. House of Representatives
Washington, DC 20515
Politician
Response Time: N/A
Received: N/A

Hunt Jr., James B.
State Capitol, 116 West Jones St.
Raleigh, NC 27603-8001
Governor
Response Time: N/A
Received: N/A

Hunter, Duncan
U.S. House of Representatives
Washington, DC 20515
Politician
Response Time: N/A
Received: N/A

Hunter, Kim
42 Commerce St.
NY, NY 10014-3711
Actress
Response Time: 15 Days
Received: Signed Photo

Hupp, Jana Marie
5555 Melrose Ave.
Hollywood, CA 90038-3197
Actress
Response Time: N/A
Received: N/A

Hurd, Michelle
1230 Ave. of Americas
NY, NY 10020
Actress
Response Time: N/A
Received: N/A

Hurley, Elizabeth
3 Cromwell Place
London SW3 2JE, England
Actress, Model
Response Time: 37 Days
Received: Signed Photo

Husband, Rick D.
2101 NASA Rd. 1
Houston, TX 77058
Astronaut
Response Time: N/A
Received: N/A

Huss, Toby
4000 Warner Blvd.
Burbank, CA 91522
Actor
Response Time: N/A
Received: N/A

Huston, Anjelica
74 Market St.
Venice, CA 90291
Actress
Response Time: N/A
Received: N/A

Huston, Anjelica
8942 Wilshire Blvd.
BH, CA 90211
Actress
Response Time: N/A
Received: N/A

Hutchins, Colleen
Two Ocean Way, Ste. 1000
Atlantic City, NJ 08401
Miss America 1952
Response Time: N/A
Received: N/A

Hutchinson, Asa
U.S. House of Representatives
Washington, DC 20515
Politician
Response Time: N/A
Received: N/A

Hutchinson, Tim
239 Dirksen Senate Office Bldg.
Washington, DC 20510
Senator
Response Time: N/A
Received: N/A

Hutchison, Kay Bailey
284 Russell Senate Office Bldg.
Washington, DC 20510
Senator
Response Time: N/A
Received: N/A

Hyde, Henry J.
U.S. House of Representatives
Washington, DC 20515
Politician
Response Time: N/A
Received: N/A

Hyde, James
4024 Radford Ave.
Studio City, CA 91604
Actor
Response Time: N/A
Received: N/A

Hyder, Brian
c/o Home Shopping Network
St. Petersburg, FL 33701
Home Shopping Network Host
Response Time: N/A
Received: N/A

Ice-T
1230 Ave. of Americas
NY, NY 10020
Actor
Response Time: N/A
Received: N/A

Iman
111 East 22nd St. #200
NY, NY 10010
Model, Singer
Response Time: 35 Days
Received: Signed Photo

Indigo Girls, The
315 West Ponce De Leon Ave.
Decatur, GA 30030
Music Duo
Response Time: 25 Days
Received: Signed Photo

Ingle, John
4151 Prospect Ave.
LA, CA 90027
Actor
Response Time: N/A
Received: N/A

Inglebright, Jim
1801 West Int'l. Spdwy. Blvd.
Daytona Beach, FL 32114
Auto Racing Personality
Response Time: 71 Days
Received: Signed Photo

Inhofe, James
453 Russell Senate Office Bldg.
Washington, DC 20510
Senator
Response Time: N/A
Received: N/A

Innes, Laura
4000 Warner Blvd.
Burbank, CA 91522
Actress
Response Time: N/A
Received: N/A

Inouye, Daniel
722 Hart Senate Office Bldg.
Washington, DC 20510
Senator
Response Time: N/A
Received: N/A

Inslee, Jay
U.S. House of Representatives
Washington, DC 20515
Politician
Response Time: N/A
Received: N/A

Ireland, Kathy
1900 Ave. of the Stars #739
LA, CA 90067
Model
Response Time: N/A
Received: N/A

Irizarry, Vincent
320 West 66th St.
NY, NY 10023
Actor
Response Time: N/A
Received: N/A

Irons, Jeremy
9830 Wilshire Blvd.
BH, CA 90212
Actor
Response Time: 194 Days
Received: Signed Photo

Irvan, Ernie
703 Performance Rd.
Mooresville, NC 28115
Auto Racing Personality
Response Time: 6 Days
Received: Signed Photo

Irvan, Ernie
1801 West Int'l. Spdwy. Blvd.
Daytona Beach, FL 32114
Auto Racing Personality
Response Time: 65 Days
Received: Signed Photo

Irwin, Hale
10726 Manchester Rd., Ste. 212
St. Louis, MO 63122-1320
Golfer
Response Time: 81 Days
Received: Signed Photo

Irwin, Hale
9909 Clayton Rd., Ste. 209
St. Louis, MO 63124-1120
Golfer
Response Time: N/A
Received: N/A

Irwin, Steve
Australia Zoo, Beerwah
Queensland 4519, Australia
Animal Expert - aka Crocodile Hunter
Response Time: N/A
Received: N/A

Irwin, Terri
c/o Australia Zoo, Beerwah
Queensland 4519, Australia
Animal Expert - Wife of Steve Irwin
Response Time: N/A
Received: N/A

Isakson, Johnny
U.S. House of Representatives
Washington, DC 20515
Politician
Response Time: N/A
Received: N/A

Israel, Steve
U.S. House of Representatives
Washington, DC 20515
Politician
Response Time: N/A
Received: N/A

Issa, Darrell E.
U.S. House of Representatives
Washington, DC 20515
Politician
Response Time: N/A
Received: N/A

Istook Jr., Ernest J.
U.S. House of Representatives
Washington, DC 20515
Politician
Response Time: N/A
Received: N/A

Ivins, Marsha S.
2101 NASA Rd. 1
Houston, TX 77058
Astronaut
Response Time: N/A
Received: N/A

Jackson Jr., Jesse L.
U.S. House of Representatives
Washington, DC 20515
Politician
Response Time: N/A
Received: N/A

Jackson, Alan
P.O. Box 121945
Nashville, TN 37212
Singer
Response Time: 78 Days
Received: Signed Photo

Jackson, Jesse
400-I Street N.W.
Washington, DC 20001
Politician
Response Time: 26 Days
Received: Signed Photo

Jackson, John M.
5555 Melrose Ave.
Hollywood, CA 90038-3197
Actor
Response Time: N/A
Received: N/A

Jackson, Joshua
4000 Warner Blvd.
Burbank, CA 91522
Actor
Response Time: N/A
Received: N/A

Jackson, Samuel L.
8942 Wilshire Blvd.
BH, CA 90211
Actor
Response Time: 68 Days
Received: Signed Photo

Jackson, Samuel L.
955 S. Carrillo., Ste. 300
LA, CA 90048
Actor
Response Time: N/A
Received: N/A

Jackson, Shar
5555 Melrose Ave.
Hollywood, CA 90038-3197
Actress
Response Time: N/A
Received: N/A

Jackson, Stonewall
6007 Cloverland Dr.
Brentwood, TN 37027-7607
Singer
Response Time: 27 Days
Received: Signed Photo

Jackson-Lee, Sheila
U.S. House of Representatives
Washington, DC 20515
Politician
Response Time: N/A
Received: N/A

James, Colton
4151 Prospect Ave.
LA, CA 90027
Actor
Response Time: N/A
Received: N/A

James, Dalton
4024 Radford Ave.
Studio City, CA 91604
Actor
Response Time: N/A
Received: N/A

James-DeMentri, Pat
c/o QVC, 1200 Wilson Dr.
West Chester, PA 19380
QVC Host
Response Time: N/A
Received: N/A

Janklow, William J.
500 East Capitol
Pierre, SD 57501
Governor
Response Time: N/A
Received: N/A

Janney, Allison
4000 Warner Blvd.
Burbank, CA 91522
Actress
Response Time: N/A
Received: N/A

Jarrett, Dale
115 Dwelle St.
Charlotte, NC 28208
Auto Racing Personality
Response Time: 78 Days
Received: Signed Photo

Jarrett, Dale
1801 West Int'l. Spdwy. Blvd.
Daytona Beach, FL 32114
Auto Racing Personality
Response Time: 359 Days
Received: Signed Photo

Jarrett, Jason
1801 West Int'l. Spdwy. Blvd.
Daytona Beach, FL 32114
Auto Racing Personality
Response Time: 201 Days
Received: Signed Photo

Jarrett, Ned
1801 West Int'l. Spdwy. Blvd.
Daytona Beach, FL 32114
Auto Racing Personality
Response Time: 240 Days
Received: Signed Photo

Jayroe, Jane
Two Ocean Way, Ste. 1000
Atlantic City, NJ 08401
Miss America 1967
Response Time: N/A
Received: N/A

Jeffcoat, Don
56 West 66th St.
NY, NY 10023
Actor
Response Time: N/A
Received: N/A

Jefferson, William J.
U.S. House of Representatives
Washington, DC 20515
Politician
Response Time: N/A
Received: N/A

Jeffords, James
728 Hart Senate Office Bldg.
Washington, DC 20510
Senator
Response Time: N/A
Received: N/A

Jeinsen, Elke
9242 Beverly Blvd.
BH, CA 90210
Playboy Playmate
Response Time: N/A
Received: N/A

Jemison, Mae C.
2101 NASA Rd. 1
Houston, TX 77058
Astronaut
Response Time: N/A
Received: N/A

Jenkins, Jackie "Butch"
Rt. #6 Box 541-G
Fairview, NC 28730
Actor
Response Time: N/A
Received: N/A

Jenkins, William L.
U.S. House of Representatives
Washington, DC 20515
Politician
Response Time: N/A
Received: N/A

Jenner, Bruce
25254 Eldorado Meadow Rd.
Hidden Hills, CA 91302
Olympian
Response Time: N/A
Received: N/A

Jenner, Bruce
P.O. Box 11137
BH, CA 90213
Olympian
Response Time: 31 Days
Received: Signed Photo

Jennings, Peter
7 West 66th St.
NY, NY 10023
News Anchor
Response Time: 12 Days
Received: Signed Photo

Jennings, Waylon
824 Old Hickory Blvd.
Brentwood, TN 37027
Singer
Response Time: 79 Days
Received: Signed Photo

Jernigan, Tamara E.
2101 NASA Rd. 1
Houston, TX 77058
Astronaut
Response Time: N/A
Received: N/A

Jett, Brent W.
2101 NASA Rd. 1
Houston, TX 77058
Astronaut
Response Time: N/A
Received: N/A

Joel, Billy
280 Elm St., 2nd Fl.
South Hampton, NY 11968
Singer
Response Time: 22 Days
Received: Signed Photo

Johanns, Mike
P.O. Box 94848
Lincoln, NE 68509-4848
Governor
Response Time: N/A
Received: N/A

John, Christopher
U.S. House of Representatives
Washington, DC 20515
Politician
Response Time: N/A
Received: N/A

John, Elton
8900 Wilshire Blvd., Ste. 370
BH, CA 90211
Singer
Response Time: N/A
Received: N/A

John, Elton
1 Blythe Rd.
London W14 0HG, England
Singer
Response Time: 31 Days
Received: Signed Photo

John, Tylyn
9242 Beverly Blvd.
BH, CA 90210
Playboy Playmate
Response Time: N/A
Received: N/A

Johnson, Amy Jo
4000 Warner Blvd.
Burbank, CA 91522
Actress
Response Time: N/A
Received: N/A

Johnson, Bryce
4000 Warner Blvd.
Burbank, CA 91522
Actor
Response Time: N/A
Received: N/A

Johnson, Don
5555 Melrose Ave.
Hollywood, CA 90038-3197
Actor
Response Time: N/A
Received: N/A

Johnson, Echo Leta
9242 Beverly Blvd.
BH, CA 90210
Playboy Playmate
Response Time: N/A
Received: N/A

Johnson, Eddie Bernice
U.S. House of Representatives
Washington, DC 20515
Politician
Response Time: N/A
Received: N/A

Johnson, Gary E.
State Capitol, 4th Fl.
Santa Fe, NM 87503
Governor
Response Time: N/A
Received: N/A

Johnson, Gregory C.
2101 NASA Rd. 1
Houston, TX 77058
Astronaut
Response Time: N/A
Received: N/A

Johnson, Gregory H.
2101 NASA Rd. 1
Houston, TX 77058
Astronaut
Response Time: N/A
Received: N/A

Johnson, Jay
3000 W. Alameda Ave.
Burbank, CA 91523
Actor
Response Time: N/A
Received: N/A

Johnson, Jimmie
1801 West Int'l. Spdwy. Blvd.
Daytona Beach, FL 32114
Auto Racing Personality
Response Time: 114 Days
Received: Signed Photo

Johnson, Nancy L.
U.S. House of Representatives
Washington, DC 20515
Politician
Response Time: N/A
Received: N/A

Johnson, Nicole
Two Ocean Way, Ste. 1000
Atlantic City, NJ 08401
Miss America 1999
Response Time: N/A
Received: N/A

Johnson, Rodney Van
4024 Radford Ave.
Studio City, CA 91604
Actor
Response Time: N/A
Received: N/A

Johnson, Russell
P.O. Box 1198
Bainbridge, WA 98110
Actor
Response Time: 13 Days
Received: Signed Photo I Sent

Johnson, Russell
P.O. Box 3135
La Jolla, CA 92038
Actor
Response Time: N/A
Received: N/A

Johnson, Sam
U.S. House of Representatives
Washington, DC 20515
Politician
Response Time: N/A
Received: N/A

Johnson, Tim
502 Hart Senate Office Bldg.
Washington, DC 20510
Senator
Response Time: N/A
Received: N/A

Johnson, Timothy V.
U.S. House of Representatives
Washington, DC 20515
Politician
Response Time: N/A
Received: N/A

Jolie, Angelina
11777 San Vicente Blvd. #880
LA, CA 90049
Actress
Response Time: N/A
Received: N/A

Jones, Bryant
7800 Beverly Blvd.
LA, CA 90036
Actor
Response Time: N/A
Received: N/A

Jones, Buckshot
1801 West Int'l. Spdwy. Blvd.
Daytona Beach, FL 32114
Auto Racing Personality
Response Time: 81 Days
Received: Signed Photo

Jones, Chipper
P.O. Box 4064
Atlanta, GA 30302
Baseball Player
Response Time: 34 Days
Received: Signed Photo

Jones, Chuck
Box 2319
Costa Mesa, CA 42628-2319
Cartoonist
Response Time: 96 Days
Received: Signed Photo

Jones, Davey
P.O. Box 400
Beavertown, PA 17813
Singer
Response Time: 410 Days
Received: Signed Photo

Jones, George
1101 17th Ave.
Nashville, TN 37212-2203
Singer
Response Time: 11 Days
Received: Signed Photo

Jones, George
296 Wine Branch Rd.
Murphy, NC 28906
Singer
Response Time: N/A
Received: N/A

Jones, James Earl
P.O. Box 610
Rawling, NY 12564-0610
Actor
Response Time: 16 Days
Received: Signed Photo

Jones, Jill Marie
5555 Melrose Ave.
Hollywood, CA 90038-3197
Actress
Response Time: N/A
Received: N/A

Jones, P.J.
1801 West Int'l. Spdwy. Blvd.
Daytona Beach, FL 32114
Auto Racing Personality
Response Time: 74 Days
Received: Signed Photo

Jones, Renee
3000 W. Alameda Ave.
Burbank, CA 91523
Actress
Response Time: N/A
Received: N/A

Jones, Stephanie Tubbs
U.S. House of Representatives
Washington, DC 20515
Politician
Response Time: N/A
Received: N/A

Jones, Summer
P.O. Box 1472
Hendersonville, TN 37077-1472
Singer
Response Time: 12 Days
Received: Signed Photo

Jones, Tamala
4000 Warner Blvd.
Burbank, CA 91522
Actress
Response Time: N/A
Received: N/A

Jones, Thomas D.
2101 NASA Rd. 1
Houston, TX 77058
Astronaut
Response Time: N/A
Received: N/A

Jones, Tommy Lee
P.O. Box 966
San Saba, TX 76877
Actor
Response Time: 211 Days
Received: Signed Photo

Jones, Walter B.
U.S. House of Representatives
Washington, DC 20515
Politician
Response Time: N/A
Received: N/A

Judd, Ashley
151 El Camino Dr.
BH, CA 90212
Actress
Response Time: N/A
Received: N/A

Judd, Ashley
P.O. Box 681828
Franklin, TN 37068
Actress
Response Time: 56 Days
Received: Signed Photo

Judd, Cledus T.
707 18th Ave. South
Nashville, TN 37203
Singer, Comedian
Response Time: N/A
Received: N/A

Judd, Naomi
P.O. Box 682068
Franklin, TN 37068
Singer
Response Time: 37 Days
Received: Signed Photo

Judd, Wynonna
P.O. Box 120777
Nashville, TN 37212
Singer
Response Time: N/A
Received: N/A

Judd, Wynonna
P.O. Box 682068
Franklin, TN 37068
Singer
Response Time: 212 Days
Received: Signed Photo

Kamano, Stacy
c/o Baywatch Productions
510-18th Ave., Honolulu, HI 96816
Actress
Response Time: N/A
Received: N/A

Kanjorski, Paul E.
U.S. House of Representatives
Washington, DC 20515
Politician
Response Time: N/A
Received: N/A

Kapoor, Ravi
500 S. Buena Vista St.
Burbank, CA 91521
Actor
Response Time: N/A
Received: N/A

Kavandi, Janet L.
2101 NASA Rd. 1
Houston, TX 77058
Astronaut
Response Time: N/A
Received: N/A

Kaptur, Marcy
U.S. House of Representatives
Washington, DC 20515
Politician
Response Time: N/A
Received: N/A

Kay, Lesli
1268 East 14th St.
Brooklyn, NY 11230
Actress
Response Time: N/A
Received: N/A

Kapture, Mitzi
3605 Sandy Plains Rd.
Marietta, GA 30066
Actress
Response Time: 177 Days
Received: Signed Photo

Kaye, Thorsten
4151 Prospect Ave.
LA, CA 90027
Actor
Response Time: N/A
Received: N/A

Kapture, Mitzi
c/o Baywatch Productions
510-18th Ave., Honolulu, HI 96816
Actress
Response Time: N/A
Received: N/A

Kaye, Wendy
9242 Beverly Blvd.
BH, CA 90210
Playboy Playmate
Response Time: N/A
Received: N/A

Kasem, Casey
138 N. Mapleton Dr.
LA, CA 90077
Radio Personality, Voice Actor
Response Time: 8 Days
Received: Signed Photo

Kazer, Beau
7800 Beverly Blvd.
LA, CA 90036
Actor
Response Time: N/A
Received: N/A

Keating, Frank
State Capitol Bldg., Ste. 212
Oklahoma City, OK 73105
Governor
Response Time: N/A
Received: N/A

Keifer, Elizabeth
51 W. 52 St.
NY, NY 10019
Actress
Response Time: N/A
Received: N/A

Keller, Jason
1801 West Int'l. Spdwy. Blvd.
Daytona Beach, FL 32114
Auto Racing Personality
Response Time: 106 Days
Received: Signed Photo

Keller, Ric
U.S. House of Representatives
Washington, DC 20515
Politician
Response Time: N/A
Received: N/A

Kellerk, Sophie
500 S. Buena Vista St.
Burbank, CA 91521
Actress
Response Time: N/A
Received: N/A

Kelley, Paul
c/o QVC, 1200 Wilson Dr.
West Chester, PA 19380
QVC Host
Response Time: N/A
Received: N/A

Kelly, James M.
2101 NASA Rd. 1
Houston, TX 77058
Astronaut
Response Time: N/A
Received: N/A

Kelly, Mark E.
2101 NASA Rd. 1
Houston, TX 77058
Astronaut
Response Time: N/A
Received: N/A

Kelly, Michael
5555 Melrose Ave.
Hollywood, CA 90038-3197
Actor
Response Time: N/A
Received: N/A

Kelly, Scott J.
2101 NASA Rd. 1
Houston, TX 77058
Astronaut
Response Time: N/A
Received: N/A

Kelly, Sue W.
U.S. House of Representatives
Washington, DC 20515
Politician
Response Time: N/A
Received: N/A

Kempthorne, Dirk
P.O. Box 83720
Boise, ID 83720-0034
Governor
Response Time: N/A
Received: N/A

Ken L.
5555 Melrose Ave.
Hollywood, CA 90038-3197
Actor
Response Time: N/A
Received: N/A

Kendall, Kerri
9242 Beverly Blvd.
BH, CA 90210
Playboy Playmate
Response Time: N/A
Received: N/A

Kennedy, Anthony
Supreme Court of the United States
Washington, DC 20543
Supreme Court Justice
Response Time: 29 Days
Received: Signed Photo

Kennedy, Edward
315 Russell Senate Office Bldg.
Washington, DC 20510
Senator
Response Time: N/A
Received: N/A

Kennedy, Mark R.
U.S. House of Representatives
Washington, DC 20515
Politician
Response Time: N/A
Received: N/A

Kennedy, Mimi
10201 West Pico Blvd.
Trailer 779, LA, CA 90035
Actress
Response Time: N/A
Received: N/A

Kennedy, Patrick J.
U.S. House of Representatives
Washington, DC 20515
Politician
Response Time: N/A
Received: N/A

Kenseth, Matt
871 Dove Court
Denver, NC 28037
Auto Racing Personality
Response Time: 51 Days
Received: Signed Photo

Kenseth, Matt
1801 West Int'l. Spdwy. Blvd.
Daytona Beach, FL 32114
Auto Racing Personality
Response Time: 228 Days
Received: Signed Photo

Kent, Heather Paige
5555 Melrose Ave.
Hollywood, CA 90038-3197
Actress
Response Time: N/A
Received: N/A

Kepler, Shell
4151 Prospect Ave.
LA, CA 90027
Actress
Response Time: N/A
Received: N/A

Kerns, Brian D.
U.S. House of Representatives
Washington, DC 20515
Politician
Response Time: N/A
Received: N/A

Kerns, Joanna
P.O. Box 49216
LA, CA 90049
Actress
Response Time: 42 Days
Received: Signed Photo

Kerr, Brook
4024 Radford Ave.
Studio City, CA 91604
Actress
Response Time: N/A
Received: N/A

Kerrigan, Nancy
7 Cedar Ave.
Stoneham, MA 02180
Figure Skater
Response Time: 46 Days
Received: Signed Photo

Kerry, John
304 Russell Senate Office Bldg.
Washington, DC 20510
Senator
Response Time: N/A
Received: N/A

Kershaw, Sammy
P.O. Box 274
Kaplan, LA 70548
Singer
Response Time: N/A
Received: N/A

Kerwin, Joseph P.
2101 NASA Rd. 1
Houston, TX 77058
Astronaut
Response Time: N/A
Received: N/A

Keselowski, Bob
1801 West Int'l. Spdwy. Blvd.
Daytona Beach, FL 32114
Auto Racing Personality
Response Time: 80 Days
Received: Signed Photo

Ketchum, Hank
P.O. Box 1997
Monterey, CA 93940
Cartoonist
Response Time: 17 Days
Received: Signed Photo

Kiel, Richard
40356 Oak Park Way #T
Oakhurst, CA 93644
Actor
Response Time: N/A
Received: N/A

Kildee, Dale E.
U.S. House of Representatives
Washington, DC 20515
Politician
Response Time: N/A
Received: N/A

Kilpatrick, Carolyn C.
U.S. House of Representatives
Washington, DC 20515
Politician
Response Time: N/A
Received: N/A

Kilrain, Susan L.
2101 NASA Rd. 1
Houston, TX 77058
Astronaut
Response Time: N/A
Received: N/A

Kincade, Thomas
c/o QVC, 1200 Wilson Dr.
West Chester, PA 19380
Artist - "Painter of Light"
Response Time: N/A
Received: N/A

Kind, Richard
100 Universal City Plaza
Universal City, CA 91608
Actor
Response Time: N/A
Received: N/A

Kind, Ron
U.S. House of Representatives
Washington, DC 20515
Politician
Response Time: N/A
Received: N/A

King Jr., Angus S.
State House, Station 1
Augusta, ME 04333
Governor
Response Time: N/A
Received: N/A

King, Ben E.
P.O. Box 1097
Teaneck, NJ 07666-2824
Singer
Response Time: 16 Days
Received: Signed Photo

King, Carole
509 Hartnell St.
Monterey, CA 93940
Singer
Response Time: N/A
Received: N/A

King, Carole
6430 Sunset Blvd.
Hollywood, CA 90028
Singer
Response Time: N/A
Received: N/A

King, Dave
c/o QVC, 1200 Wilson Dr.
West Chester, PA 19380
QVC Host
Response Time: N/A
Received: N/A

King, Larry
111 Massachusetts
Washington, DC 20001
CNN News Anchor
Response Time: 38 Days
Received: Signed Photo

King, Larry
c/o CNN, 820 1st St. N.E.
Washington, DC 20002-4243
CNN News Anchor
Response Time: N/A
Received: N/A

King, Perry
5700 Wilshire, Ste. 575
LA, CA 90036
Actor
Response Time: N/A
Received: N/A

King, Peter T.
U.S. House of Representatives
Washington, DC 20515
Politician
Response Time: N/A
Received: N/A

King, Rebecca
Two Ocean Way, Ste. 1000
Atlantic City, NJ 08401
Miss America 1974
Response Time: N/A
Received: N/A

Kingsley, Ben
Pabworth House, Stratford-on-Avon
Warwickshire, CV37 8XQ, England
Actor
Response Time: N/A
Received: N/A

Kingston, Alex
4000 Warner Blvd.
Burbank, CA 91522
Actress
Response Time: N/A
Received: N/A

Kingston, Jack
U.S. House of Representatives
Washington, DC 20515
Politician
Response Time: N/A
Received: N/A

Kinleys, The
P.O. Box 128501
Nashville, TN 37212
Music Group
Response Time: 32 Days
Received: Signed Photo

Kinney, Kathy
4000 Warner Blvd.
Burbank, CA 91522
Actress
Response Time: N/A
Received: N/A

Kirby, Andy
1801 West Int'l. Spdwy. Blvd.
Daytona Beach, FL 32114
Auto Racing Personality
Response Time: 91 Days
Received: Signed Photo

Kirk, Justin
4000 Warner Blvd.
Burbank, CA 91522
Actor
Response Time: N/A
Received: N/A

Kirk, Mark Steven
U.S. House of Representatives
Washington, DC 20515
Politician
Response Time: N/A
Received: N/A

Kirk, Pat
c/o Home Shopping Network
St. Petersburg, FL 33701
Home Shopping Network Host
Response Time: N/A
Received: N/A

Kitt, Eartha
125 Boulder Ridge Rd.
Scarsdale, NY 10583
Actress
Response Time: 71 Days
Received: Signed Photo

Kitzhaber, John A.
254 State Capitol
Salem, OR 97310
Governor
Response Time: N/A
Received: N/A

Kleczka, Gerald D.
U.S. House of Representatives
Washington, DC 20515
Politician
Response Time: N/A
Received: N/A

Klemperer, Werner
44 W. 62nd St., 10th Fl.
NY, NY 10023
Actor
Response Time: N/A
Received: N/A

Klugman, Jack
22548 Pacific Coast Hwy.
Malibu, CA 90205
Actor
Response Time: 46 Days
Received: Signed Photo

Klum, Heidi
c/o Elite Model Management
111 E. 22nd St., NY, NY 10010
Model
Response Time: 45 Days
Received: Signed Photo

Klum, Heidi
c/o IMG, 304 Park Avenue S.
Penthouse North, NY, NY 10010
Model
Response Time: 39 Days
Received: Signed Photo

Knight, Jonathan
90 Apple St.
Essex, MA 01929
Singer
Response Time: N/A
Received: N/A

Knight, Jordan
27 Dudley St.
Roxbury, MA 02132
Singer
Response Time: N/A
Received: N/A

Knight, Michael E.
320 West 66th St.
NY, NY 10023
Actor
Response Time: N/A
Received: N/A

Knollenberg, Joe
U.S. House of Representatives
Washington, DC 20515
Politician
Response Time: N/A
Received: N/A

Knowles, Tony
P.O. Box 110001
Juneau, AK 99811-0001
Governor
Response Time: N/A
Received: N/A

Koch, Ed
1290 Ave. of the Americas
NY, NY 10101
Politician
Response Time: 45 Days
Received: Signed Photo

Kodjoe, Boris
5555 Melrose Ave.
Hollywood, CA 90038-3197
Actor
Response Time: N/A
Received: N/A

Koenig, Walter
P.O. Box 4395
N. Hollywood, CA 91607
Actor
Response Time: 14 Days
Received: Signed Photo

Kohl, Herb
330 Hart Senate Office Bldg.
Washington, DC 20510
Senator
Response Time: N/A
Received: N/A

Kolbe, Jim
U.S. House of Representatives
Washington, DC 20515
Politician
Response Time: N/A
Received: N/A

Koontz, Dean
P.O. Box 9529
Newport Beach, CA 92658-9529
Writer
Response Time: N/A
Received: N/A

Korman, Lindsay
4024 Radford Ave.
Studio City, CA 91604
Actor
Response Time: N/A
Received: N/A

Korver, Paul
1268 East 14th St.
Brooklyn, NY 11230
Actor
Response Time: N/A
Received: N/A

Kosar, Bernie
6969 Rin Park Place
Youngstown, OH 44512
Football Player
Response Time: 16 Days
Received: Signed Photo

Koslow, Lauren
3000 W. Alameda Ave.
Burbank, CA 91523
Actress
Response Time: N/A
Received: N/A

Kozar, Heather
9242 Beverly Blvd.
BH, CA 90210
Playboy Playmate
Response Time: N/A
Received: N/A

Kramer, Steven E.
4000 Warner Blvd.
Burbank, CA 91522
Actor
Response Time: N/A
Received: N/A

Kravits, Jason
10201 West Pico Blvd.
LA, CA 90035
Actor
Response Time: N/A
Received: N/A

Kregel Kevin R.
2101 NASA Rd. 1
Houston, TX 77058
Astronaut
Response Time: N/A
Received: N/A

Krumholtz, David
5555 Melrose Ave.
Hollywood, CA 90038-3197
Actor
Response Time: N/A
Received: N/A

Kurth, Wallace
4151 Prospect Ave.
LA, CA 90027
Actor
Response Time: N/A
Received: N/A

Kucinich, Dennis J.
U.S. House of Representatives
Washington, DC 20515
Politician
Response Time: N/A
Received: N/A

Kwan, Michelle
44450 Pinetree Dr. #103
Plymouth, MI 48170
Figure Skater
Response Time: 161 Days
Received: Signed Photo

Kudrow, Lisa
4000 Warner Blvd.
Burbank, CA 91522
Actress
Response Time: N/A
Received: N/A

Kyl, Jon
724 Hart Senate Office Bldg.
Washington, DC 20510
Senator
Response Time: N/A
Received: N/A

La Motta, Jake
400 E. 57th St.
NY, NY 10022
Boxer
Response Time: N/A
Received: N/A

LaBelle, Patti
1212 Grennox Rd.
Wynnewood, PA 19096
Singer
Response Time: 65 Days
Received: Signed Photo

Labonte, Bobby
1801 West Int'l. Spdwy. Blvd.
Daytona Beach, FL 32114
Auto Racing Personality
Response Time: 371 Days
Received: Signed Photo

Labonte, Bobby
P.O. Box 358
Trinity, NC 27370
Auto Racing Personality
Response Time: 74 Days
Received: STC

Labonte, Terry
1801 West Int'l. Spdwy. Blvd.
Daytona Beach, FL 32114
Auto Racing Personality
Response Time: 400 Days
Received: Signed Photo

Labonte, Terry
P.O. Box 843
Trinity, NC 27370
Auto Racing Personality
Response Time: 120 Days
Received: STC

Labyorteaux, Patrick
5555 Melrose Ave.
Hollywood, CA 90038-3197
Actor
Response Time: N/A
Received: N/A

LaFalce, John J.
U.S. House of Representatives
Washington, DC 20515
Politician
Response Time: N/A
Received: N/A

Lafayette, John
5555 Melrose Ave.
Hollywood, CA 90038-3197
Actor
Response Time: N/A
Received: N/A

Lago, David
7800 Beverly Blvd.
LA, CA 90036
Actor
Response Time: N/A
Received: N/A

LaHood, Ray
U.S. House of Representatives
Washington, DC 20515
Politician
Response Time: N/A
Received: N/A

Lahti, Christine
1122 S. Robertson Blvd. #15
LA, CA 90069
Actress
Response Time: N/A
Received: N/A

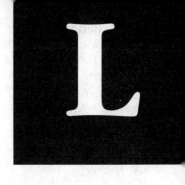

LaJoie, Randy
1801 West Int'l. Spdwy. Blvd.
Daytona Beach, FL 32114
Auto Racing Personality
Response Time: 67 Days
Received: Signed Photo

Lake, Ricki
226 West 26th St.
NY, NY 10001
Actress, Television Personality
Response Time: 57 Days
Received: Signed Photo

Lampson, Nick
U.S. House of Representatives
Washington, DC 20515
Politician
Response Time: N/A
Received: N/A

Landrieu, Mary
702 Hart Senate Office Bldg.
Washington, DC 20510
Senator
Response Time: N/A
Received: N/A

Lane, Kenneth J.
c/o QVC, 1200 Wilson Dr.
West Chester, PA 19380
Celebrity Jewelry Designer
Response Time: N/A
Received: N/A

Lang, Katherine Kelly
7800 Beverly Blvd.
LA, CA 90036
Actress
Response Time: N/A
Received: N/A

Lange, Artie
300 Television Plaza, Bldg. 137
Burbank, CA 91505
Actor
Response Time: N/A
Received: N/A

Langevin, James R.
U.S. House of Representatives
Washington, DC 20515
Politician
Response Time: N/A
Received: N/A

Langley, Neva
Two Ocean Way, Ste. 1000
Atlantic City, NJ 08401
Miss America 1953
Response Time: N/A
Received: N/A

Lansbury, Angela
635 N. Bonhill Rd.
LA, CA 90049-2301
Actress
Response Time: 45 Days
Received: Signed Photo

Lantos, Tom
U.S. House of Representatives
Washington, DC 20515
Politician
Response Time: N/A
Received: N/A

Lapaglia, Jonathan
5555 Melrose Ave.
Hollywood, CA 90038-3197
Actor
Response Time: N/A
Received: N/A

LaPlanche, Rosemary
Two Ocean Way, Ste. 1000
Atlantic City, NJ 08401
Miss America 1941
Response Time: N/A
Received: N/A

Largent, Steve
U.S. House of Representatives
Washington, DC 20515
Politician
Response Time: N/A
Received: N/A

Larsen, Rick
U.S. House of Representatives
Washington, DC 20515
Politician
Response Time: N/A
Received: N/A

Larson, Jill
320 West 66th St.
NY, NY 10023
Actress
Response Time: N/A
Received: N/A

Larson, John B.
U.S. House of Representatives
Washington, DC 20515
Politician
Response Time: N/A
Received: N/A

LaSalle, Eriq
4000 Warner Blvd.
Burbank, CA 91522
Actor
Response Time: N/A
Received: N/A

Lascher, David
5555 Melrose Ave.
Hollywood, CA 90038-3197
Actor
Response Time: N/A
Received: N/A

Lasswell, Fred
1111 N. Westshore Blvd. #604
Tampa, FL 33607
Cartoonist
Response Time: 7 Days
Received: Signed Sketch

Latham, Tom
U.S. House of Representatives
Washington, DC 20515
Politician
Response Time: N/A
Received: N/A

LaTourette, Steven C.
U.S. House of Representatives
Washington, DC 20515
Politician
Response Time: N/A
Received: N/A

Lau, Michele
c/o Home Shopping Network
St. Petersburg, FL 33701
Home Shopping Network Host
Response Time: N/A
Received: N/A

Laver, Rod
P.O. Box 4798
Hilton Head, SC 29938-4798
Singer
Response Time: N/A
Received: N/A

Lavin, Linda
321 Front St.
Wilmington, NC 28401
Actress
Response Time: 30 Days
Received: Signed Photo

Lavoie, Jennifer J.
9242 Beverly Blvd.
BH, CA 90210
Playboy Playmate
Response Time: N/A
Received: N/A

Lawler, Jerry
5190 Walnut Grove Rd.
Memphis, TN 38117-2876
Politician, Wrestler, Actor
Response Time: 29 Days
Received: Signed Photo

Lawler, Patrick
1801 West Int'l. Spdwy. Blvd.
Daytona Beach, FL 32114
Auto Racing Personality
Response Time: 81 Days
Received: Signed Photo

Lawlor, Craig
1268 East 14th St.
Brooklyn, NY 11230
Actor
Response Time: N/A
Received: N/A

Lawrence, Tracy
1100 17th Ave. South
Nashville, TN 37212
Singer
Response Time: N/A
Received: N/A

Lawrence, Vicki
9255 Sunset Blvd., Ste. 106
LA, CA 91608
Actress
Response Time: 26 Days
Received: Signed Photo

Lawrence, Wendy B.
2101 NASA Rd. 1
Houston, TX 77058
Astronaut
Response Time: N/A
Received: N/A

Lazzaro, Anthony
1801 West Int'l. Spdwy. Blvd.
Daytona Beach, FL 32114
Auto Racing Personality
Response Time: 72 Days
Received: Signed Photo

Leach, James A.
U.S. House of Representatives
Washington, DC 20515
Politician
Response Time: N/A
Received: N/A

Leahy, Patrick
433 Russell Senate Office Bldg.
Washington, DC 20510
Senator
Response Time: N/A
Received: N/A

Leardini, Christina Marie
9242 Beverly Blvd.
BH, CA 90210
Playboy Playmate
Response Time: N/A
Received: N/A

Leary, Denis
9560 Wilshire Blvd. #516
BH, CA 90212
Comedian
Response Time: 18 Days
Received: Signed Photo

Leavitt, Michael O.
210 State Capitol
Salt Lake City, UT 84114
Governor
Response Time: N/A
Received: N/A

LeBlanc, Christian
7800 Beverly Blvd.
LA, CA 90036
Actor
Response Time: N/A
Received: N/A

LeBlanc, Matt
4000 Warner Blvd.
Burbank, CA 91522
Actor
Response Time: N/A
Received: N/A

LeBrock, Kelly
P.O. Box 57593
Sherman Oaks, CA 91403
Actress
Response Time: N/A
Received: N/A

Ledford, Brandy
c/o Baywatch Productions
510-18th Ave., Honolulu, HI 96816
Actress
Response Time: N/A
Received: N/A

Lee, Anna
4151 Prospect Ave.
LA, CA 90027
Actress
Response Time: N/A
Received: N/A

Lee, Barbara
U.S. House of Representatives
Washington, DC 20515
Politician
Response Time: N/A
Received: N/A

Lee, Jessica
9242 Beverly Blvd.
BH, CA 90210
Playboy Playmate
Response Time: N/A
Received: N/A

Lee, Mark C.
2101 NASA Rd. 1
Houston, TX 77058
Astronaut
Response Time: N/A
Received: N/A

Lee, Stan
387 Park Ave. South
NY, NY 10016
Comic Book Illustrator
Response Time: 37 Days
Received: Signed Photo

Leestma, David C.
2101 NASA Rd. 1
Houston, TX 77058
Astronaut
Response Time: N/A
Received: N/A

Leeves, Jane
5555 Melrose Ave.
Hollywood, CA 90038-3197
Actress
Response Time: N/A
Received: N/A

Leffler, Jason
1801 West Int'l. Spdwy. Blvd.
Daytona Beach, FL 32114
Auto Racing Personality
Response Time: 61 Days
Received: Signed Photo

Leigh, Janet
1625 Summit Ridge Dr.
BH, CA 90210
Actress
Response Time: 43 Days
Received: Signed Photo

Lemus, Eva Tamargo
4024 Radford Ave.
Studio City, CA 91604
Actress
Response Time: N/A
Received: N/A

Leno, Jay
3000 W. Alameda Ave.
Burbank, CA 91523
Television Personality
Response Time: 24 Days
Received: Signed Photo

Lenoir, William B.
2101 NASA Rd. 1
Houston, TX 77058
Astronaut
Response Time: N/A
Received: N/A

Lenz, Nicole Marie
9242 Beverly Blvd.
BH, CA 90210
Playboy Playmate
Response Time: N/A
Received: N/A

Leonard, Sugar Ray
4401 East-West Hwy., Ste. 303
Bethesda, MD 20814
Boxer
Response Time: 92 Days
Received: Signed Photo

Leoni, Tea
2300 W. Victory Blvd. #384
Burbank, CA 91506-1200
Actress
Response Time: N/A
Received: N/A

Lepage, Kevin
1801 West Int'l. Spdwy. Blvd.
Daytona Beach, FL 32114
Auto Racing Personality
Response Time: 91 Days
Received: Signed Photo

LeRoy, Jennifer
9242 Beverly Blvd.
BH, CA 90210
Playboy Playmate
Response Time: N/A
Received: N/A

Lesser, Len
934 N. Evergreen St.
Burbank, CA 91505
Actor
Response Time: N/A
Received: N/A

Lester, Ron
4000 Warner Blvd.
Burbank, CA 91522
Actor
Response Time: N/A
Received: N/A

Lesure, James
4000 Warner Blvd.
Burbank, CA 91522
Actor
Response Time: N/A
Received: N/A

Levin, Carl
459 Russell Senate Office Bldg.
Washington, DC 20510
Senator
Response Time: N/A
Received: N/A

Levin, Sander M.
U.S. House of Representatives
Washington, DC 20515
Politician
Response Time: N/A
Received: N/A

Levine, Kathy
1325 Ave. of the Americas
5th Fl., NY, NY 10019
Television Personality
Response Time: N/A
Received: N/A

Lewis Jr., Ashton
1801 West Int'l. Spdwy. Blvd.
Daytona Beach, FL 32114
Auto Racing Personality
Response Time: 67 Days
Received: Signed Photo

Lewis, Carl
P.O. Box 571990
Houston, TX 77257-1990
Track & Field Athlete
Response Time: N/A
Received: N/A

Lewis, Jenifer
4000 Warner Blvd.
Burbank, CA 91522
Actress
Response Time: N/A
Received: N/A

Lewis, Jerry Lee
P.O. Box 384
Nesbit, MS 38651
Singer
Response Time: 33 Days
Received: Signed Photo

Lewis, Jerry
3160 W. Sahara Ave. #816
Las Vegas, NV 89102
Actor
Response Time: 137 Days
Received: Signed Photo

Lewis, Jerry
U.S. House of Representatives
Washington, DC 20515
Politician
Response Time: N/A
Received: N/A

Lewis, John
U.S. House of Representatives
Washington, DC 20515
Politician
Response Time: N/A
Received: N/A

Lewis, Ron
U.S. House of Representatives
Washington, DC 20515
Politician
Response Time: N/A
Received: N/A

Leyden, Paul
1268 East 14th St.
Brooklyn, NY 11230
Actor
Response Time: N/A
Received: N/A

Lieberman, Joseph
706 Hart Senate Office Bldg.
Washington, DC 20510
Senator
Response Time: N/A
Received: N/A

Light, Judith
8942 Wilshire Blvd.
BH, CA 90211
Actress
Response Time: 120 Days
Received: Signed Photo

Light, Judith
c/o QVC, 1200 Wilson Dr.
West Chester, PA 19380
Actress
Response Time: N/A
Received: N/A

Limbaugh, Rush
2 Penn Plaza
NY, NY 10121
Radio Personality
Response Time: N/A
Received: N/A

Lincoln, Blanche
708 Hart Senate Office Bldg.
Washington, DC 20510
Senator
Response Time: N/A
Received: N/A

Lind, Don L.
2101 NASA Rd. 1
Houston, TX 77058
Astronaut
Response Time: N/A
Received: N/A

Linder, John
U.S. House of Representatives
Washington, DC 20515
Politician
Response Time: N/A
Received: N/A

Linder, Kate
7800 Beverly Blvd.
LA, CA 90036
Actress
Response Time: N/A
Received: N/A

Lindsey, George
1350 Ave. of the Americas
NY, NY 10019
Actor
Response Time: 58 Days
Received: Signed Photo

Lindsey, Steven W.
2101 NASA Rd. 1
Houston, TX 77058
Astronaut
Response Time: N/A
Received: N/A

Linenger, Jerry M.
2101 NASA Rd. 1
Houston, TX 77058
Astronaut
Response Time: N/A
Received: N/A

Linklater, Hamish
500 S. Buena Vista St.
Burbank, CA 91521
Actor
Response Time: N/A
Received: N/A

Linnehan, Richard M.
2101 NASA Rd. 1
Houston, TX 77058
Astronaut
Response Time: N/A
Received: N/A

Linssen, Saskia
9242 Beverly Blvd.
BH, CA 90210
Playboy Playmate
Response Time: N/A
Received: N/A

Liotta, Ray
955 S. Carrillo Dr. #300
LA, CA 90048
Actor
Response Time: 36 Days
Received: Signed Photo

Liotta, Ray
P.O. Box 4632
Tequesta, FL 33469-1024
Actor
Response Time: 36 Days
Received: Signed Photo

Lipinski, Tara
P.O. Box 472288
Charlotte, NC 28247-2288
Gymnast
Response Time: 80 Days
Received: Signed Photo

Lipinski, William O.
U.S. House of Representatives
Washington, DC 20515
Politician
Response Time: N/A
Received: N/A

Lissauer, Trevor
5555 Melrose Ave.
Hollywood, CA 90038-3197
Actor
Response Time: N/A
Received: N/A

Little, Angela
9242 Beverly Blvd.
BH, CA 90210
Playboy Playmate
Response Time: N/A
Received: N/A

Little, Chad
1801 West Int'l. Spdwy. Blvd.
Daytona Beach, FL 32114
Auto Racing Personality
Response Time: 151 Days
Received: Signed Photo

Littler, Gene
P.O. Box 1949
Rancho Santa Fe, CA 92067-1949
Golfer
Response Time: N/A
Received: N/A

Livier, Ruth
5555 Melrose Ave.
Hollywood, CA 90038-3197
Actress
Response Time: N/A
Received: N/A

Llewellyn, John A.
2101 NASA Rd. 1
Houston, TX 77058
Astronaut
Response Time: N/A
Received: N/A

Lloyd, Sabrina
34-12 36th St.
Astoria, NY 11106
Actress
Response Time: N/A
Received: N/A

LoBiondo, Frank A.
U.S. House of Representatives
Washington, DC 20515
Politician
Response Time: N/A
Received: N/A

Locke, Gary
P.O. Box 40002, Legislative Bldg.
Olympia, WA 98504-0002
Governor
Response Time: N/A
Received: N/A

Lockhart, Paul S.
2101 NASA Rd. 1
Houston, TX 77058
Astronaut
Response Time: N/A
Received: N/A

Locklear, Heather
100 Universal City Plaza
Universal City, CA 91608
Actress
Response Time: N/A
Received: N/A

Lofgren, Zoe
U.S. House of Representatives
Washington, DC 20515
Politician
Response Time: N/A
Received: N/A

Lonestar
P.O. Box 128467
Nashville, TN 37212
Music Group
Response Time: 20 Days
Received: Unsigned Photo

Loomis, Robbie
1801 West Int'l. Spdwy. Blvd.
Daytona Beach, FL 32114
Auto Racing Personality
Response Time: 123 Days
Received: Signed Photo

Lopez, Colleen
c/o Home Shopping Network
St. Petersburg, FL 33701
Home Shopping Network Host
Response Time: N/A
Received: N/A

Lopez, Jennifer
9560 Wilshire Blvd. #500
BH, CA 90212
Actress, Singer
Response Time: N/A
Received: N/A

Lopez, Jennifer
9200 Sunset Blvd. #625
LA, CA 90069
Actress, Singer
Response Time: N/A
Received: N/A

Lopez, Jennifer
P.O. Box 57593
Sherman Oaks, CA 91403
Actress, Singer
Response Time: 52 Days
Received: Signed Photo

Lopez, Nancy
2308 Tara Dr.
Albany, GA 31707-9111
Golfer
Response Time: 91 Days
Received: Signed Photo

Lopez-Alegria, Michael E.
2101 NASA Rd. 1
Houston, TX 77058
Astronaut
Response Time: N/A
Received: N/A

Loren, Sophia
1151 Hidden Valley Rd.
Thousand Oaks, CA 91361
Actress
Response Time: 21 Days
Received: Signed Photo

Loria, Christopher J.
2101 NASA Rd. 1
Houston, TX 77058
Astronaut
Response Time: N/A
Received: N/A

Lott, Trent
487 Russell Senate Office Bldg.
Washington, DC 20510
Senator
Response Time: N/A
Received: N/A

Louganis, Greg
P.O. Box 4068
Malibu, CA 90265
Swimmer
Response Time: 16 Days
Received: Signed Photo

Loughlin, Lori
1122 S. Robertson Blvd. #15
LA, CA 90035
Actress
Response Time: N/A
Received: N/A

Louise, Tina
310 E. 46th St. #18-T
NY, NY 10017
Actress
Response Time: 14 Days
Received: Signed Photo I Sent

Lounge, John M.
2101 NASA Rd. 1
Houston, TX 77058
Astronaut
Response Time: N/A
Received: N/A

Lousma, Jack R.
2101 NASA Rd. 1
Houston, TX 77058
Astronaut
Response Time: N/A
Received: N/A

Love, Stanley G.
2101 NASA Rd. 1
Houston, TX 77058
Astronaut
Response Time: N/A
Received: N/A

Lovell Jr., James A.
2101 NASA Rd. 1
Houston, TX 77058
Astronaut
Response Time: N/A
Received: N/A

Low, G. David
2101 NASA Rd. 1
Houston, TX 77058
Astronaut
Response Time: N/A
Received: N/A

Lowder, Kyle
3000 W. Alameda Ave.
Burbank, CA 91523
Actor
Response Time: N/A
Received: N/A

Lowe, Rob
4000 Warner Blvd.
Burbank, CA 91522
Actor
Response Time: N/A
Received: N/A

Lowey, Nita M.
U.S. House of Representatives
Washington, DC 20515
Politician
Response Time: N/A
Received: N/A

Lu, Edward T.
2101 NASA Rd. 1
Houston, TX 77058
Astronaut
Response Time: N/A
Received: N/A

Lucas, Frank D.
U.S. House of Representatives
Washington, DC 20515
Politician
Response Time: N/A
Received: N/A

Lucas, Ken
U.S. House of Representatives
Washington, DC 20515
Politician
Response Time: N/A
Received: N/A

Lucci, Susan
320 West 66th St.
NY, NY 10023
Actress, Hair Care Creator
Response Time: 30 Days
Received: Signed Photo

Lucci, Susan
c/o QVC, 1200 Wilson Dr.
West Chester, PA 19380
Actress, Hair Care Creator
Response Time: N/A
Received: N/A

Lucci, Susan
P.O. Box 621
Quogue, NY 10019
Actress, Hair Care Creator
Response Time: 31 Days
Received: Signed Photo

Lucid, Shannon W.
2101 NASA Rd. 1
Houston, TX 77058
Astronaut
Response Time: N/A
Received: N/A

Lugar, Richard
306 Hart Senate Office Bldg.
Washington, DC 20510
Senator
Response Time: N/A
Received: N/A

Lundgren, Dolph
151 El Camino Dr.
BH, CA 90212
Actor
Response Time: 39 Days
Received: Signed Photo

LuPone, Patti
P.O. Box 2520
New Preston, CT 06777
Singer
Response Time: 27 Days
Received: Signed Photo

Luther, Bill
U.S. House of Representatives
Washington, DC 20515
Politician
Response Time: N/A
Received: N/A

Lydon, Jimmy
1317 Los Arboles Ave. N.W.
Albuquerque, NM 87107
Actor
Response Time: N/A
Received: N/A

Lyman, Dorothy
8899 Beverly Blvd. #510
LA, CA 90048
Actress
Response Time: 140 Days
Received: Signed Photo

Lynch, John Carroll
4000 Warner Blvd.
Burbank, CA 91522
Actor
Response Time: N/A
Received: N/A

Lynn, Loretta
4900 Claycut Rd. #51
Baton Rouge, LA 70806
Singer
Response Time: N/A
Received: N/A

Lynn, Loretta
P.O. Box 120369
Nashville, TN 37212
Singer
Response Time: 18 Days
Received: SIC

Macdonald, David Andrew
51 W. 52 St.
NY, NY 10019
Actor
Response Time: N/A
Received: N/A

Macdonald, Norm
300 Television Plaza, Bldg. 137
Burbank, CA 91505
Actor
Response Time: N/A
Received: N/A

MacDonald, Randy
1801 West Int'l. Spdwy. Blvd.
Daytona Beach, FL 32114
Auto Racing Personality
Response Time: 119 Days
Received: Signed Photo

MacDonnell, Ray
320 West 66th St.
NY, NY 10023
Actor
Response Time: N/A
Received: N/A

Mackinnon, Simmone
c/o Baywatch Productions
510-18th Ave., Honolulu, HI 96816
Actress
Response Time: N/A
Received: N/A

MacLaine, Shirley
25200 Old Malibu Rd.
Malibu, CA 90265
Actress
Response Time: 21 Days
Received: Signed Photo

MacLean, Steven G.
2101 NASA Rd. 1
Houston, TX 77058
Astronaut
Response Time: N/A
Received: N/A

MacPherson, Elle
414 E. 52nd St. #PHB
NY, NY 10022
Actress, Model
Response Time: 92 Days
Received: Signed Photo

Madden, John
5955 Coronado Blvd.
Pleasanton, CA 94588-8518
Football Coach
Response Time: N/A
Received: N/A

Madonna
3029 Brickell Ave.
Miami, FL 33129
Singer, Actress
Response Time: N/A
Received: N/A

Madonna
8000 Beverly Blvd.
LA, CA 90048
Singer, Actress
Response Time: N/A
Received: N/A

Maffett, Debra
Two Ocean Way, Ste. 1000
Atlantic City, NJ 08401
Miss America 1983
Response Time: N/A
Received: N/A

Maggart, Garett
5555 Melrose Ave.
Hollywood, CA 90038-3197
Actor
Response Time: N/A
Received: N/A

Magnus, Sandra H.
2101 NASA Rd. 1
Houston, TX 77058
Astronaut
Response Time: N/A
Received: N/A

Mahoney, John
5555 Melrose Ave.
Hollywood, CA 90038-3197
Actor
Response Time: N/A
Received: N/A

Majors, Lee
3000 Holiday Dr. PH-1
Ft. Lauderdale, FL 33316
Actor
Response Time: 63 Days
Received: Signed Photo

Makar, Jimmy
1801 West Int'l. Spdwy. Blvd.
Daytona Beach, FL 32114
Auto Racing Personality
Response Time: 81 Days
Received: Signed Photo

Malco, Roman
5555 Melrose Ave.
Hollywood, CA 90038-3197
Actor
Response Time: N/A
Received: N/A

Maloney, Carolyn B.
U.S. House of Representatives
Washington, DC 20515
Politician
Response Time: N/A
Received: N/A

Maloney, James H.
U.S. House of Representatives
Washington, DC 20515
Politician
Response Time: N/A
Received: N/A

Mancini, Ray
12524 Indianapolis St.
LA, CA 90066
Boxer
Response Time: 14 Days
Received: Signed Photo

Mandel, Howie
23679 Calabasas Rd. #180
Calabasas, CA 91302
Actor, Comedian
Response Time: 53 Days
Received: Signed Photo

Mandrell, Barbara
9830 Wilshire Blvd.
BH, CA 90212
Singer
Response Time: 43 Days
Received: Signed Photo

Mandrell, Barbara
P.O. Box 620
Hendersonville, TN 37077-0620
Singer
Response Time: 38 Days
Received: Signed Photo

Mandrell, Irlene
544 Nashville Pike, Ste. 244
Gallatin, TN 37066
Singer
Response Time: 183 Days
Received: Signed Photo

Mandrell, Louise
2046 Parkway
Pigeon Forge, TN 37863-2959
Singer
Response Time: 10 Days
Received: Signed Photo

Manheim, Camryn
10201 West Pico Blvd.
LA, CA 90035
Actress
Response Time: 26 Days
Received: Signed Photo

Manilow, Barry
5443 Beethoven St.
LA, CA 90066
Singer
Response Time: N/A
Received: N/A

Manzullo, Donald A.
U.S. House of Representatives
Washington, DC 20515
Politician
Response Time: N/A
Received: N/A

March Karlsen, Alexandria
9242 Beverly Blvd.
BH, CA 90210
Playboy Playmate
Response Time: N/A
Received: N/A

March, Stephanie
1230 Ave. of Americas
NY, NY 10020
Actress
Response Time: N/A
Received: N/A

Marcis, Dave
1801 West Int'l. Spdwy. Blvd.
Daytona Beach, FL 32114
Auto Racing Personality
Response Time: 65 Days
Received: Signed Photo

Marin, Cheech
5555 Melrose Ave.
Hollywood, CA 90038-3197
Actor
Response Time: N/A
Received: N/A

Marino, Bonnie
9242 Beverly Blvd.
BH, CA 90210
Playboy Playmate
Response Time: N/A
Received: N/A

Mark, Heidi
9242 Beverly Blvd.
BH, CA 90210
Playboy Playmate
Response Time: N/A
Received: N/A

Markey, Edward J.
U.S. House of Representatives
Washington, DC 20515
Politician
Response Time: N/A
Received: N/A

Marks, Shae
9242 Beverly Blvd.
BH, CA 90210
Playboy Playmate
Response Time: N/A
Received: N/A

Marlin, Sterling
1801 West Int'l. Spdwy. Blvd.
Daytona Beach, FL 32114
Auto Racing Personality
Response Time: 57 Days
Received: Signed Photo

Marshall, Garry
4252 W. Riverside Dr.
Burbank, CA 91505-4145
Director
Response Time: 137 Days
Received: Signed Photo

Marshall, Penny
8942 Wilshire Blvd.
LA, CA 90212
Actress
Response Time: 48 Days
Received: Signed Photo

Marsters, James
4000 Warner Blvd.
Burbank, CA 91522
Actor
Response Time: N/A
Received: N/A

Marteen, Rachel Jean
9242 Beverly Blvd.
BH, CA 90210
Playboy Playmate
Response Time: N/A
Received: N/A

Martin, Jesse L.
1230 Ave. of Americas
NY, NY 10020
Actor
Response Time: N/A
Received: N/A

Martin, Kellie
5918 Van Nuys Blvd.
Van Nuys, CA 91401
Actress
Response Time: 29 Days
Received: Signed Photo

Martin, Kenny
1801 West Int'l. Spdwy. Blvd.
Daytona Beach, FL 32114
Auto Racing Personality
Response Time: 66 Days
Received: Signed Photo

Martin, Mark
112 Knob Hill Rd.
Mooresville, NC 28115
Auto Racing Personality
Response Time: 136 Days
Received: Signed Photo

Martin, Mark
1801 West Int'l. Spdwy. Blvd.
Daytona Beach, FL 32114
Auto Racing Personality
Response Time: 217 Days
Received: Signed Photo

Martin, Steve
P.O. Box 929
BH, CA 90210
Actor
Response Time: 21 Days
Received: Signed Photo

Martindale, Wink
5744 New Castle
Calabasas, CA 90302
Game Show Host
Response Time: 26 Days
Received: Signed Photo

Martinez, A.
4151 Prospect Ave.
LA, CA 90027
Actor
Response Time: N/A
Received: N/A

Martini, Max
5555 Melrose Ave.
Hollywood, CA 90038-3197
Actor
Response Time: N/A
Received: N/A

Martz, Judy
P.O. Box 0801
Helena, MT 59620
Governor
Response Time: N/A
Received: N/A

Marville, Barbara
c/o Home Shopping Network
St. Petersburg, FL 33701
Home Shopping Network Host
Response Time: N/A
Received: N/A

Mascara, Frank
U.S. House of Representatives
Washington, DC 20515
Politician
Response Time: N/A
Received: N/A

Mascolo, Joe
3000 W. Alameda Ave.
Burbank, CA 91523
Actor
Response Time: N/A
Received: N/A

Mason, Lisa
c/o QVC, 1200 Wilson Dr.
West Chester, PA 19380
QVC Host
Response Time: N/A
Received: N/A

Massimino, Michael J.
2101 NASA Rd. 1
Houston, TX 77058
Astronaut
Response Time: N/A
Received: N/A

Mast, Rick
1801 West Int'l. Spdwy. Blvd.
Daytona Beach, FL 32114
Auto Racing Personality
Response Time: 81 Days
Received: Signed Photo

Masters, Ben
4024 Radford Ave.
Studio City, CA 91604
Actor
Response Time: N/A
Received: N/A

Masters, Marie
1268 East 14th St.
Brooklyn, NY 11230
Actress
Response Time: N/A
Received: N/A

Mastracchio, Richard A.
2101 NASA Rd. 1
Houston, TX 77058
Astronaut
Response Time: N/A
Received: N/A

Matheson, Jim
U.S. House of Representatives
Washington, DC 20515
Politician
Response Time: N/A
Received: N/A

Matheson, Tim
1187 Coast Village Rd., Ste. 504
Santa Barbara, CA 93108-2749
Actor
Response Time: 41 Days
Received: Signed Photo

Mathias, Bob
7469 E. Pine Ave.
Fresno, CA 93727-9520
Singer
Response Time: N/A
Received: N/A

Mathison, Cameron
320 West 66th St.
NY, NY 10023
Actress
Response Time: N/A
Received: N/A

Matsui, Robert T.
U.S. House of Representatives
Washington, DC 20515
Politician
Response Time: N/A
Received: N/A

Mattea, Kathy
P.O. Box 158482
Nashville, TN 37215
Singer
Response Time: 270 Days
Received: Signed Photo

Matthews, Lisa
9242 Beverly Blvd.
BH, CA 90210
Playboy Playmate
Response Time: N/A
Received: N/A

Mattingly, Thomas K.
2101 NASA Rd. 1
Houston, TX 77058
Astronaut
Response Time: N/A
Received: N/A

Mauceri, Patricia
56 West 66th St.
NY, NY 10023
Actress
Response Time: N/A
Received: N/A

Maule, Brad
4151 Prospect Ave.
LA, CA 90027
Actor
Response Time: N/A
Received: N/A

Max, Peter
c/o QVC, 1200 Wilson Dr.
West Chester, PA 19380
Artist
Response Time: N/A
Received: N/A

May Yazel, Carrie Jean
9242 Beverly Blvd.
BH, CA 90210
Playboy Playmate
Response Time: N/A
Received: N/A

Mayer, Jacquelyn
Two Ocean Way, Ste. 1000
Atlantic City, NJ 08401
Miss America 1963
Response Time: N/A
Received: N/A

Mayfield, Jeremy
1801 West Int'l. Spdwy. Blvd.
Daytona Beach, FL 32114
Auto Racing Personality
Response Time: 92 Days
Received: Signed Photo

Mazar, Debi
5555 Melrose Ave.
Hollywood, CA 90038-3197
Actress
Response Time: N/A
Received: N/A

McArthur Jr., William S.
2101 NASA Rd. 1
Houston, TX 77058
Astronaut
Response Time: N/A
Received: N/A

McBride, Jon A.
2101 NASA Rd. 1
Houston, TX 77058
Astronaut
Response Time: N/A
Received: N/A

McBride, Martina
P.O. Box 291627
Nashville, TN 37229
Singer
Response Time: 61 Days
Received: Signed Photo

McCaan, Lila
3800-A Bridgeport Way West
University Place, WA 98466
Singer
Response Time: 13 Days
Received: Signed Photo

McCain, John
241 Russell Senate Office Bldg.
Washington, DC 20510
Senator
Response Time: N/A
Received: N/A

McCandless, Bruce
2101 NASA Rd. 1
Houston, TX 77058
Astronaut
Response Time: N/A
Received: N/A

McCarthy, Carolyn
U.S. House of Representatives
Washington, DC 20515
Politician
Response Time: N/A
Received: N/A

McCarthy, Jenny
8424-A Santa Monica Blvd., PMB 804
W. Hollywood, CA 90069
Actress, Playboy Playmate
Response Time: 16 Days
Received: Signed Photo

McCarthy, Jenny
9242 Beverly Blvd.
BH, CA 90210
Actress, Playboy Playmate
Response Time: N/A
Received: N/A

McCarthy, Karen
U.S. House of Representatives
Washington, DC 20515
Politician
Response Time: N/A
Received: N/A

McCarthy, Melissa
4000 Warner Blvd.
Burbank, CA 91522
Actress
Response Time: N/A
Received: N/A

McCay, Peggy
3000 W. Alameda Ave.
Burbank, CA 91523
Actress
Response Time: N/A
Received: N/A

McClain, Cady
320 West 66th St.
NY, NY 10023
Actress
Response Time: N/A
Received: N/A

McClannahan, Rue
1185 Ave. of the Americas
NY, NY 10036-2602
Actress
Response Time: 90 Days
Received: Signed Photo

McCollum, Betty
U.S. House of Representatives
Washington, DC 20515
Politician
Response Time: N/A
Received: N/A

McConnell, Mitch
361-A Russell Senate Office Bldg.
Washington, DC 20510
Senator
Response Time: N/A
Received: N/A

McCoo, Marilyn
2639 Lavery Court #5
Newbury Park, CA 91320
Singer
Response Time: N/A
Received: N/A

McCook, John
7800 Beverly Blvd.
LA, CA 90036
Actor
Response Time: N/A
Received: N/A

McCool, William C.
2101 NASA Rd. 1
Houston, TX 77058
Astronaut
Response Time: N/A
Received: N/A

McCortney, Mindy
c/o Home Shopping Network
St. Petersburg, FL 33701
Home Shopping Network Host
Response Time: N/A
Received: N/A

McCoy, Neal
3196 Royal Lane #204
Dallas, TX 75229
Singer
Response Time: 24 Days
Received: Signed Photo

McCoy, Neal
P.O. Box 9610
Longview, TX 75608
Singer
Response Time: N/A
Received: N/A

McCrane, Paul
4000 Warner Blvd.
Burbank, CA 91522
Actor
Response Time: N/A
Received: N/A

McCray, Rick
1801 West Int'l. Spdwy. Blvd.
Daytona Beach, FL 32114
Auto Racing Personality
Response Time: 80 Days
Received: Signed Photo

McCrery, Jim
U.S. House of Representatives
Washington, DC 20515
Politician
Response Time: N/A
Received: N/A

McCulley, Michael J.
2101 NASA Rd. 1
Houston, TX 77058
Astronaut
Response Time: N/A
Received: N/A

McDaniel, James
10201 West Pico Blvd.
LA, CA 90035
Actor
Response Time: N/A
Received: N/A

McDermott, Dylan
10201 West Pico Blvd.
LA, CA 90035
Actor
Response Time: 31 Days
Received: Signed Photo

McDermott, Jim
U.S. House of Representatives
Washington, DC 20515
Politician
Response Time: N/A
Received: N/A

McDivitt, James A.
2101 NASA Rd. 1
Houston, TX 77058
Astronaut
Response Time: N/A
Received: N/A

McDonald, Christopher
151 El Camino Dr.
BH, CA 90212
Actor
Response Time: 59 Days
Received: Signed Photo

McDougal, Karen
9242 Beverly Blvd.
BH, CA 90210
Playboy Playmate
Response Time: N/A
Received: N/A

McEnroe, John
194 Bellevue Ave.
Newport, RI 02840
Tennis Player
Response Time: 38 Days
Received: Signed Photo

McEntire, Reba
40 Music Sq. West
Nashville, TN 37203
Singer
Response Time: 151 Days
Received: Signed Photo

McGlynn, Ryan
1801 West Int'l. Spdwy. Blvd.
Daytona Beach, FL 32114
Auto Racing Personality
Response Time: 74 Days
Received: Signed Photo

McGovern, George
P.O. Box 3339
Washington, DC 20033
Politician
Response Time: N/A
Received: N/A

McGovern, James P.
U.S. House of Representatives
Washington, DC 20515
Politician
Response Time: N/A
Received: N/A

McGovern, Maureen
163 Amsterdam Ave. #174
NY, NY 10023
Singer
Response Time: N/A
Received: N/A

McGraw, Ali
10345 W. Olympic Blvd. #200
LA, CA 90064
Actress
Response Time: 94 Days
Received: Signed Photo

McGraw, Tim
209 10th Ave. South, Ste. 229
Nashville, TN 37203
Singer
Response Time: N/A
Received: N/A

McGraw, Tim
P.O. Box 128138
Nashville, TN 37212
Singer
Response Time: N/A
Received: N/A

McGregor, Ewan
503/504 Lotts Rd., The Chambers
Chelsea Harbour, SW10 0XF, England
Actor
Response Time: 45 Days
Received: Signed Photo

McHugh, John M.
U.S. House of Representatives
Washington, DC 20515
Politician
Response Time: N/A
Received: N/A

McIlwain, Lena
c/o QVC, 1200 Wilson Dr.
West Chester, PA 19380
QVC Host
Response Time: N/A
Received: N/A

McInnis, Scott
U.S. House of Representatives
Washington, DC 20515
Politician
Response Time: N/A
Received: N/A

McIntaggart, Peggy
9242 Beverly Blvd.
BH, CA 90210
Playboy Playmate
Response Time: N/A
Received: N/A

McIntyre, Joe
215 Warren St.
Brookline, MA 02146
Singer
Response Time: N/A
Received: N/A

McIntyre, Mike
U.S. House of Representatives
Washington, DC 20515
Politician
Response Time: N/A
Received: N/A

McKellar, Danica
10635 Santa Monica Blvd. #130
LA, CA 90025
Actress
Response Time: N/A
Received: N/A

McKeon, Howard P. "Buck"
U.S. House of Representatives
Washington, DC 20515
Politician
Response Time: N/A
Received: N/A

McKinney, Cynthia A.
U.S. House of Representatives
Washington, DC 20515
Politician
Response Time: N/A
Received: N/A

McKnight, Marian
Two Ocean Way, Ste. 1000
Atlantic City, NJ 08401
Miss America 1957
Response Time: N/A
Received: N/A

McLaughlin, Mike
1801 West Int'l. Spdwy. Blvd.
Daytona Beach, FL 32114
Auto Racing Personality
Response Time: 68 Days
Received: Signed Photo

McMahon, Linda
c/o WWF, 1241 East Main St.
P.O. Box 3857, Stamford, CT 06902
Wrestling Personality
Response Time: 18 Days
Received: Signed Photo

McMahon, Shane
c/o WWF, 1241 East Main St.
P.O. Box 3857, Stamford, CT 06902
Wrestling Personality
Response Time: 18 Days
Received: Signed Photo

McMahon, Stephanie
c/o WWF, 1241 East Main St.
P.O. Box 3857, Stamford, CT 06902
Wrestling Personality
Response Time: 18 Days
Received: Signed Photo

McMahon, Vince
c/o WWF, 1241 East Main St.
P.O. Box 3857, Stamford, CT 06902
Wrestling Personality
Response Time: 18 Days
Received: Signed Photo

McMonagle, Donald R.
2101 NASA Rd. 1
Houston, TX 77058
Astronaut
Response Time: N/A
Received: N/A

McMurray, Jamie
1801 West Int'l. Spdwy. Blvd.
Daytona Beach, FL 32114
Auto Racing Personality
Response Time: 81 Days
Received: Signed Photo

McNally, Kerry
c/o Home Shopping Network
St. Petersburg, FL 33701
Home Shopping Network Host
Response Time: N/A
Received: N/A

McNamara, Robert
2412 Tracy Place N.W.
Washington, DC 20008-1627
Politician
Response Time: 120 Days
Received: Signed Photo

McNamara, Robert
700 New Hampshire Ave. N.W. #101
Washington, DC 20037-2406
Politician
Response Time: 140 Days
Received: Signed Photo

McNulty, Michael R.
U.S. House of Representatives
Washington, DC 20515
Politician
Response Time: N/A
Received: N/A

McReynolds, Larry
1801 West Int'l. Spdwy. Blvd.
Daytona Beach, FL 32114
Auto Racing Personality
Response Time: 341 Days
Received: Signed Photo

McVicar, Daniel
7800 Beverly Blvd.
LA, CA 90036
Actor
Response Time: N/A
Received: N/A

Mead, Lynda
Two Ocean Way, Ste. 1000
Atlantic City, NJ 08401
Miss America 1960
Response Time: N/A
Received: N/A

Meade, Carl J.
2101 NASA Rd. 1
Houston, TX 77058
Astronaut
Response Time: N/A
Received: N/A

Meehan, Martin T.
U.S. House of Representatives
Washington, DC 20515
Politician
Response Time: N/A
Received: N/A

Meek, Carrie P.
U.S. House of Representatives
Washington, DC 20515
Politician
Response Time: N/A
Received: N/A

Meeks, Aaron
5555 Melrose Ave.
Hollywood, CA 90038-3197
Actor
Response Time: N/A
Received: N/A

Meeks, Gregory W.
U.S. House of Representatives
Washington, DC 20515
Politician
Response Time: N/A
Received: N/A

Meeuwsen, Terry
Two Ocean Way, Ste. 1000
Atlantic City, NJ 08401
Miss America 1973
Response Time: N/A
Received: N/A

Melini, Angela
9242 Beverly Blvd.
BH, CA 90210
Playboy Playmate
Response Time: N/A
Received: N/A

Mello, Tamara
4000 Warner Blvd.
Burbank, CA 91522
Actress
Response Time: N/A
Received: N/A

Mellons, Ken
Box 158732
Nashville, TN 37215
Singer
Response Time: 31 Days
Received: Signed Photo

Melnick, Bruce E.
2101 NASA Rd. 1
Houston, TX 77058
Astronaut
Response Time: N/A
Received: N/A

Meloni, Christopher
1230 Ave. of Americas
NY, NY 10020
Actor
Response Time: N/A
Received: N/A

Melroy, Pamela A.
2101 NASA Rd. 1
Houston, TX 77058
Astronaut
Response Time: N/A
Received: N/A

Melvin, Leland D.
2101 NASA Rd. 1
Houston, TX 77058
Astronaut
Response Time: N/A
Received: N/A

Mendoza, Alex
4151 Prospect Ave.
LA, CA 90027
Actor
Response Time: N/A
Received: N/A

Mendoza, Mauricio
5555 Melrose Ave.
Hollywood, CA 90038-3197
Actor
Response Time: N/A
Received: N/A

Menendez, Robert
U.S. House of Representatives
Washington, DC 20515
Politician
Response Time: N/A
Received: N/A

Meriwether, Lee
Two Ocean Way, Ste. 1000
Atlantic City, NJ 08401
Miss America 1955
Response Time: N/A
Received: N/A

Merkerson, Epatha
1230 Ave. of Americas
NY, NY 10020
Actress
Response Time: N/A
Received: N/A

Mero, Rena
P.O. Box 1210
Geneva, FL 32732-1210
Actress, Model
Response Time: N/A
Received: N/A

Messina, Jo Dee
P.O. Box 8031
Hermitage, TN 37076
Singer
Response Time: 29 Days
Received: Signed Photo

Metcalf, Laurie
300 Television Plaza, Bldg. 137
Burbank, CA 91505
Actress
Response Time: N/A
Received: N/A

Metcalfe, Jesse
4024 Radford Ave.
Studio City, CA 91604
Actor
Response Time: N/A
Received: N/A

Mica, John L.
U.S. House of Representatives
Washington, DC 20515
Politician
Response Time: N/A
Received: N/A

Michaels, Tammy Lynn
4000 Warner Blvd.
Burbank, CA 91522
Actress
Response Time: N/A
Received: N/A

Michel, F. Curtis
2101 NASA Rd. 1
Houston, TX 77058
Astronaut
Response Time: N/A
Received: N/A

Michele, Michael
4000 Warner Blvd.
Burbank, CA 91522
Actor
Response Time: N/A
Received: N/A

Michelle, Cara
9242 Beverly Blvd.
BH, CA 90210
Playboy Playmate
Response Time: N/A
Received: N/A

Mickelson, Phil
2515 Mckinney Ave. #940
Dallas, TX 75201
Golfer
Response Time: 51 Days
Received: Signed Photo

Mickelson, Phil
7373 N. Scottsdale Rd., Ste. C-134
Scottsdale, AZ 85253-3557
Golfer
Response Time: N/A
Received: N/A

Middleton, Mae
5555 Melrose Ave.
Hollywood, CA 90038-3197
Actress
Response Time: N/A
Received: N/A

Midler, Bette
1222 16th Ave. South, 3rd Fl.
Nashville, TN 37212
Actress, Singer
Response Time: 116 Days
Received: Signed Photo

Midler, Bette
500 S. Buena Vista #102
Burbank, CA 91521
Actress, Singer
Response Time: N/A
Received: N/A

Mikulski, Barbara
709 Hart Senate Office Bldg.
Washington, DC 20510
Senator
Response Time: N/A
Received: N/A

Milano, Alyssa
5555 Melrose Ave.
Hollywood, CA 90038-3197
Actress
Response Time: N/A
Received: N/A

Millender-McDonald, Juanita
U.S. House of Representatives
Washington, DC 20515
Politician
Response Time: N/A
Received: N/A

Miller, Christa
4000 Warner Blvd.
Burbank, CA 91522
Actress
Response Time: N/A
Received: N/A

Miller, Dan
U.S. House of Representatives
Washington, DC 20515
Politician
Response Time: N/A
Received: N/A

Miller, Gary G.
U.S. House of Representatives
Washington, DC 20515
Politician
Response Time: N/A
Received: N/A

Miller, George
U.S. House of Representatives
Washington, DC 20515
Politician
Response Time: N/A
Received: N/A

Miller, Nolan
c/o QVC, 1200 Wilson Dr.
West Chester, PA 19380
Celebrity Jewelry Designer
Response Time: N/A
Received: N/A

Miller, Shannon
2136 N. 13th St.
Reading, PA 19604-1200
Gymnast
Response Time: N/A
Received: N/A

Miller, Tangi
4000 Warner Blvd.
Burbank, CA 91522
Actress
Response Time: N/A
Received: N/A

Miller, Zell
United States Senate
Washington, DC 20510
Senator
Response Time: N/A
Received: N/A

Mills, Billy
632 S. 2nd St., P.O. Box 670
Raton, NM 87740-4110
Olympian
Response Time: N/A
Received: N/A

Mills, Juliet
4024 Radford Ave.
Studio City, CA 91604
Actress
Response Time: N/A
Received: N/A

Ming-Na
4000 Warner Blvd.
Burbank, CA 91522
Actress
Response Time: N/A
Received: N/A

Mink, Patsy T.
U.S. House of Representatives
Washington, DC 20515
Politician
Response Time: N/A
Received: N/A

Minnelli, Liza
150 E. 69th St. #21-G
NY, NY 10021
Actress, Singer
Response Time: N/A
Received: N/A

Minnelli, Liza
200 W. 57th St. #908
NY, NY 10019
Actress, Singer
Response Time: 57 Days
Received: Signed Photo

Minner, Ruth Ann
Tatnall Bldg., William Penn St.
Dover, DE 19901
Governor
Response Time: N/A
Received: N/A

Miriam, Jennifer
9242 Beverly Blvd.
BH, CA 90210
Playboy Playmate
Response Time: N/A
Received: N/A

Mitchell, Beverly
c/o The WB Network, 3701 Oak St.
Bldg. 34R, Burbank, CA 91505
Actress
Response Time: N/A
Received: N/A

Mitchell, Edgar D.
2101 NASA Rd. 1
Houston, TX 77058
Astronaut
Response Time: N/A
Received: N/A

Mitchell, James
320 West 66th St.
NY, NY 10023
Actor
Response Time: N/A
Received: N/A

Mitra, Rhona
500 S. Buena Vista St.
Burbank, CA 91521
Actress
Response Time: N/A
Received: N/A

Moakley, John Joseph
U.S. House of Representatives
Washington, DC 20515
Politician
Response Time: N/A
Received: N/A

Mobley, Mary Ann
Two Ocean Way, Ste. 1000
Atlantic City, NJ 08401
Miss America 1959
Response Time: N/A
Received: N/A

Moceanu, Dominique
5959 FM 1960 Rd. W. #1437
Houston, TX 77069
Gymnast
Response Time: N/A
Received: N/A

Mochrie, Colin
10201 West Pico Blvd.
LA, CA 90035
Actor
Response Time: N/A
Received: N/A

Moffett, D.W.
4000 Warner Blvd.
Burbank, CA 91522
Actor
Response Time: N/A
Received: N/A

Mohr, Jay
1776 Broadway, Ste. 2001
NY, NY 10019
Actor
Response Time: 13 Days
Received: Signed Photo

Mohri, Mamoru
2101 NASA Rd. 1
Houston, TX 77058
Astronaut
Response Time: N/A
Received: N/A

Mollohan, Alan B.
U.S. House of Representatives
Washington, DC 20515
Politician
Response Time: N/A
Received: N/A

Molloy, Irene
4000 Warner Blvd.
Burbank, CA 91522
Actress
Response Time: N/A
Received: N/A

Moloney, Janel
4000 Warner Blvd.
Burbank, CA 91522
Actress
Response Time: N/A
Received: N/A

Momoa, Jason
c/o Baywatch Productions
510-18th Ave., Honolulu, HI 96816
Actor
Response Time: N/A
Received: N/A

Monaco, Kelly Marie
9242 Beverly Blvd.
BH, CA 90210
Playboy Playmate
Response Time: N/A
Received: N/A

Monaco, Kelly
4151 Prospect Ave.
LA, CA 90027
Actress
Response Time: N/A
Received: N/A

Mondale, Walter
220 S. 6th St.
Minneapolis, MN 55402-4502
Former Vice President; Politician
Response Time: 31 Days
Received: Signed Photo

Mondale, Walter
2200 First Bank Place East
Minneapolis, MN 55402
Former Vice President; Politician
Response Time: 10 Days
Received: SIC

Mo'Nique
5555 Melrose Ave.
Hollywood, CA 90038-3197
Actress
Response Time: N/A
Received: N/A

Montalbon, Ricardo
1423 Oriole Dr.
LA, CA 90069
Actor
Response Time: 103 Days
Received: Signed Photo

Montana, Joe
801 W. 47th St. #200
Kansas City, MO 64112
Football Player
Response Time: 150 Days
Received: STC

Montgomery Gentry
P.O. Box 283
Danville, KY 40423
Music Group
Response Time: 36 Days
Received: Signed Photo

Montgomery, John Michael
P.O. Box 128229
Nashville, TN 37212
Singer
Response Time: N/A
Received: N/A

Moore, Barbara
9242 Beverly Blvd.
BH, CA 90210
Playboy Playmate
Response Time: N/A
Received: N/A

Moore, Demi
375 Greenwich St. #725
NY, NY 10013
Actress
Response Time: 30 Days
Received: Signed Photo

Moore, Dennis
U.S. House of Representatives
Washington, DC 20515
Politician
Response Time: N/A
Received: N/A

Moore, Dickie
150 West End Ave. #26C
NY, NY 10023-5743
Actor
Response Time: N/A
Received: N/A

Moore, Mary Tyler
510 E. 86th St. #21A
NY, NY 10028
Actress
Response Time: 17 Days
Received: Signed Photo

Moore, Roger
2-4 Noel St. #43
London W1V 3RB, England
Actor
Response Time: 19 Days
Received: Signed Photo

Moore, Shemar
7800 Beverly Blvd.
LA, CA 90036
Actor
Response Time: N/A
Received: N/A

Moran, Erin
P.O. Box 3261
Quartz Hill, CA 93586
Actress
Response Time: 52 Days
Received: Signed Photo

Moran, James P.
U.S. House of Representatives
Washington, DC 20515
Politician
Response Time: N/A
Received: N/A

Moran, Jerry
U.S. House of Representatives
Washington, DC 20515
Politician
Response Time: N/A
Received: N/A

Moranis, Rick
101 Central Park W. #12B
NY, NY 10023
Actor
Response Time: N/A
Received: N/A

Moranis, Rick
1325 Ave. of the Americas, 15th Fl.
NY, NY 10019-6026
Actor
Response Time: 24 Days
Received: Signed Photo

Morella, Constance A.
U.S. House of Representatives
Washington, DC 20515
Politician
Response Time: N/A
Received: N/A

Morgan, Barbara R.
2101 NASA Rd. 1
Houston, TX 77058
Astronaut
Response Time: N/A
Received: N/A

Morgan, Harry
13172 Boca de Canyon Dr.
LA, CA 90049
Actor
Response Time: 13 Days
Received: Signed Photo

Morgan, Lorrie
P.O. Box 78
Spencer, TN 38585
Singer
Response Time: 29 Days
Received: Signed Photo

Morgan, Michele
4000 Warner Blvd.
Burbank, CA 91522
Actress
Response Time: N/A
Received: N/A

Morgan, Rob
1801 West Int'l. Spdwy. Blvd.
Daytona Beach, FL 32114
Auto Racing Personality
Response Time: 62 Days
Received: Signed Photo

Morin, Lee M.
2101 NASA Rd. 1
Houston, TX 77058
Astronaut
Response Time: N/A
Received: N/A

Morris, Garrett
4000 Warner Blvd.
Burbank, CA 91522
Actor
Response Time: N/A
Received: N/A

Morris, Julianne
3000 W. Alameda Ave.
Burbank, CA 91523
Actress
Response Time: N/A
Received: N/A

Morrow, Joshua
7800 Beverly Blvd.
LA, CA 90036
Actor
Response Time: N/A
Received: N/A

Mortensen, Viggo
11244 Huntley Place
Culver City, CA 90230
Actor
Response Time: 60 Days
Received: SIC

Moss, Ronn
7800 Beverly Blvd.
LA, CA 90036
Actor
Response Time: N/A
Received: N/A

Mulkey, Chris
5555 Melrose Ave.
Hollywood, CA 90038-3197
Actor
Response Time: N/A
Received: N/A

Mullane, Richard M.
2101 NASA Rd. 1
Houston, TX 77058
Astronaut
Response Time: N/A
Received: N/A

Murkowski, Frank
322 Hart Senate Office Bldg.
Washington, DC 20510
Senator
Response Time: N/A
Received: N/A

Murphy, Eddie
152 West 57th St., 47th Fl.
NY, NY 10019
Actor
Response Time: N/A
Received: N/A

Murphy, Eddie
4000 Warner Blvd.
Burbank, CA 91522
Actor
Response Time: N/A
Received: N/A

Murphy, Kim
5555 Melrose Ave.
Hollywood, CA 90038-3197
Actress
Response Time: N/A
Received: N/A

Murphy, Lynn
c/o Home Shopping Network
St. Petersburg, FL 33701
Home Shopping Network Host
Response Time: N/A
Received: N/A

Murray, Anne
12 St. Clair Ave. East
Box 69030, Toronto, ON M4T 1K0
Singer
Response Time: N/A
Received: N/A

Murray, Joel
10201 West Pico Blvd.
Trailer 779, LA, CA 90035
Actor
Response Time: N/A
Received: N/A

Murray, Patty
173 Russell Senate Office Bldg.
Washington, DC 20510
Senator
Response Time: N/A
Received: N/A

Murtha, John P.
U.S. House of Representatives
Washington, DC 20515
Politician
Response Time: N/A
Received: N/A

Musgrave, Story
2101 NASA Rd. 1
Houston, TX 77058
Astronaut
Response Time: N/A
Received: N/A

Musgrove, Ronnie
P.O. Box 139
Jackson, MS 39205
Governor
Response Time: N/A
Received: N/A

Musial, Stan
1655 Des Peres Rd. #125
St. Louis, MO 63131
Baseball Player
Response Time: 36 Days
Received: Signed Photo

Musial, Stan
85 Trent Dr.
Ladue, MO 63124
Baseball Player
Response Time: 59 Days
Received: Signed Photo

Myerson, Bess
Two Ocean Way, Ste. 1000
Atlantic City, NJ 08401
Miss America 1945
Response Time: N/A
Received: N/A

Myrick, Sue Wilkins
U.S. House of Representatives
Washington, DC 20515
Politician
Response Time: N/A
Received: N/A

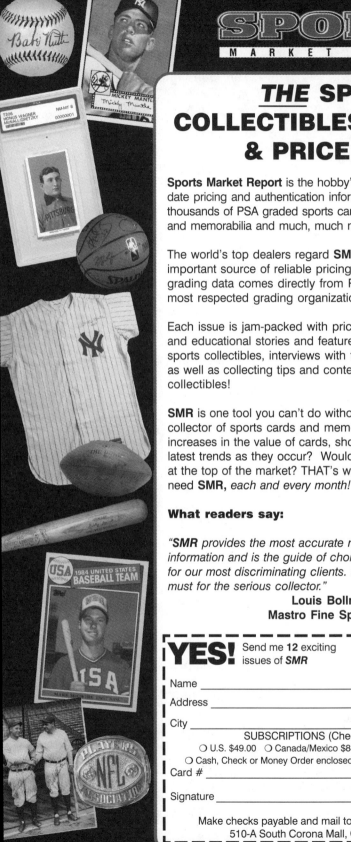

Nabors, Jim
215 Kulamanu Pl.
Honolulu, HI 96816
Actor
Response Time: 85 Days
Received: Signed Photo

Nadeau, Jerry
1801 West Int'l. Spdwy. Blvd.
Daytona Beach, FL 32114
Auto Racing Personality
Response Time: 76 Days
Received: Signed Photo

Nadeau, Jerry
P.O. Box 9
Harrisburg, NC 28075
Auto Racing Personality
Response Time: 26 Days
Received: Signed Photo

Najimy, Kathy
120 W. 45th St., 36th Fl.
NY, NY 10036
Actress
Response Time: 365 Days
Received: Signed Photo

Nader, Michael
320 West 66th St.
NY, NY 10023
Actor
Response Time: N/A
Received: N/A

Napolitano, Grace F.
U.S. House of Representatives
Washington, DC 20515
Politician
Response Time: N/A
Received: N/A

Nadler, Jerrold
U.S. House of Representatives
Washington, DC 20515
Politician
Response Time: N/A
Received: N/A

Neal, Richard E.
U.S. House of Representatives
Washington, DC 20515
Politician
Response Time: N/A
Received: N/A

Nagel, Steven R.
2101 NASA Rd. 1
Houston, TX 77058
Astronaut
Response Time: N/A
Received: N/A

Nelson, Ben
United States Senate
Washington, DC 20510
Senator
Response Time: N/A
Received: N/A

Nagler, Morgan
5555 Melrose Ave.
Hollywood, CA 90038-3197
Actress
Response Time: N/A
Received: N/A

Nelson, Bill
United States Senate
Washington, DC 20510
Senator
Response Time: N/A
Received: N/A

Nelson, Christen
4000 Warner Blvd.
Burbank, CA 91522
Actress
Response Time: N/A
Received: N/A

Nelson, Craig T.
150 W. 65th St.
NY, NY 10023-6975
Actor
Response Time: 31 Days
Received: Signed Photo

Nelson, Craig T.
28872 Boniface Dr.
Malibu, CA 90265
Actor
Response Time: N/A
Received: N/A

Nelson, Craig T.
9171 Wilshire Blvd. #436
BH, CA 90210
Actor
Response Time: N/A
Received: N/A

Nelson, George D.
2101 NASA Rd. 1
Houston, TX 77058
Astronaut
Response Time: N/A
Received: N/A

Nelson, Willie
P.O. Box 2689
Danbury, CT 06813
Singer
Response Time: 365 Days
Received: Signed Photo

Nemechek, Joe
1801 West Int'l. Spdwy. Blvd.
Daytona Beach, FL 32114
Auto Racing Personality
Response Time: 23 Days
Received: STC

Nespoli, Paolo
2101 NASA Rd. 1
Houston, TX 77058
Astronaut
Response Time: N/A
Received: N/A

Nethercutt Jr., George R.
U.S. House of Representatives
Washington, DC 20515
Politician
Response Time: N/A
Received: N/A

Newhart, Bob
420 Anapolo Dr.
LA, CA 90077-3411
Actor
Response Time: 48 Days
Received: Signed Photo

Newman, James H.
2101 NASA Rd. 1
Houston, TX 77058
Astronaut
Response Time: N/A
Received: N/A

Newman, Michael
c/o Baywatch Productions
510-18th Ave., Honolulu, HI 96816
Actor
Response Time: N/A
Received: N/A

Newman, Robert
51 W. 52 St.
NY, NY 10019
Actor
Response Time: N/A
Received: N/A

Newton, Wayne
3422 Happy Ln.
Las Vegas, NV 89120
Singer, Entertainer
Response Time: 30 Days
Received: Signed Photo

Newton, Wayne
6629 South Pecos
Las Vegas, NV 89120
Singer, Entertainer
Response Time: 30 Days
Received: Signed Photo

Newton-John, Olivia
P.O. Box 2710
Malibu, CA 90265
Actress
Response Time: 365 Days
Received: Signed Photo

Ney, Robert W.
U.S. House of Representatives
Washington, DC 20515
Politician
Response Time: N/A
Received: N/A

Nichols, Marisol
5555 Melrose Ave.
Hollywood, CA 90038-3197
Actress
Response Time: N/A
Received: N/A

Nichols, Stephen
4151 Prospect Ave.
LA, CA 90027
Actor
Response Time: N/A
Received: N/A

Nicholson, Jack
11500 W. Olympic Blvd., Ste. 510
LA, CA 90064
Actor
Response Time: 29 Days
Received: Signed Photo

Nicholson, Jack
9911 W. Pico Blvd. PH-A
LA, CA 90035
Actor
Response Time: N/A
Received: N/A

Nicklaus, Jack
11760 U.S. Highway #1
North Palm Beach, FL 33408-3023
Golfer
Response Time: 27 Days
Received: Signed Photo

Nickles, Don
133 Hart Senate Office Bldg.
Washington, DC 20510
Senator
Response Time: N/A
Received: N/A

Nicollier, Claude
2101 NASA Rd. 1
Houston, TX 77058
Astronaut
Response Time: N/A
Received: N/A

Nielsen, Leslie
1622 Viewmont Dr.
LA, CA 90069
Actor
Response Time: 26 Days
Received: Signed Photo

Nimoy, Leonard
2300 W. Victory Blvd. #C-384
Burbank, CA 91506-1200
Actor
Response Time: N/A
Received: N/A

Nimoy, Leonard
c/o Rumbleseat Productions
501 S. Beverly Dr., BH, CA 90212
Actor
Response Time: 48 Days
Received: Signed Photo

Nixon, Cynthia
c/o Sex and the City
1100 6th Ave., NY, NY 10036
Actress
Response Time: N/A
Received: N/A

No Doubt
c/o ND Friend Club
P.O. Box 8899, Anaheim, CA 92812
Music Group
Response Time: 14 Days
Received: Signed Photo

Noguchi, Soichi
2101 NASA Rd. 1
Houston, TX 77058
Astronaut
Response Time: N/A
Received: N/A

Nolin, Gena Lee
2135 Groveland Dr.
LA, CA 90046
Actress
Response Time: N/A
Received: N/A

Nolin, Gena Lee
c/o Baywatch Productions
510-18th Ave., Honolulu, HI 96816
Actress
Response Time: N/A
Received: N/A

Nolte, Nick
6174 Bonsall Dr.
Malibu, CA 90265
Actor
Response Time: 280 Days
Received: Signed Photo

Nordling, Jeffrey
8660 Hayden Place
Culver City, CA 90232
Actor
Response Time: N/A
Received: N/A

Norick, Lance
1801 West Int'l. Spdwy. Blvd.
Daytona Beach, FL 32114
Auto Racing Personality
Response Time: 73 Days
Received: Signed Photo

Noriega, Carlos I.
2101 NASA Rd. 1
Houston, TX 77058
Astronaut
Response Time: N/A
Received: N/A

Norris, Chuck
P.O. Box 872
Navasota, TX 77868
Actor, Martial Arts Expert
Response Time: 154 Days
Received: Signed Photo

North, Nolan
4151 Prospect Ave.
LA, CA 90027
Actor
Response Time: N/A
Received: N/A

North, Oliver
c/o NAE, 22570 Markey St. #220
Sterling, VA 20166
Politician, Radio Host
Response Time: 33 Days
Received: Signed Photo

North, Oliver
P.O. Box 9771
McLean, VA 22102
Politician, Radio Host
Response Time: 78 Days
Received: Signed Photo

Northagen, Callie
c/o Home Shopping Network
St. Petersburg, FL 33701
Home Shopping Network Host
Response Time: N/A
Received: N/A

Northup, Anne M.
U.S. House of Representatives
Washington, DC 20515
Politician
Response Time: N/A
Received: N/A

Norton, Eleanor Holmes
U.S. House of Representatives
Washington, DC 20515
Politician
Response Time: N/A
Received: N/A

Norwood, Charlie
U.S. House of Representatives
Washington, DC 20515
Politician
Response Time: N/A
Received: N/A

Nowak, Lisa M.
2101 NASA Rd. 1
Houston, TX 77058
Astronaut
Response Time: N/A
Received: N/A

Nussle, Jim
U.S. House of Representatives
Washington, DC 20515
Politician
Response Time: N/A
Received: N/A

O'Bannon, Frank
206 State Capitol
Indianapolis, IN 46204
Governor
Response Time: N/A
Received: N/A

Oak Ridge Boys, The
88 New Shackel Island Rd.
Hendersonville, TN 37075-2306
Music Group
Response Time: 17 Days
Received: Signed Photo

Oberstar, James L.
U.S. House of Representatives
Washington, DC 20515
Politician
Response Time: N/A
Received: N/A

Obey, David R.
U.S. House of Representatives
Washington, DC 20515
Politician
Response Time: N/A
Received: N/A

O'Brien, Conan
30 Rockefeller Plaza
NY, NY 10112
Television Personality
Response Time: 280 Days
Received: Signed Photo

O'Brien, Parry
73285 Goldflower St.
Palm Desert, CA 92260-5718
Track & Field Athlete
Response Time: N/A
Received: N/A

Ochoa, Ellen
2101 NASA Rd. 1
Houston, TX 77058
Astronaut
Response Time: N/A
Received: N/A

Ockels, Wubbo J.
2101 NASA Rd. 1
Houston, TX 77058
Astronaut
Response Time: N/A
Received: N/A

O'Connor, Bryan D.
2101 NASA Rd. 1
Houston, TX 77058
Astronaut
Response Time: N/A
Received: N/A

O'Connor, Carroll
30826 Broad Beach Rd.
Malibu, CA 90265
Actor
Response Time: 99 Days
Received: Signed Photo

O'Connor, Kevin
500 S. Buena Vista St.
Burbank, CA 91521
Actor
Response Time: N/A
Received: N/A

O'Connor, Sandra Day
1 First St. N.E.
Washington, DC 20543
Supreme Court Justice
Response Time: 21 Days
Received: Signed Photo

October Bachman, Cheryl
9242 Beverly Blvd.
BH, CA 90210
Playboy Playmate
Response Time: N/A
Received: N/A

October Paterson, Jodi Ann
9242 Beverly Blvd.
BH, CA 90210
Playboy Playmate
Response Time: N/A
Received: N/A

O'Donnell, Rosie
30 Rockefeller Plaza
NY, NY 10112-0002
Actress, Television Personality
Response Time: N/A
Received: N/A

Oefelein, William A.
2101 NASA Rd. 1
Houston, TX 77058
Astronaut
Response Time: N/A
Received: N/A

O'Keefe, Jodi Lyn
5555 Melrose Ave.
Hollywood, CA 90038-3197
Actress
Response Time: N/A
Received: N/A

O'Leary, Brian T.
2101 NASA Rd. 1
Houston, TX 77058
Astronaut
Response Time: N/A
Received: N/A

Olivas, John D.
2101 NASA Rd. 1
Houston, TX 77058
Astronaut
Response Time: N/A
Received: N/A

Olivia, Lorraine
9242 Beverly Blvd.
BH, CA 90210
Playboy Playmate
Response Time: N/A
Received: N/A

Olson, Kalin
9242 Beverly Blvd.
BH, CA 90210
Playboy Playmate
Response Time: N/A
Received: N/A

Olver, John W.
U.S. House of Representatives
Washington, DC 20515
Politician
Response Time: N/A
Received: N/A

Onasch, Kim
1268 East 14th St.
Brooklyn, NY 11230
Actress
Response Time: N/A
Received: N/A

Ono, Yoko
c/o Studio One, 1 W. 72nd St.
NY, NY 10023
Author; Widow of John Lennon
Response Time: N/A
Received: N/A

Orbach, Jerry
10100 Santa Monica Blvd. #2490
LA, CA 90067
Actor
Response Time: N/A
Received: N/A

Orbach, Jerry
1325 Ave. of the Americas, 15th Fl.
NY, NY 10019
Actor
Response Time: 41 Days
Received: Signed Photo

Orbach, Jerry
301 W. 53rd St. #20A
NY, NY 10019
Actor
Response Time: 41 Days
Received: Signed Photo

Orbach, Jerry
1230 Ave. of Americas
NY, NY 10020
Actor
Response Time: N/A
Received: N/A

Oreskovich, Alesha M.
9242 Beverly Blvd.
BH, CA 90210
Playboy Playmate
Response Time: N/A
Received: N/A

Orman, Suze
c/o QVC, 1200 Wilson Dr.
West Chester, PA 19380
Financial Expert, Author
Response Time: N/A
Received: N/A

Ortiz, Solomon P.
U.S. House of Representatives
Washington, DC 20515
Politician
Response Time: N/A
Received: N/A

Osborne, Tom
U.S. House of Representatives
Washington, DC 20515
Politician
Response Time: N/A
Received: N/A

Ose, Doug
U.S. House of Representatives
Washington, DC 20515
Politician
Response Time: N/A
Received: N/A

Osmond, Ken
9863 Wornam Ave.
Sunland, CA 91040
Actor
Response Time: 25 Days
Received: Signed Photo

Osmond, Marie
3325 North University, Ste. 375
Provo, UT 84605
Singer, Doll Designer
Response Time: 23 Days
Received: Signed Photo

Oswald, Stephen S.
2101 NASA Rd. 1
Houston, TX 77058
Astronaut
Response Time: N/A
Received: N/A

O'Toole, Annette
1230 Ave. of Americas
NY, NY 10020
Actress
Response Time: N/A
Received: N/A

Otter, C. L. "Butch"
U.S. House of Representatives
Washington, DC 20515
Politician
Response Time: N/A
Received: N/A

Overall, Park
4843 Arcola Ave.
N. Hollywood, CA 91601
Actress
Response Time: N/A
Received: N/A

Overman, Ion
4151 Prospect Ave.
LA, CA 90027
Actress
Response Time: N/A
Received: N/A

Overstreet, Paul
P.O. Box 320
Pegram, TN 37143
Singer
Response Time: 7 Days
Received: Signed Photo

Owens, Bill
136 State Capitol
Denver, CO 80203-1792
Governor
Response Time: N/A
Received: N/A

Owens, Major R.
U.S. House of Representatives
Washington, DC 20515
Politician
Response Time: N/A
Received: N/A

Oxley, Michael G.
U.S. House of Representatives
Washington, DC 20515
Politician
Response Time: N/A
Received: N/A

Oz, Frank
P.O. Box 20750
NY, NY 10023-1488
Actor
Response Time: 15 Days
Received: Signed Photo

Pacino, Al
301 W. 57th St. #10C
NY, NY 10017
Actor
Response Time: 25 Days
Received: Signed Photo

Pacino, Al
350 Park Ave. #900
NY, NY 10023
Actor
Response Time: 21 Days
Received: Signed Photo

Packard, Kelly
c/o Baywatch Productions
510-18th Ave., Honolulu, HI 96816
Actress
Response Time: N/A
Received: N/A

Page, Erika
56 West 66th St.
NY, NY 10023
Actress
Response Time: N/A
Received: N/A

Page, LaWanda
1056 W. 84th St.
LA, CA 90044
Actress
Response Time: 18 Days
Received: Signed Photo

Paget, Debra
737 Kuhlman Rd.
Houston, TX 77024
Actress
Response Time: N/A
Received: N/A

Paisley, Brad
P.O. Box 121113
Nashville, TN 37212
Singer
Response Time: 37 Days
Received: Signed Photo

Palladino, Erik
4000 Warner Blvd.
Burbank, CA 91522
Actor
Response Time: 46 Days
Received: Signed Photo

Pallone Jr., Frank
U.S. House of Representatives
Washington, DC 20515
Politician
Response Time: N/A
Received: N/A

Palmer, Arnold
P.O. Box 52
Youngstown, PA 15696
Golfer
Response Time: 15 Days
Received: Signed Photo

Palmer, Betsy
4040 Farmdale Ave.
Studio City, CA 91604
Actress
Response Time: 18 Days
Received: Signed Photo

Panettiere, Hayden
51 W. 52 St.
NY, NY 10019
Actress
Response Time: N/A
Received: N/A

Parazynski, Scott E.
2101 NASA Rd. 1
Houston, TX 77058
Astronaut
Response Time: N/A
Received: N/A

Parisse, Annie
1268 East 14th St.
Brooklyn, NY 11230
Actress
Response Time: N/A
Received: N/A

Park, Michael
1268 East 14th St.
Brooklyn, NY 11230
Actor
Response Time: N/A
Received: N/A

Park, Steve
1675 Coddle Creek Hwy.
Mooresville, NC 28115
Auto Racing Personality
Response Time: 180 Days
Received: Signed Photo

Park, Steve
1801 West Int'l. Spdwy. Blvd.
Daytona Beach, FL 32114
Auto Racing Personality
Response Time: 291 Days
Received: Signed Photo

Park, Susie
5555 Melrose Ave.
Hollywood, CA 90038-3197
Actress
Response Time: N/A
Received: N/A

Parker Jr., Hank
1801 West Int'l. Spdwy. Blvd.
Daytona Beach, FL 32114
Auto Racing Personality
Response Time: 71 Days
Received: Signed Photo

Parker, Fess
P.O. Box 908
Los Olivos, CA 93411
Actor
Response Time: 39 Days
Received: Signed Photo

Parker, Frank
3000 W. Alameda Ave.
Burbank, CA 91523
Actor
Response Time: N/A
Received: N/A

Parker, Nicole Ari
5555 Melrose Ave.
Hollywood, CA 90038-3197
Actress
Response Time: N/A
Received: N/A

Parker, Robert A. R.
2101 NASA Rd. 1
Houston, TX 77058
Astronaut
Response Time: N/A
Received: N/A

Parker, Sarah Jessica
P.O. Box 69646
LA, CA 90069
Actress
Response Time: 22 Days
Received: Signed Photo

Parker, Trey
South Park, c/o Comedy Central
1775 Broadway, NY, NY 10019
Creator, Southpark
Response Time: 50 Days
Received: Signed Photo

Parrilla, Lana
100 Universal City Plaza
Universal City, CA 91608
Actress
Response Time: N/A
Received: N/A

Parrish, Kimberly
c/o QVC, 1200 Wilson Dr.
West Chester, PA 19380
QVC Host
Response Time: N/A
Received: N/A

Parros, Peter
1268 East 14th St.
Brooklyn, NY 11230
Actor
Response Time: N/A
Received: N/A

Parrott, Todd
1801 West Int'l. Spdwy. Blvd.
Daytona Beach, FL 32114
Auto Racing Personality
Response Time: 216 Days
Received: Signed Photo

Parsons, Benny
1801 West Int'l. Spdwy. Blvd.
Daytona Beach, FL 32114
Auto Racing Personality
Response Time: 109 Days
Received: Signed Photo

Parsons, Phil
1801 West Int'l. Spdwy. Blvd.
Daytona Beach, FL 32114
Auto Racing Personality
Response Time: 90 Days
Received: Signed Photo

Parton, Julia
1350 E. Flamingo Rd. #105
Las Vegas, NV 89109
Model, Actress
Response Time: 70 Days
Received: Signed Photo

Parton, Stella
P.O. Box 120871
Nashville, TN 37212
Singer
Response Time: 16 Days
Received: Signed Photo

Pascrell Jr., Bill
U.S. House of Representatives
Washington, DC 20515
Politician
Response Time: N/A
Received: N/A

Pastor, Ed
U.S. House of Representatives
Washington, DC 20515
Politician
Response Time: N/A
Received: N/A

Pataki, George E.
State Capitol
AlbaNY, NY 12224
Governor
Response Time: N/A
Received: N/A

Patrick, Nicholas J. M.
2101 NASA Rd. 1
Houston, TX 77058
Astronaut
Response Time: N/A
Received: N/A

Patterson, Scott
4000 Warner Blvd.
Burbank, CA 91522
Actor
Response Time: N/A
Received: N/A

Patton, Paul E.
State Capitol, 700 Capitol Ave.
Frankfort, KY 40601
Governor
Response Time: N/A
Received: N/A

Paul, Alexandra
c/o Baywatch Productions
510-18th Ave., Honolulu, HI 96816
Actress
Response Time: N/A
Received: N/A

Paul, Ron
U.S. House of Representatives
Washington, DC 20515
Politician
Response Time: N/A
Received: N/A

Paulk, Marcus T.
5555 Melrose Ave.
Hollywood, CA 90038-3197
Actor
Response Time: N/A
Received: N/A

Paulson, Sarah
4000 Warner Blvd.
Burbank, CA 91522
Actress
Response Time: N/A
Received: N/A

Payette, Julie
2101 NASA Rd. 1
Houston, TX 77058
Astronaut
Response Time: N/A
Received: N/A

Payne, Donald M.
U.S. House of Representatives
Washington, DC 20515
Politician
Response Time: N/A
Received: N/A

Pearlman, Rhea
P.O. Box 491246
LA, CA 90049
Actress
Response Time: 180 Days
Received: Signed Photo

Peck, Austin
3000 W. Alameda Ave.
Burbank, CA 91523
Actor
Response Time: N/A
Received: N/A

Peck, J. Eddie
320 West 66th St.
NY, NY 10023
Actor
Response Time: N/A
Received: N/A

Peet, Amanda
4000 Warner Blvd.
Burbank, CA 91522
Actress
Response Time: N/A
Received: N/A

Peete, Holly Robinson
4000 Warner Blvd.
Burbank, CA 91522
Actress
Response Time: N/A
Received: N/A

Pelligrini, Margaret
5018 N. 61st St.
Glendale, AZ 85301
Actress
Response Time: N/A
Received: N/A

Pelosi, Nancy
U.S. House of Representatives
Washington, DC 20515
Politician
Response Time: N/A
Received: N/A

Pemberton, Robin
1801 West Int'l. Spdwy. Blvd.
Daytona Beach, FL 32114
Auto Racing Personality
Response Time: 156 Days
Received: Signed Photo

Pena, Anthony
7800 Beverly Blvd.
LA, CA 90036
Actor
Response Time: N/A
Received: N/A

Pena, Elizabeth
5555 Melrose Ave.
Hollywood, CA 90038-3197
Actress
Response Time: N/A
Received: N/A

Pence, Mike
U.S. House of Representatives
Washington, DC 20515
Politician
Response Time: N/A
Received: N/A

Pennington, Janice
5757 Wilshire Blvd. #206
LA, CA 90036
Television Personality
Response Time: N/A
Received: N/A

Penske, Roger
136 Knob Hill Rd.
Mooresville, NC 28115
NASCAR Team Owner
Response Time: 180 Days
Received: STC

Perfect Stranger
P.O. Box 773
Chanute, KS 66720
Music Group
Response Time: 120 Days
Received: Signed Photo

Perkins, Susan
Two Ocean Way, Ste. 1000
Atlantic City, NJ 08401
Miss America 1978
Response Time: N/A
Received: N/A

Perkovic, Diana
c/o Home Shopping Network
St. Petersburg, FL 33701
Home Shopping Network Host
Response Time: N/A
Received: N/A

Perot, H. Ross
1700 Lakeside Square
Dallas, TX 75251
Politician
Response Time: N/A
Received: N/A

Perreau, Gigi
268 N. Bowling Green Way
LA, CA 90049
Actress
Response Time: N/A
Received: N/A

Perrin, Philippe
2101 NASA Rd. 1
Houston, TX 77058
Astronaut
Response Time: N/A
Received: N/A

Perry, Donna
9242 Beverly Blvd.
BH, CA 90210
Playboy Playmate
Response Time: N/A
Received: N/A

Perry, Jeff
5555 Melrose Ave.
Hollywood, CA 90038-3197
Actor
Response Time: N/A
Received: N/A

Perry, Matthew
4000 Warner Blvd.
Burbank, CA 91522
Actor
Response Time: N/A
Received: N/A

Perry, Rick
P.O. Box 12428
Austin, TX 78711
Governor
Response Time: N/A
Received: N/A

Perry, Shari Dyon
5555 Melrose Ave.
Hollywood, CA 90038-3197
Actress
Response Time: N/A
Received: N/A

Pesci, Joe
P.O. Box 6
Lavallette, NJ 08735
Actor
Response Time: 8 Days
Received: SIC

Peter, Paul & Mary
301 W. 53rd St.
NY, NY 10023
Music Group
Response Time: N/A
Received: N/A

Peters, Bernadette
323 W. 80th St.
NY, NY 10024
Actress, Singer
Response Time: 77 Days
Received: Signed Photo

Peterson, Collin C.
U.S. House of Representatives
Washington, DC 20515
Politician
Response Time: N/A
Received: N/A

Peterson, Donald H.
2101 NASA Rd. 1
Houston, TX 77058
Astronaut
Response Time: N/A
Received: N/A

Peterson, John E.
U.S. House of Representatives
Washington, DC 20515
Politician
Response Time: N/A
Received: N/A

Peterson, Michael
P.O. Box 120205
Nashville, TN 37212
Singer
Response Time: 14 Days
Received: Signed Photo

Petree, Andy
1801 West Int'l. Spdwy. Blvd.
Daytona Beach, FL 32114
Auto Racing Personality
Response Time: 133 Days
Received: Signed Photo

Petri, Thomas E.
U.S. House of Representatives
Washington, DC 20515
Politician
Response Time: N/A
Received: N/A

Petrone, Shana
209 10th Ave. S. #229
Nashville, TN 37230
Singer
Response Time: 15 Days
Received: Signed Photo

Pettiford, Atonia
c/o Home Shopping Network
St. Petersburg, FL 33701
Home Shopping Network Host
Response Time: N/A
Received: N/A

Pettit, Donald R.
2101 NASA Rd. 1
Houston, TX 77058
Astronaut
Response Time: N/A
Received: N/A

Petty, Kyle
1801 West Int'l. Spdwy. Blvd.
Daytona Beach, FL 32114
Auto Racing Personality
Response Time: 217 Days
Received: Signed Photo

Petty, Kyle
Rt. 4 Box 86
Randleman, NC 27317
Auto Racing Personality
Response Time: 130 Days
Received: Signed Photo

Petty, Richard
311 Branson Mill Rd.
Randleman, NC 27317
Auto Racing Personality
Response Time: 11 Days
Received: Signed Photo

Petty, Richard
1801 West Int'l. Spdwy. Blvd.
Daytona Beach, FL 32114
Auto Racing Personality
Response Time: 90 Days
Received: Signed Photo

Pfeiffer, Dedee
4000 Warner Blvd.
Burbank, CA 91522
Actress
Response Time: N/A
Received: N/A

Phelps, David D.
U.S. House of Representatives
Washington, DC 20515
Politician
Response Time: N/A
Received: N/A

Philbin, Regis
7 Lincoln Square, 5th Fl.
NY, NY 10023
Television Personality
Response Time: 64 Days
Received: Signed Photo

Phillips, John L.
2101 NASA Rd. 1
Houston, TX 77058
Astronaut
Response Time: N/A
Received: N/A

Phillips, Michelle
4350 Berryman Ave., Apt. 4
LA, CA 90066
Singer
Response Time: 94 Days
Received: Signed Photo

Piazza, Mike
61 Fox Ln.
Dix Hills, NY 11746-5928
Baseball Player
Response Time: 41 Days
Received: STC

Piazza, Mike
P.O. Box 864, Oakwood Ln.
Valley Forge, PA 19481
Baseball Player
Response Time: 15 Days
Received: STC

Picatto, Antoinette
1230 Ave. of Americas
NY, NY 10020
Actress
Response Time: N/A
Received: N/A

Pickering, Charles W. "Chip"
U.S. House of Representatives
Washington, DC 20515
Politician
Response Time: N/A
Received: N/A

Pickett, Jay
4151 Prospect Ave.
LA, CA 90027
Actor
Response Time: N/A
Received: N/A

Pierce, David Hyde
5555 Melrose Ave.
Hollywood, CA 90038-3197
Actor
Response Time: N/A
Received: N/A

Pinson, Julie
4151 Prospect Ave.
LA, CA 90027
Actress
Response Time: N/A
Received: N/A

Pinter, Colleen Zenk
1268 East 14th St.
Brooklyn, NY 11230
Actress
Response Time: N/A
Received: N/A

Pitt, Brad
9150 Wilshire Blvd. #350
BH, CA 90212
Actor
Response Time: N/A
Received: N/A

Pitts, Joseph R.
U.S. House of Representatives
Washington, DC 20515
Politician
Response Time: N/A
Received: N/A

Plana, Tony
5555 Melrose Ave.
Hollywood, CA 90038-3197
Actor
Response Time: N/A
Received: N/A

Platt, Victoria
51 W. 52 St.
NY, NY 10019
Actress
Response Time: N/A
Received: N/A

Platters, The
990 Mass Ave.
Arlington, MA 02476
Music Group
Response Time: 8 Days
Received: Signed Photo

Platts, Todd Russell
U.S. House of Representatives
Washington, DC 20515
Politician
Response Time: N/A
Received: N/A

Pogue, William R.
2101 NASA Rd. 1
Houston, TX 77058
Astronaut
Response Time: N/A
Received: N/A

Poindexter, Alan G.
2101 NASA Rd. 1
Houston, TX 77058
Astronaut
Response Time: N/A
Received: N/A

Poitier, Sidney
9255 Doheny Rd.
LA, CA 90069-3201
Actor
Response Time: 85 Days
Received: Signed Photo

Polansky, Mark L.
2101 NASA Rd. 1
Houston, TX 77058
Astronaut
Response Time: N/A
Received: N/A

Pombo, Richard W.
U.S. House of Representatives
Washington, DC 20515
Politician
Response Time: N/A
Received: N/A

Pomeroy, Earl
U.S. House of Representatives
Washington, DC 20515
Politician
Response Time: N/A
Received: N/A

Pontes, Marcos
2101 NASA Rd. 1
Houston, TX 77058
Astronaut
Response Time: N/A
Received: N/A

Pope, Carly
4000 Warner Blvd.
Burbank, CA 91522
Actress
Response Time: N/A
Received: N/A

Portman, Rob
U.S. House of Representatives
Washington, DC 20515
Politician
Response Time: N/A
Received: N/A

Post, Markie
10152 - 1/2 Riverside Dr. #333
Toluca Lake, CA 91602
Actress
Response Time: 59 Days
Received: Signed Photo

Postlethwaite, Pete
Julian House, 4 Windmill St.
London W1P 1HF, United Kingdom
Actor
Response Time: 27 Days
Received: Signed Photo

Poston, Tom
2930 Deep Canyon
BH, CA 90210
Actor
Response Time: N/A
Received: N/A

Potter, Chris
1230 Ave. of Americas
NY, NY 10020
Actor
Response Time: N/A
Received: N/A

Potter, Monica
9830 Wilshire Blvd.
BH, CA 90212
Actress
Response Time: N/A
Received: N/A

Potts, Annie
5555 Melrose Ave.
Hollywood, CA 90038-3197
Actress
Response Time: N/A
Received: N/A

Potts, Annie
P.O. Box 29400
LA, CA 90029
Actress
Response Time: 19 Days
Received: Signed Photo

Poundstone, Paula
1223 Broadway #162
Santa Monica, CA 90404
Comedian
Response Time: 55 Days
Received: Signed Photo

Powell, Colin
909 W. Washington St., Ste. 767
Alexandria, VA 22314
Politician
Response Time: 30 Days
Received: Signed Photo

Powell, Esteban
5555 Melrose Ave.
Hollywood, CA 90038-3197
Actor
Response Time: N/A
Received: N/A

Powell, Susan
Two Ocean Way, Ste. 1000
Atlantic City, NJ 08401
Miss America 1981
Response Time: N/A
Received: N/A

Powers, Tommy
1801 West Int'l. Spdwy. Blvd.
Daytona Beach, FL 32114
Auto Racing Personality
Response Time: 62 Days
Received: Signed Photo

Precourt Jr., Charles J.
2101 NASA Rd. 1
Houston, TX 77058
Astronaut
Response Time: N/A
Received: N/A

Presley, Brian
4151 Prospect Ave.
LA, CA 90027
Actor
Response Time: N/A
Received: N/A

Pressley, Robert
1801 West Int'l. Spdwy. Blvd.
Daytona Beach, FL 32114
Auto Racing Personality
Response Time: 78 Days
Received: Signed Photo

Pressly, Jamie
4000 Warner Blvd.
Burbank, CA 91522
Actress
Response Time: N/A
Received: N/A

Preston, Kelly
15821 Ventura Blvd. #460
Encino CA 91436
Actress
Response Time: 90 Days
Received: Signed Photo

Prewitt, Cheryl
Two Ocean Way, Ste. 1000
Atlantic City, NJ 08401
Miss America 1980
Response Time: N/A
Received: N/A

Price, David E.
U.S. House of Representatives
Washington, DC 20515
Politician
Response Time: N/A
Received: N/A

Price, Molly
4000 Warner Blvd.
Burbank, CA 91522
Actress
Response Time: N/A
Received: N/A

Price, Ray
P.O. Box 61
Harrisburg, PA 17108
Singer
Response Time: 11 Days
Received: Signed Photo

Pride, Charlie
3198 Royal Ln.
Dallas, TX 75229
Singer
Response Time: 60 Days
Received: Signed Photo

Principal, Victoria
c/o QVC, 1200 Wilson Dr.
West Chester, PA 19380
Actress, Skincare Creator
Response Time: N/A
Received: N/A

Principal, Victoria
5700 Wilshire, Ste. 575
LA, CA 90036
Actress, Skincare Creator
Response Time: N/A
Received: N/A

Prinze Jr., Freddie
9830 Wilshire Blvd.
BH, CA 90212
Actor
Response Time: 391 Days
Received: Signed Photo

Pruett, Jeanne
2804 Opryland Dr.
Nashville, TN 37214
Singer
Response Time: N/A
Received: N/A

Pruett, Scott
1801 West Int'l. Spdwy. Blvd.
Daytona Beach, FL 32114
Auto Racing Personality
Response Time: 82 Days
Received: Signed Photo

Pryce, Deborah
U.S. House of Representatives
Washington, DC 20515
Politician
Response Time: N/A
Received: N/A

Pryor, Nicholas
4151 Prospect Ave.
LA, CA 90027
Actor
Response Time: N/A
Received: N/A

Puck, Wolfgang
c/o Home Shopping Network
St. Petersburg, FL 33701
World-Renowned Chef
Response Time: N/A
Received: N/A

Purdee, Nathan
56 West 66th St.
NY, NY 10023
Actor
Response Time: N/A
Received: N/A

Purvis, Jeff
1801 West Int'l. Spdwy. Blvd.
Daytona Beach, FL 32114
Auto Racing Personality
Response Time: 173 Days
Received: Signed Photo

Putnam, Adam H.
U.S. House of Representatives
Washington, DC 20515
Politician
Response Time: N/A
Received: N/A

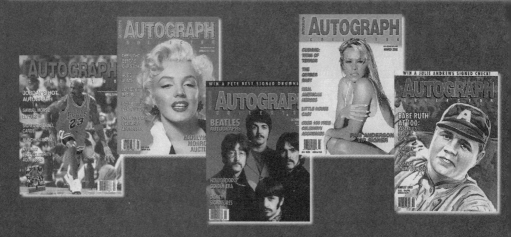

Quaid, Dennis
9665 Wilshire Blvd. #200
BH, CA 90212
Actor
Response Time: 35 Days
Received: Signed Photo

Quaid, Randy
270 N. Canon Dr., Ste. 1064
BH, CA 90210
Actor
Response Time: N/A
Received: N/A

Quayle, Dan
2929 E. Camelback Rd. #124
Phoenix, AZ 85016-4425
Politician
Response Time: 54 Days
Received: Signed Photo

Quinlan, Maeve
7800 Beverly Blvd.
LA, CA 90036
Actress
Response Time: N/A
Received: N/A

Quinn, Adian
8383 Wilshire Blvd. #340
BH, CA 90211
Actor
Response Time: 70 Days
Received: Signed Photo

Quinn, Anthony
420 Poppasquash Rd.
Bristol, RI 02809-1008
Actor
Response Time: 43 Days
Received: Signed Photo

Quinn, Francesco
7800 Beverly Blvd.
LA, CA 90036
Actor
Response Time: N/A
Received: N/A

Quinn, Jack
U.S. House of Representatives
Washington, DC 20515
Politician
Response Time: N/A
Received: N/A

Raabe, Meinhardt
P.O. Box 913
Penney Farms, FL 32079
Actor
Response Time: N/A
Received: N/A

Rachins, Alan
10201 West Pico Blvd.
Trailer 779, LA, CA 90035
Actor
Response Time: N/A
Received: N/A

Radanovich, George
U.S. House of Representatives
Washington, DC 20515
Politician
Response Time: N/A
Received: N/A

Rademacher, Ingo
5700 Wilshire, Ste. 575
LA, CA 90036
Actor
Response Time: N/A
Received: N/A

Radko, Christopher
c/o QVC, 1200 Wilson Dr.
West Chester, PA 19380
Radko Ornaments Creator
Response Time: N/A
Received: N/A

Rafko, Kaye Lani Rae
Two Ocean Way, Ste. 1000
Atlantic City, NJ 08401
Miss America 1988
Response Time: N/A
Received: N/A

Ragland, Michelle
c/o Home Shopping Network
St. Petersburg, FL 33701
Home Shopping Network Host
Response Time: N/A
Received: N/A

Ragsdale, William
4000 Warner Blvd.
Burbank, CA 91522
Actor
Response Time: N/A
Received: N/A

Rahall II, Nick J.
U.S. House of Representatives
Washington, DC 20515
Politician
Response Time: N/A
Received: N/A

Raider, Brad
5555 Melrose Ave.
Hollywood, CA 90038-3197
Actor
Response Time: N/A
Received: N/A

Rainer, Luise
34 Eton Mews North
London, SW1 XAS, England
Actress
Response Time: N/A
Received: N/A

Raines, Ron
51 W. 52 St.
NY, NY 10019
Actor
Response Time: N/A
Received: N/A

Raines, Tony
1801 West Int'l. Spdwy. Blvd.
Daytona Beach, FL 32114
Auto Racing Personality
Response Time: 190 Days
Received: Signed Photo

Ralph, Sheryl Lee
5555 Melrose Ave.
Hollywood, CA 90038-3197
Actress
Response Time: N/A
Received: N/A

Ramey, Venus
Two Ocean Way, Ste. 1000
Atlantic City, NJ 08401
Miss America 1944
Response Time: N/A
Received: N/A

Ramirez, Marisa
4151 Prospect Ave.
LA, CA 90027
Actress
Response Time: N/A
Received: N/A

Ramos, Luis Antonio
1230 Ave. of Americas
NY, NY 10020
Actor
Response Time: N/A
Received: N/A

Ramstad, Jim
U.S. House of Representatives
Washington, DC 20515
Politician
Response Time: N/A
Received: N/A

Randall, Josh
5555 Melrose Ave.
Hollywood, CA 90038-3197
Actor
Response Time: N/A
Received: N/A

Randall, Tony
1 West 81st St. #6-D
NY, NY 10024
Actor
Response Time: 6 Days
Received: Signed Photo

Randolph, Joyce
295 Central Park W. #18A
NY, NY 10024
Actress
Response Time: 22 Days
Received: Signed Photo

Randy Savage
13300 Indian Rocks Rd. #304
Largo, FL 33774-2008
Wrestler
Response Time: 30 Days
Received: Signed Photo

Rangel, Charles B.
U.S. House of Representatives
Washington, DC 20515
Politician
Response Time: N/A
Received: N/A

Rascal Flatts
P.O. Box 330427
Nashville, TN 37203
Music Group
Response Time: N/A
Received: N/A

Rauch, Paul
51 W. 52 St.
NY, NY 10019
Actor
Response Time: N/A
Received: N/A

Raven, Eddy
P.O. Box 2476
Hendersonville, TN 37077
Singer
Response Time: 30 Days
Received: Signed Photo

Ravencroft, Thurl
500 S. Buena Vista
Burbank, CA 91521
Voice of "Tony the Tiger"
Response Time: 21 Days
Received: Signed Photo

Raver, Kim
4000 Warner Blvd.
Burbank, CA 91522
Actress
Response Time: N/A
Received: N/A

Ray J
5555 Melrose Ave.
Hollywood, CA 90038-3197
Actor
Response Time: N/A
Received: N/A

Ray, Robert W.
1001 Pennsylvania Ave. N.W.
Ste. 490-N., Washington, DC 20004
Independent Counsel
Response Time: 35 Days
Received: Signed Photo

Raye, Collin
P.O. Box 530
Reno, NV 89509
Singer
Response Time: 35 Days
Received: Signed Photo

Readdy, William F.
2101 NASA Rd. 1
Houston, TX 77058
Astronaut
Response Time: N/A
Received: N/A

Reckell, Peter
3000 W. Alameda Ave.
Burbank, CA 91523
Actor
Response Time: N/A
Received: N/A

Reddy, Helen
820 Stanford Dr.
Santa Monica, CA 90403
Singer
Response Time: N/A
Received: N/A

Redford, Robert
1101 East Montana Ave.
Santa Monica, CA 90403
Actor
Response Time: 37 Days
Received: Signed Photo

Reed, Jack
320 Hart Senate Office Bldg.
Washington, DC 20510
Senator
Response Time: N/A
Received: N/A

Reeves, Julie
P.O. Box 300
Russell, KY 41169
Singer
Response Time: 9 Days
Received: Signed Photo

Reeves, Scott
7800 Beverly Blvd.
LA, CA 90036
Actor
Response Time: N/A
Received: N/A

Reffner, Bryan
1801 West Int'l. Spdwy. Blvd.
Daytona Beach, FL 32114
Auto Racing Personality
Response Time: 78 Days
Received: Signed Photo

Regula, Ralph
U.S. House of Representatives
Washington, DC 20515
Politician
Response Time: N/A
Received: N/A

Rehberg, Dennis R.
U.S. House of Representatives
Washington, DC 20515
Politician
Response Time: N/A
Received: N/A

Rehnquist, William
Supreme Court of the United States
Washington, DC 20543
Supreme Court Justice
Response Time: 30 Days
Received: Signed Photo

Reid, Francis
3000 W. Alameda Ave.
Burbank, CA 91523
Actress
Response Time: N/A
Received: N/A

Reid, Harry
528 Hart Senate Office Bldg.
Washington, DC 20510
Senator
Response Time: N/A
Received: N/A

Reightler Jr., Kenneth S.
2101 NASA Rd. 1
Houston, TX 77058
Astronaut
Response Time: N/A
Received: N/A

Reilly, James F.
2101 NASA Rd. 1
Houston, TX 77058
Astronaut
Response Time: N/A
Received: N/A

Reilly, Patti
c/o QVC, 1200 Wilson Dr.
West Chester, PA 19380
QVC Host
Response Time: N/A
Received: N/A

Reiner, Rob
335 N. Maple Dr., Ste. 135
BH, CA 90210
Actor, Director
Response Time: 32 Days
Received: Signed Photo

Reiser, Robbie
1801 West Int'l. Spdwy. Blvd.
Daytona Beach, FL 32114
Auto Racing Personality
Response Time: 167 Days
Received: Signed Photo

Reisman, Garrett E.
2101 NASA Rd. 1
Houston, TX 77058
Astronaut
Response Time: N/A
Received: N/A

Remar, James
1230 Ave. of Americas
NY, NY 10020
Actor
Response Time: N/A
Received: N/A

Remini, Leah
10202 W. Washington Blvd.
Culver City, CA 90232
Actress
Response Time: 47 Days
Received: Signed Photo

Renfrow, Randy
1801 West Int'l. Spdwy. Blvd.
Daytona Beach, FL 32114
Auto Racing Personality
Response Time: 133 Days
Received: Signed Photo

Reno, Janet
10th & Constitution N.W.
Washington, DC 20530
Politician
Response Time: 45 Days
Received: Signed Photo

Retton, Mary Lou
114 White Ave.
Fairmont, WV 26554
Gymnast
Response Time: 9 Days
Received: Signed Photo

Rex, Simon
4000 Warner Blvd.
Burbank, CA 91522
Actor
Response Time: N/A
Received: N/A

Reyes, Silvestre
U.S. House of Representatives
Washington, DC 20515
Politician
Response Time: N/A
Received: N/A

Reynolds, Burt
16133 Jupiter Farms
Jupiter, FL 33478
Actor
Response Time: 41 Days
Received: Signed Photo

Reynolds, Debbie
6514 Lankership
N. Hollywood, CA 91606
Actress
Response Time: 16 Days
Received: Signed Photo

Reynolds, James
3000 W. Alameda Ave.
Burbank, CA 91523
Actor
Response Time: N/A
Received: N/A

Reynolds, Ryan
10201 West Pico Blvd.
LA, CA 90035
Actor
Response Time: N/A
Received: N/A

Reynolds, Thomas M.
U.S. House of Representatives
Washington, DC 20515
Politician
Response Time: N/A
Received: N/A

Rhea, Caroline
5555 Melrose Ave.
Hollywood, CA 90038-3197
Actress
Response Time: N/A
Received: N/A

Rice, Anne
1239 First St.
New Orleans, LA 70130
Author
Response Time: 39 Days
Received: Signed Photo

Richards, Brooke
9242 Beverly Blvd.
BH, CA 90210
Playboy Playmate
Response Time: N/A
Received: N/A

Richards, Denise
c/o The Gersh Agency
P.O. Box 5617, BH, CA 90210
Actress
Response Time: 54 Days
Received: Signed Photo

Richards, J. August
4000 Warner Blvd.
Burbank, CA 91522
Actor
Response Time: N/A
Received: N/A

Richards, Paul W.
2101 NASA Rd. 1
Houston, TX 77058
Astronaut
Response Time: N/A
Received: N/A

Richards, Richard N.
2101 NASA Rd. 1
Houston, TX 77058
Astronaut
Response Time: N/A
Received: N/A

Richardson, Cameron
1230 Ave. of Americas
NY, NY 10020
Actress
Response Time: N/A
Received: N/A

Richardson, Patricia
196 Granvill Ave.
LA, CA 90049
Actress
Response Time: N/A
Received: N/A

Richardson, Patricia
253 26th St. #A-312
Santa Monica, CA 90402-2523
Actress
Response Time: 30 Days
Received: Signed Photo

Rickles, Don
10249 Century Woods Dr.
LA, CA 90067-6312
Comedian
Response Time: 31 Days
Received: Signed Photo

Rickter, Alicia
c/o Baywatch Productions
510-18th Ave., Honolulu, HI 96816
Actress, Playboy Playmate
Response Time: N/A
Received: N/A

Rickter, Alicia
9242 Beverly Blvd.
BH, CA 90210
Actress, Playboy Playmate
Response Time: N/A
Received: N/A

Ricochet
P.O. Box 128468
Nashville, TN 37212
Music Group
Response Time: 17 Days
Received: Signed Photo - $7

Ride, Sally K.
2101 NASA Rd. 1
Houston, TX 77058
Astronaut
Response Time: 31 Days
Received: Signed Photo

Ride, Sally K.
9500 Gilmar Dr.
La Jolla, CA 92093
Astronaut
Response Time: 24 Days
Received: Signed Photo - $10

Ridge, Tom
225 Main Capitol Bldg.
Harrisburg, PA 17120
Governor
Response Time: N/A
Received: N/A

Riegel, Eden
320 West 66th St.
NY, NY 10023
Actress
Response Time: N/A
Received: N/A

Rigby, Cathy
110 E. Wilshire #200
Fullerton, CA 92632
Gymnast, Actress
Response Time: 42 Days
Received: Signed Photo

Righteous Brothers, The
9841 Hot Springs Dr.
Huntington Beach, CA 92646
Music Group
Response Time: 33 Days
Received: Signed Photo

Riley, Bob
U.S. House of Representatives
Washington, DC 20515
Politician
Response Time: N/A
Received: N/A

Rimes, LeAnn
6060 N. Central ExpressWay, Ste. 816
Dallas, TX 75206
Singer
Response Time: N/A
Received: N/A

Rimes, LeAnn
P.O. Box 743668
Dallas, TX 75374
Singer
Response Time: N/A
Received: N/A

Ripa, Kelly
320 West 66th St.
NY, NY 10023
Actress
Response Time: N/A
Received: N/A

Ritch, Michael
1801 West Int'l. Spdwy. Blvd.
Daytona Beach, FL 32114
Auto Racing Personality
Response Time: 90 Days
Received: Signed Photo

Ritchie, Sharon
Two Ocean Way, Ste. 1000
Atlantic City, NJ 08401
Miss America 1956
Response Time: N/A
Received: N/A

Rivers Edge
P.O. Box 2375
Winchester, VA 22604
Music Group
Response Time: 10 Days
Received: Signed Photo

Rivers, Joan
c/o QVC, 1200 Wilson Dr.
West Chester, PA 19380
Television Personality
Response Time: N/A
Received: N/A

Rivers, Joan
P.O. Box 49774
LA, CA 90049
Television Personality
Response Time: 68 Days
Received: Signed Photo

Rivers, Lynn N.
U.S. House of Representatives
Washington, DC 20515
Politician
Response Time: N/A
Received: N/A

Rivers, Melissa
c/o QVC, 1200 Wilson Dr.
West Chester, PA 19380
Television Personality
Response Time: N/A
Received: N/A

Roberts, Cokie
1350 Ave. of the Americas
NY, NY 10019
News Anchor
Response Time: 31 Days
Received: Signed Photo

Roberts, Cokie
1717 DeSales St. N.W.
Washington, DC 20036
News Anchor
Response Time: N/A
Received: N/A

Roberts, Julia
6220 Del Valle Dr.
LA, CA 90048
Actress
Response Time: N/A
Received: N/A

Roberts, Julia
8942 Wilshire Blvd.
LA, CA 90211
Actress
Response Time: N/A
Received: N/A

Roberts, Julia
9701 Wilshire Blvd., 10th Fl.
BH, CA 90212
Actress
Response Time: 49 Days
Received: Signed Photo I Sent

Roberts, Layla Harvest
9242 Beverly Blvd.
BH, CA 90210
Playboy Playmate
Response Time: N/A
Received: N/A

Roberts, Nora
344 Cedar Ave.
Ridgewood, NJ 07450
Author
Response Time: N/A
Received: N/A

Roberts, Pat
302 Hart Senate Office Bldg.
Washington, DC 20510
Senator
Response Time: N/A
Received: N/A

Robertson, Lisa
c/o QVC, 1200 Wilson Dr.
West Chester, PA 19380
QVC Host
Response Time: N/A
Received: N/A

Robertson, Pat
1000 Centerville Turnpike
Virginia Beach, VA 23463
Televangelist
Response Time: N/A
Received: N/A

Robinson, Larry
3211 Stevenson St.
Plant City, FL 33567
Basketball Player
Response Time: N/A
Received: N/A

Robinson, Stephen K.
2101 NASA Rd. 1
Houston, TX 77058
Astronaut
Response Time: N/A
Received: N/A

Robinson, Wendy Raquel
4000 Warner Blvd.
Burbank, CA 91522
Actress
Response Time: N/A
Received: N/A

Rockefeller IV, John
531 Hart Senate Office Bldg.
Washington, DC 20510
Politician
Response Time: 20 Days
Received: Signed Photo

Roddy, Rod
5757 Wilshire Blvd. #206
LA, CA 90036
Television Personality
Response Time: N/A
Received: N/A

Roderick, Brande Nicole
9242 Beverly Blvd.
BH, CA 90210
Playboy Playmate
Response Time: N/A
Received: N/A

Roderick, Brande
c/o Baywatch Productions
510-18th Ave., Honolulu, HI 96816
Actress
Response Time: N/A
Received: N/A

Rodriguez, Chi Chi
1720 Merriman Rd.
Box 5118, Akron, OH 44334
Boxer
Response Time: 20 Days
Received: Signed Photo

Rodriguez, Ciro D.
U.S. House of Representatives
Washington, DC 20515
Politician
Response Time: N/A
Received: N/A

Roe, Mary Beth
c/o QVC, 1200 Wilson Dr.
West Chester, PA 19380
QVC Host
Response Time: N/A
Received: N/A

Roemer, Tim
U.S. House of Representatives
Washington, DC 20515
Politician
Response Time: N/A
Received: N/A

Rogers, Fred
4802 5th Ave.
Pittsburgh, PA 15213
Television Personality
Response Time: 28 Days
Received: Signed Photo

Rogers, Harold
U.S. House of Representatives
Washington, DC 20515
Politician
Response Time: N/A
Received: N/A

Rogers, Kenny
2910 Poston Ave.
Nashville, TN 37203
Singer
Response Time: N/A
Received: N/A

Rogers, Kenny
P.O. Box 100, Route 1
Colbert, CA 30628
Singer
Response Time: N/A
Received: N/A

Rogers, Mike
U.S. House of Representatives
Washington, DC 20515
Politician
Response Time: N/A
Received: N/A

Rogers, Mimi
500 S. Buena Vista St.
Burbank, CA 91521
Actress
Response Time: N/A
Received: N/A

Rogers, Suzanne
3000 W. Alameda Ave.
Burbank, CA 91523
Actress
Response Time: N/A
Received: N/A

Rohrabacher, Dana
U.S. House of Representatives
Washington, DC 20515
Politician
Response Time: N/A
Received: N/A

Roker, Al
30 Rockerfeller Plaza
NY, NY 10122
Author, Weatherman
Response Time: 18 Days
Received: Signed Photo

Rominger, Kent V.
2101 NASA Rd. 1
Houston, TX 77058
Astronaut
Response Time: N/A
Received: N/A

Roof, Michael
4000 Warner Blvd.
Burbank, CA 91522
Actor
Response Time: N/A
Received: N/A

Rooney, Mickey
1400 Red Sail Circle
Westlake Village, CA 91361
Actor
Response Time: N/A
Received: N/A

Rooney, Mickey
P.O. Box 5028
Westlake Village, CA 91362
Actor
Response Time: 65 Days
Received: Signed Photo

Roper, Tony
1801 West Int'l. Spdwy. Blvd.
Daytona Beach, FL 32114
Auto Racing Personality
Response Time: 56 Days
Received: Signed Photo

Rose, Pete
8144 Glades Rd.
Boca Raton, FL 33434-4073
Baseball Player
Response Time: N/A
Received: N/A

Ros-Lehtinen, Ileana
U.S. House of Representatives
Washington, DC 20515
Politician
Response Time: N/A
Received: N/A

Rosman, Mackenzie
c/o The WB Network, 3701 Oak St.
Bldg. 34R, Burbank, CA 91505
Actress
Response Time: N/A
Received: N/A

Ross, Jerry L.
2101 NASA Rd. 1
Houston, TX 77058
Astronaut
Response Time: N/A
Received: N/A

Ross, Marion
20929-47 Ventura Blvd. #144
Woodland Hills, CA 91364
Actress
Response Time: 57 Days
Received: Signed Photo

Ross, Marion
21755 Ventura Blvd. #144
Woodland Hills, CA 91364
Actress
Response Time: 89 Days
Received: Signed Photo

Ross, Mike
U.S. House of Representatives
Washington, DC 20515
Politician
Response Time: N/A
Received: N/A

Ross, Tracee Ellis
5555 Melrose Ave.
Hollywood, CA 90038-3197
Actress
Response Time: N/A
Received: N/A

Ross, Tracey
4024 Radford Ave.
Studio City, CA 91604
Actress
Response Time: N/A
Received: N/A

Roszell, Jennifer
51 W. 52 St.
NY, NY 10019
Actress
Response Time: N/A
Received: N/A

Rothman, Steven R.
U.S. House of Representatives
Washington, DC 20515
Politician
Response Time: N/A
Received: N/A

Rotondi, Todd
1268 East 14th St.
Brooklyn, NY 11230
Actor
Response Time: N/A
Received: N/A

Roukema, Marge
U.S. House of Representatives
Washington, DC 20515
Politician
Response Time: N/A
Received: N/A

Rovero, Jennifer
9242 Beverly Blvd.
BH, CA 90210
Playboy Playmate
Response Time: N/A
Received: N/A

Rowell, Victoria
5555 Melrose Ave.
Hollywood, CA 90038-3197
Actress
Response Time: N/A
Received: N/A

Rowland, John G.
210 Capitol Ave.
Hartford, CT 06106
Governor
Response Time: N/A
Received: N/A

Rowlands, Gena
7917 Woodrow Wilson Dr.
LA, CA 90046
Actress
Response Time: N/A
Received: N/A

Rowling, J.K.
c/o Arthur A. Levine Books
555 Broadway, NY, NY 10012
Author
Response Time: 41 Days
Received: Signed Photo

Roybal-Allard, Lucille
U.S. House of Representatives
Washington, DC 20515
Politician
Response Time: N/A
Received: N/A

Royce, Edward R.
U.S. House of Representatives
Washington, DC 20515
Politician
Response Time: N/A
Received: N/A

Ruccolo, Richard
10201 West Pico Blvd.
LA, CA 90035
Actor
Response Time: N/A
Received: N/A

Ruck, Alan
100 Universal City Plaza
Universal City, CA 91608
Actor
Response Time: N/A
Received: N/A

Rudd, Ricky
1801 West Int'l. Spdwy. Blvd.
Daytona Beach, FL 32114
Auto Racing Personality
Response Time: 83 Days
Received: Signed Photo

Rudie, Evelyn
7514 Hollywood Blvd.
LA, CA 90046
Actress
Response Time: N/A
Received: N/A

Rue, Sara
4000 Warner Blvd.
Burbank, CA 91522
Actress
Response Time: N/A
Received: N/A

Ruivivar, Anthony
4000 Warner Blvd.
Burbank, CA 91522
Actor
Response Time: N/A
Received: N/A

Runco Jr., Mario
2101 NASA Rd. 1
Houston, TX 77058
Astronaut
Response Time: N/A
Received: N/A

Ru-Paul
6671 Sunset Blvd. #1590
Hollywood, CA 90028
Actor
Response Time: 61 Days
Received: Signed Photo

Rush, Bobby L.
U.S. House of Representatives
Washington, DC 20515
Politician
Response Time: N/A
Received: N/A

Russell, Keri
4000 Warner Blvd.
Burbank, CA 91522
Actress
Response Time: N/A
Received: N/A

Russell, Theresa
9454 Lloyd Crest Dr.
BH, CA 90212
Actress
Response Time: N/A
Received: N/A

Russo, Rene
253-A 26th St. #199
Santa Monica, CA 90402-2523
Actress
Response Time: N/A
Received: N/A

Russo, Rene
400 S. Beverly Blvd. #216
BH, CA 90212
Actress
Response Time: 30 Days
Received: Signed Photo

Ruttman, Joe
1801 West Int'l. Spdwy. Blvd.
Daytona Beach, FL 32114
Auto Racing Personality
Response Time: 152 Days
Received: Signed Photo

Ryan, George H.
State Capitol
Springfield, IL 62706
Governor
Response Time: N/A
Received: N/A

Ryan, Meg
11718 Barrington Court #508
LA, CA 90049
Actress
Response Time: N/A
Received: N/A

Ryan, Mitchell
10201 West Pico Blvd.
Trailer 779, LA, CA 90035
Actor
Response Time: N/A
Received: N/A

Ryan, Nolan
P.O. Box 670
Alvin, TX 77512
Baseball Player
Response Time: 39 Days
Received: Signed Photo

Ryan, Paul
U.S. House of Representatives
Washington, DC 20515
Politician
Response Time: N/A
Received: N/A

Rydell, Bobby
917 Bryn Mawr Ave.
Narberth, PA 19072
Singer
Response Time: 30 Days
Received: Signed Photo

Ryun, Jim
U.S. House of Representatives
Washington, DC 20515
Politician
Response Time: N/A
Received: N/A

Sabato Jr., Antonio
13029 Mindanao Way #5
Marina del Ray, CA 90295
Actor, Model
Response Time: 94 Days
Received: Signed Photo

Sabato Jr., Antonio
P.O. Box 480012
LA, CA 90048
Actor, Model
Response Time: 94 Days
Received: Signed Photo

Sabo, Martin Olav
U.S. House of Representatives
Washington, DC 20515
Politician
Response Time: N/A
Received: N/A

Sadler, Elliott
1801 West Int'l. Spdwy. Blvd.
Daytona Beach, FL 32114
Auto Racing Personality
Response Time: 191 Days
Received: Signed Photo

Sadler, William
4000 Warner Blvd.
Burbank, CA 91522
Actor
Response Time: N/A
Received: N/A

Safer, Morley
51 W. 52nd St.
NY, NY 10019
Television Personality
Response Time: N/A
Received: N/A

Sagona, Katie
51 W. 52 St.
NY, NY 10019
Actress
Response Time: N/A
Received: N/A

Sajak, Pat
3400 Riverside Dr., 2nd Fl.
Burbank, CA 91505
Television Personality
Response Time: N/A
Received: N/A

Sajak, Pat
10202 W. Washington Blvd.
Culver City, CA 90232
Television Personality
Response Time: 8 Days
Received: Signed Photo

Sales, Soupy
245 35th St.
NY, NY 10016
Actor, Comedian
Response Time: 8 Days
Received: Signed Photo

Samuels, Melissa
5555 Melrose Ave.
Hollywood, CA 90038-3197
Actress
Response Time: N/A
Received: N/A

Samuelson, Joan Benoit
RR #1 Box 1455-A
Freeport, ME 04032
Track & Field Athlete
Response Time: N/A
Received: N/A

Sanches, Stacy
9242 Beverly Blvd.
BH, CA 90210
Playboy Playmate
Response Time: N/A
Received: N/A

Sanchez, Loretta
U.S. House of Representatives
Washington, DC 20515
Politician
Response Time: N/A
Received: N/A

Sand, Shauna
9242 Beverly Blvd.
BH, CA 90210
Playboy Playmate
Response Time: N/A
Received: N/A

Sanders, Bernard
U.S. House of Representatives
Washington, DC 20515
Politician
Response Time: N/A
Received: N/A

Sanders, Ricky
1801 West Int'l. Spdwy. Blvd.
Daytona Beach, FL 32114
Auto Racing Personality
Response Time: 62 Days
Received: Signed Photo

Sandlin, Max
U.S. House of Representatives
Washington, DC 20515
Politician
Response Time: N/A
Received: N/A

Sands, Lee
c/o QVC, 1200 Wilson Dr.
West Chester, PA 19380
Jewelry & Fashion Designer
Response Time: N/A
Received: N/A

Santana, Merlin
4000 Warner Blvd.
Burbank, CA 91522
Actor
Response Time: N/A
Received: N/A

Santerre, Andy
1801 West Int'l. Spdwy. Blvd.
Daytona Beach, FL 32114
Auto Racing Personality
Response Time: 65 Days
Received: Signed Photo

Santiago, Saundra
51 W. 52 St.
NY, NY 10019
Actress
Response Time: N/A
Received: N/A

Santorum, Rick
120 Russell Senate Office Bldg.
Washington, DC 20510
Senator
Response Time: N/A
Received: N/A

Santos, Al
4000 Warner Blvd.
Burbank, CA 91522
Actor
Response Time: N/A
Received: N/A

Sapp, Carolyn
Two Ocean Way, Ste. 1000
Atlantic City, NJ 08401
Miss America 1992
Response Time: N/A
Received: N/A

Sarandon, Susan
40 W. 57th St.
NY, NY 10019
Actress
Response Time: 54 Days
Received: Signed Photo

Sarbanes, Paul
309 Hart Senate Office Bldg.
Washington, DC 20510
Senator
Response Time: N/A
Received: N/A

Sarna, Shivan
c/o Home Shopping Network
St. Petersburg, FL 33701
Home Shopping Network Host
Response Time: N/A
Received: N/A

Saucedo, Michael
4151 Prospect Ave.
LA, CA 90027
Actor
Response Time: N/A
Received: N/A

Sauter, Jay
1801 West Int'l. Spdwy. Blvd.
Daytona Beach, FL 32114
Auto Racing Personality
Response Time: 81 Days
Received: Signed Photo

Sawyer Brown
5200 Old Harding Pike
Franklin, TN 37064
Music Group
Response Time: 9 Days
Received: Signed Photo

Sawyer, Diane
147 Columbus Ave.
NY, NY 10023-5900
News Anchor
Response Time: 29 Days
Received: Signed Photo

Sawyer, Elton
1801 West Int'l. Spdwy. Blvd.
Daytona Beach, FL 32114
Auto Racing Personality
Response Time: 83 Days
Received: Signed Photo

Sawyer, Tom
U.S. House of Representatives
Washington, DC 20515
Politician
Response Time: N/A
Received: N/A

Saxton, Jim
U.S. House of Representatives
Washington, DC 20515
Politician
Response Time: N/A
Received: N/A

Scales, Crystal
4000 Warner Blvd.
Burbank, CA 91522
Actress
Response Time: N/A
Received: N/A

Scalia, Antonin
Supreme Court of the United States
Washington, DC 20543
Supreme Court Justice
Response Time: 23 Days
Received: Signed Photo

Scanlon, Chris
c/o Home Shopping Network
St. Petersburg, FL 33701
Home Shopping Network Host
Response Time: N/A
Received: N/A

Scarborough, Joe
U.S. House of Representatives
Washington, DC 20515
Politician
Response Time: N/A
Received: N/A

Scarfe, Alan
5555 Melrose Ave.
Hollywood, CA 90038-3197
Actor
Response Time: N/A
Received: N/A

Schaefer, Laurel
Two Ocean Way, Ste. 1000
Atlantic City, NJ 08401
Miss America 1972
Response Time: N/A
Received: N/A

Schaffer, Bob
U.S. House of Representatives
Washington, DC 20515
Politician
Response Time: N/A
Received: N/A

Schakowsky, Janice D.
U.S. House of Representatives
Washington, DC 20515
Politician
Response Time: N/A
Received: N/A

Schieler, Nikki
9242 Beverly Blvd.
BH, CA 90210
Playboy Playmate
Response Time: N/A
Received: N/A

Schiff, Adam B.
U.S. House of Representatives
Washington, DC 20515
Politician
Response Time: N/A
Received: N/A

Schiff, Richard
4000 Warner Blvd.
Burbank, CA 91522
Actor
Response Time: N/A
Received: N/A

Schirra Jr., Walter M.
2101 NASA Rd. 1
Houston, TX 77058
Astronaut
Response Time: N/A
Received: N/A

Schlatter, Charlie
5555 Melrose Ave.
Hollywood, CA 90038-3197
Actor
Response Time: N/A
Received: N/A

Schlegel, Hans
2101 NASA Rd. 1
Houston, TX 77058
Astronaut
Response Time: N/A
Received: N/A

Schmitt, Harrison H.
2101 NASA Rd. 1
Houston, TX 77058
Astronaut
Response Time: N/A
Received: N/A

Schrader, Ken
1801 West Int'l. Spdwy. Blvd.
Daytona Beach, FL 32114
Auto Racing Personality
Response Time: 200 Days
Received: Signed Photo

Schrock, Edward L.
U.S. House of Representatives
Washington, DC 20515
Politician
Response Time: N/A
Received: N/A

Schroder, Rick
10201 West Pico Blvd.
LA, CA 90035
Actor
Response Time: N/A
Received: N/A

Schroeder, Carly
4151 Prospect Ave.
LA, CA 90027
Actress
Response Time: N/A
Received: N/A

Schuldt, Travis
4024 Radford Ave.
Studio City, CA 91604
Actor
Response Time: N/A
Received: N/A

Schuler, Jason
1801 West Int'l. Spdwy. Blvd.
Daytona Beach, FL 32114
Auto Racing Personality
Response Time: 169 Days
Received: Signed Photo

Schultz, Julia
9242 Beverly Blvd.
BH, CA 90210
Playboy Playmate
Response Time: N/A
Received: N/A

Schumer, Charles
313 Hart Senate Office Bldg.
Washington, DC 20510
Senator
Response Time: N/A
Received: N/A

Schwartz, Sherwood
1865 Carla Ridge Dr.
BH, CA 90212
Director
Response Time: 38 Days
Received: Signed Photo

Schwarzenegger, Arnold
3110 Main St. #300
Santa Monica, CA 90405
Actor
Response Time: N/A
Received: N/A

Schwarzkopf, Norman
400 N. Ashley Dr. #3050
Tampa, FL 33609
Military General
Response Time: 12 Days
Received: Signed Photo

Schweickart, Russell L.
2101 NASA Rd. 1
Houston, TX 77058
Astronaut
Response Time: N/A
Received: N/A

Schwimmer, David
4000 Warner Blvd.
Burbank, CA 91522
Actor
Response Time: N/A
Received: N/A

Scott, Coltin
4151 Prospect Ave.
LA, CA 90027
Actor
Response Time: N/A
Received: N/A

Scott, David R.
2101 NASA Rd. 1
Houston, TX 77058
Astronaut
Response Time: N/A
Received: N/A

Scott, Esther
500 S. Buena Vista St.
Burbank, CA 91521
Actress
Response Time: N/A
Received: N/A

Scott, Jason-Shane
56 West 66th St.
NY, NY 10023
Actor
Response Time: N/A
Received: N/A

Scott, Lisa Marie
9242 Beverly Blvd.
BH, CA 90210
Playboy Playmate
Response Time: N/A
Received: N/A

Scott, Melody Thomas
7800 Beverly Blvd.
LA, CA 90036
Actress
Response Time: N/A
Received: N/A

Scott, Rebecca
9242 Beverly Blvd.
BH, CA 90210
Playboy Playmate
Response Time: N/A
Received: N/A

Scott, Robert C.
U.S. House of Representatives
Washington, DC 20515
Politician
Response Time: N/A
Received: N/A

Scott, William Lee
4000 Warner Blvd.
Burbank, CA 91522
Actor
Response Time: N/A
Received: N/A

Scott, Winston E.
2101 NASA Rd. 1
Houston, TX 77058
Astronaut
Response Time: N/A
Received: N/A

Searcy, Nick
5555 Melrose Ave.
Hollywood, CA 90038-3197
Actor
Response Time: N/A
Received: N/A

Searfoss, Richard A.
2101 NASA Rd. 1
Houston, TX 77058
Astronaut
Response Time: N/A
Received: N/A

Secada, Jon
420 Jefferson Ave.
Miami Beach, FL 33139
Singer
Response Time: 225 Days
Received: Signed Photo

Seddon, Margaret Rhea
2101 NASA Rd. 1
Houston, TX 77058
Astronaut
Response Time: N/A
Received: N/A

Sega, Ronald M.
2101 NASA Rd. 1
Houston, TX 77058
Astronaut
Response Time: N/A
Received: N/A

Seles, Monica
c/o IMG, Erieview Plaza #1300
Cleveland, OH 44114
Tennis Player
Response Time: 120 Days
Received: Signed Photo

Selleca, Connie
15030 Ventura Blvd. #355
Sherman Oaks, CA 91403
Actress
Response Time: N/A
Received: N/A

Selleck, Tom
331 Sage Ln.
Santa Monica, CA 90402-1119
Actor
Response Time: 210 Days
Received: Signed Photo

Sellers, Piers J.
2101 NASA Rd. 1
Houston, TX 77058
Astronaut
Response Time: N/A
Received: N/A

Sensenbrenner Jr., F. James
U.S. House of Representatives
Washington, DC 20515
Politician
Response Time: N/A
Received: N/A

September Fare, Kerissa
9242 Beverly Blvd.
BH, CA 90210
Playboy Playmate
Response Time: N/A
Received: N/A

Sergei, Ivan
4000 Warner Blvd.
Burbank, CA 91522
Actor
Response Time: N/A
Received: N/A

Serrano, Jose E.
U.S. House of Representatives
Washington, DC 20515
Politician
Response Time: N/A
Received: N/A

Sessions, Jeff
493 Russell Senate Office Bldg.
Washington, DC 20510
Senator
Response Time: N/A
Received: N/A

Sessions, Pete
U.S. House of Representatives
Washington, DC 20515
Politician
Response Time: N/A
Received: N/A

Setzer, Dennis
1801 West Int'l. Spdwy. Blvd.
Daytona Beach, FL 32114
Auto Racing Personality
Response Time: 203 Days
Received: Signed Photo

Shadegg, John B.
U.S. House of Representatives
Washington, DC 20515
Politician
Response Time: N/A
Received: N/A

Shaheen, Jeanne
State House, Room 208
Concord, NH 03301
Governor
Response Time: N/A
Received: N/A

Sharp, Kevin
P.O. Box 888
Camino, CA 95709
Singer
Response Time: N/A
Received: N/A

Shaud, Grant
34-12 36th St.
Astoria, NY 11106
Actor
Response Time: N/A
Received: N/A

Shaw Jr., Brewster H.
2101 NASA Rd. 1
Houston, TX 77058
Astronaut
Response Time: N/A
Received: N/A

Shaw Jr., E. Clay
U.S. House of Representatives
Washington, DC 20515
Politician
Response Time: N/A
Received: N/A

Shays, Christopher
U.S. House of Representatives
Washington, DC 20515
Politician
Response Time: N/A
Received: N/A

Shearer, Harry
c/o KCRW, 1900 Pico Blvd.
Santa Monica, CA 90405
Voice Actor
Response Time: N/A
Received: N/A

SheDaisy
P.O. Box 150638
Nashville, TN 37215-0638
Music Group
Response Time: 78 Days
Received: Signed Photo

Sheedy, Ally
P.O. Box 523
Topanga, CA 90290
Actress
Response Time: N/A
Received: N/A

Sheen, Charlie
6916 Dune Dr.
Malibu, CA 90265
Actor
Response Time: 31 Days
Received: Signed Photo

Sheen, Charlie
100 Universal City Plaza
Universal City, CA 91608
Actor
Response Time: N/A
Received: N/A

Sheen, Jacqueline
9242 Beverly Blvd.
BH, CA 90210
Playboy Playmate
Response Time: N/A
Received: N/A

Sheen, Martin
6916 Dune Dr.
Malibu, CA 90265
Actor
Response Time: 41 Days
Received: Signed Photo

Sheen, Martin
4000 Warner Blvd.
Burbank, CA 91522
Actor
Response Time: N/A
Received: N/A

Shelby, Richard
110 Hart Senate Office Bldg.
Washington, DC 20510
Senator
Response Time: N/A
Received: N/A

Shelton, Ricky Van
P.O. Box 120548
Nashville, TN 37212
Singer
Response Time: 11 Days
Received: Signed Photo

Shepard, Jean
2802 Opryland Dr.
Nashville, TN 37214
Singer
Response Time: N/A
Received: N/A

Shepherd, Neferteri
9242 Beverly Blvd.
BH, CA 90210
Playboy Playmate
Response Time: N/A
Received: N/A

Shepherd, William M.
2101 NASA Rd. 1
Houston, TX 77058
Astronaut
Response Time: N/A
Received: N/A

Sheridan, Leisa
9242 Beverly Blvd.
BH, CA 90210
Playboy Playmate
Response Time: N/A
Received: N/A

Sherman, Brad
U.S. House of Representatives
Washington, DC 20515
Politician
Response Time: N/A
Received: N/A

Sherwood, Don
U.S. House of Representatives
Washington, DC 20515
Politician
Response Time: N/A
Received: N/A

Shimkus, Dave
c/o Home Shopping Network
St. Petersburg, FL 33701
Home Shopping Network Host
Response Time: N/A
Received: N/A

Shimkus, John
U.S. House of Representatives
Washington, DC 20515
Politician
Response Time: N/A
Received: N/A

Shindle, Kate
Two Ocean Way, Ste. 1000
Atlantic City, NJ 08401
Miss America 1998
Response Time: N/A
Received: N/A

Shopp, BeBe
Two Ocean Way, Ste. 1000
Atlantic City, NJ 08401
Miss America 1949
Response Time: N/A
Received: N/A

Shore, Pauly
1375 N. Doheny Dr.
LA, CA 96169
Actor
Response Time: N/A
Received: N/A

Shore, Pauly
8491 Sunset Blvd. #700
W. Hollywood, CA 90069
Actor
Response Time: 44 Days
Received: Signed Photo

Shows, Ronnie
U.S. House of Representatives
Washington, DC 20515
Politician
Response Time: N/A
Received: N/A

Shriner, Kin
4151 Prospect Ave.
LA, CA 90027
Actor
Response Time: N/A
Received: N/A

Shriver, Loren J.
2101 NASA Rd. 1
Houston, TX 77058
Astronaut
Response Time: N/A
Received: N/A

Shriver, Maria
3110 Main St. #300
Santa Monica, CA 90405
Journalist, Author
Response Time: 91 Days
Received: Signed Photo

Shuster, Bud
U.S. House of Representatives
Washington, DC 20515
Politician
Response Time: N/A
Received: N/A

Siegelman, Don
State Capitol, 600 Dexter Ave.
Montgomery, AL 36130-2751
Governor
Response Time: N/A
Received: N/A

Siegfried & Roy
1639 N. Valley Dr.
Las Vegas, NV 89108
Illusionists
Response Time: 27 Days
Received: Signed Photo

Siegfried & Roy
c/o The Mirage
Las Vegas, NV 89103
Illusionists
Response Time: 27 Days
Received: Signed Photo

Silverstone, Alicia
8899 Beverly Blvd. #510
LA, CA 90048
Actress
Response Time: N/A
Received: N/A

Silvstedt, Victoria
9242 Beverly Blvd.
BH, CA 90210
Playboy Playmate
Response Time: N/A
Received: N/A

Simmons, Henry
10201 West Pico Blvd.
LA, CA 90035
Actor
Response Time: N/A
Received: N/A

Simmons, Richard
P.O. Box 5403
BH, CA 90209
Fitness Expert
Response Time: 46 Days
Received: Signed Photo

Simmons, Rob
U.S. House of Representatives
Washington, DC 20515
Politician
Response Time: N/A
Received: N/A

Simon, Carly
135 Central Park West
NY, NY 10023
Singer
Response Time: N/A
Received: N/A

Simon, Neil
10745 Chalon Rd.
LA, CA 90077
Singer
Response Time: N/A
Received: N/A

Simpson, Michael K.
U.S. House of Representatives
Washington, DC 20515
Politician
Response Time: N/A
Received: N/A

Simpson, Suzi
9242 Beverly Blvd.
BH, CA 90210
Playboy Playmate
Response Time: N/A
Received: N/A

Sinatra, Nancy
c/o Bootleggers
P.O. Box 10236, BH, CA 90213
Singer
Response Time: 17 Days
Received: Signed Photo

Sinbad
11330 Ventura Blvd.
Studio City, CA 91604
Actor, Comedian
Response Time: 27 Days
Received: Signed Photo

Sinbad
21704 Devonshire #13
Chatsworth, CA 91311-2949
Actor, Comedian
Response Time: 120 Days
Received: Signed Photo

Sinden, Harry
9 Old Village Dr.
Winchester, MA 01890-2213
Hockey Player
Response Time: N/A
Received: N/A

Singletary, Daryl
607 W. Church Dr.
Sugarland, TX 77478
Singer
Response Time: 10 Days
Received: Signed Photo

Sinise, Gary
9830 Wilshire Blvd.
BH, CA 90212
Actor
Response Time: 106 Days
Received: Signed Photo

Sisco, Kristina
1268 East 14th St.
Brooklyn, NY 11230
Actress
Response Time: N/A
Received: N/A

Sisisky, Norman
U.S. House of Representatives
Washington, DC 20515
Politician
Response Time: N/A
Received: N/A

Skaggs, Ricky
P.O. Box 2478
Hendersonville, TN 37075
Singer
Response Time: 64 Days
Received: Signed Photo

Skeen, Joe
U.S. House of Representatives
Washington, DC 20515
Politician
Response Time: N/A
Received: N/A

Skelton, Ike
U.S. House of Representatives
Washington, DC 20515
Politician
Response Time: N/A
Received: N/A

Skinner, Jamie
1801 West Int'l. Spdwy. Blvd.
Daytona Beach, FL 32114
Auto Racing Personality
Response Time: 196 Days
Received: Signed Photo

Skinner, Mike
1801 West Int'l. Spdwy. Blvd.
Daytona Beach, FL 32114
Auto Racing Personality
Response Time: 219 Days
Received: Signed Photo

Slater, Christian
2029 Century Park E. #1190
LA, CA 90067
Actor
Response Time: 63 Days
Received: Signed Photo

Slater, Perry
c/o Home Shopping Network
St. Petersburg, FL 33701
Home Shopping Network Host
Response Time: N/A
Received: N/A

Slattery, John
5555 Melrose Ave.
Hollywood, CA 90038-3197
Actor
Response Time: N/A
Received: N/A

Slaughter, Enos
959 Lawson Chapel Church Rd.
Roxboro, NC 27573-6401
Baseball Player
Response Time: 14 Days
Received: Signed Photo

Slaughter, Enos
P.O. Box 590
Cooperstown, NY 13326
Baseball Player
Response Time: N/A
Received: N/A

Slaughter, Louise McIntosh
U.S. House of Representatives
Washington, DC 20515
Politician
Response Time: N/A
Received: N/A

Slezak, Erika
56 West 66th St.
NY, NY 10023
Actress
Response Time: N/A
Received: N/A

Sloan, Tiffany M.
9242 Beverly Blvd.
BH, CA 90210
Playboy Playmate
Response Time: N/A
Received: N/A

Sloan, Tina
51 W. 52 St.
NY, NY 10019
Actress
Response Time: N/A
Received: N/A

Sloane, Lindsay
4000 Warner Blvd.
Burbank, CA 91522
Actress
Response Time: N/A
Received: N/A

Smiley, Tava
4151 Prospect Ave.
LA, CA 90027
Actress
Response Time: N/A
Received: N/A

Smith, Adam
U.S. House of Representatives
Washington, DC 20515
Politician
Response Time: N/A
Received: N/A

Smith, Anna Nicole
9242 Beverly Blvd.
BH, CA 90210
Playboy Playmate
Response Time: N/A
Received: N/A

Smith, Bob
307 Dirksen Senate Office Bldg.
Washington, DC 20510
Senator
Response Time: N/A
Received: N/A

Smith, Christopher H.
U.S. House of Representatives
Washington, DC 20515
Politician
Response Time: N/A
Received: N/A

Smith, Gordon
404 Russell Senate Office Bldg.
Washington, DC 20510
Senator
Response Time: N/A
Received: N/A

Smith, Hillary B.
56 West 66th St.
NY, NY 10023
Actress
Response Time: N/A
Received: N/A

Smith, Jaclyn
10398 Sunset Blvd.
LA, CA 90049
Actress
Response Time: 160 Days
Received: Signed Photo

Smith, Lamar S.
U.S. House of Representatives
Washington, DC 20515
Politician
Response Time: N/A
Received: N/A

Smith, Marlo
c/o Home Shopping Network
St. Petersburg, FL 33701
Home Shopping Network Host
Response Time: N/A
Received: N/A

Smith, Nick
U.S. House of Representatives
Washington, DC 20515
Politician
Response Time: N/A
Received: N/A

Smith, Shannon
c/o Home Shopping Network
St. Petersburg, FL 33701
Home Shopping Network Host
Response Time: N/A
Received: N/A

Smith, Shawnee
5555 Melrose Ave.
Hollywood, CA 90038-3197
Actress
Response Time: N/A
Received: N/A

Smith, Shawntel
Two Ocean Way, Ste. 1000
Atlantic City, NJ 08401
Miss America 1996
Response Time: N/A
Received: N/A

Smith, Steven L.
2101 NASA Rd. 1
Houston, TX 77058
Astronaut
Response Time: N/A
Received: N/A

Smits, Jimmy
Box 49922, Barrington Station
LA, CA 90049
Actor
Response Time: 104 Days
Received: Signed Photo

Snipes, Wesley
9701 Wilshire Blvd. #1000
BH, CA 90212
Actor
Response Time: 143 Days
Received: Signed Photo

Snow, Brittany
51 W. 52 St.
NY, NY 10019
Actress
Response Time: N/A
Received: N/A

Snowe, Olympia
250 Russell Senate Office Bldg.
Washington, DC 20510
Senator
Response Time: N/A
Received: N/A

Snyder, Vic
U.S. House of Representatives
Washington, DC 20515
Politician
Response Time: N/A
Received: N/A

Sockwell, Brian
1801 West Int'l. Spdwy. Blvd.
Daytona Beach, FL 32114
Auto Racing Personality
Response Time: 190 Days
Received: Signed Photo

Sokoloff, Marla
10201 West Pico Blvd.
LA, CA 90035
Actress
Response Time: N/A
Received: N/A

Solano, Jose
c/o Baywatch Productions
510-18th Ave., Honolulu, HI 96816
Actor
Response Time: N/A
Received: N/A

Solis, Hilda L.
U.S. House of Representatives
Washington, DC 20515
Politician
Response Time: N/A
Received: N/A

Somers, Suzanne
c/o Home Shopping Network
St. Petersburg, FL 33701
Actress, Jewelry Designer
Response Time: N/A
Received: N/A

Somerville, Bonnie
4000 Warner Blvd.
Burbank, CA 91522
Actress
Response Time: N/A
Received: N/A

Sorvino, Mira
308 West 48th St.
NY, NY 10036
Actress
Response Time: N/A
Received: N/A

Sorvino, Mira
41 W. 86th St.
NY, NY 10024
Actress
Response Time: 180 Days
Received: Signed Photo

Sorvino, Paul
5555 Melrose Ave.
Hollywood, CA 90038-3197
Actor
Response Time: N/A
Received: N/A

Souder, Mark E.
U.S. House of Representatives
Washington, DC 20515
Politician
Response Time: N/A
Received: N/A

Souter, David Hackett
Supreme Court of the United States
Washington, DC 20543
Supreme Court Justice
Response Time: 19 Days
Received: Signed Photo

Southbound
Box 617373
Orlando, FL 32861-7373
Music Group
Response Time: 23 Days
Received: Signed Photo

Spacek, Sissy
Route 22
Cobham, VA 22929
Actress
Response Time: 38 Days
Received: Signed Photo

Spacey, Kevin
120 W. 45th St., 36th Fl.
NY, NY 10036
Actor
Response Time: N/A
Received: N/A

Spade, David
9150 Wilshire Blvd. #350
BH, CA 90212
Actor
Response Time: N/A
Received: N/A

Spade, David
c/o Jonas PR, 240 26th St., Ste. 3
Santa Monica, CA 90402
Actor
Response Time: 72 Days
Received: Signed Photo

Sparks, Dana
4024 Radford Ave.
Studio City, CA 91604
Actress
Response Time: N/A
Received: N/A

Specter, Arlen
711 Hart Senate Office Bldg.
Washington, DC 20510
Senator
Response Time: N/A
Received: N/A

Speedman, Scott
4000 Warner Blvd.
Burbank, CA 91522
Actor
Response Time: N/A
Received: N/A

Spence, Floyd
U.S. House of Representatives
Washington, DC 20515
Politician
Response Time: N/A
Received: N/A

Spencer, Abigail
320 West 66th St.
NY, NY 10023
Actress
Response Time: N/A
Received: N/A

Spencer, Jimmy
1801 West Int'l. Speedway. Blvd.
Daytona Beach, FL 32114
Auto Racing Personality
Response Time: 299 Days
Received: Signed Photo

Spencer, John
4000 Warner Blvd.
Burbank, CA 91522
Actor
Response Time: N/A
Received: N/A

Spicer, Kimberly
9242 Beverly Blvd.
BH, CA 90210
Playboy Playmate
Response Time: N/A
Received: N/A

Spielberg, Steven
P.O. Box 8520
Universal City, CA 91608
Director
Response Time: 123 Days
Received: Signed Photo

Spiro, Jordana
1230 Ave. of Americas
NY, NY 10020
Actress
Response Time: N/A
Received: N/A

Spirtas, Kevin
3000 W. Alameda Ave.
Burbank, CA 91523
Actor
Response Time: N/A
Received: N/A

Sprague, Jack
1801 West Int'l. Spdwy. Blvd.
Daytona Beach, FL 32114
Auto Racing Personality
Response Time: 250 Days
Received: Signed Photo

Spraker, Jeff
1801 West Int'l. Spdwy. Blvd.
Daytona Beach, FL 32114
Auto Racing Personality
Response Time: 153 Days
Received: Signed Photo

Spratt Jr., John M.
U.S. House of Representatives
Washington, DC 20515
Politician
Response Time: N/A
Received: N/A

Spring, Sherwood C.
2101 NASA Rd. 1
Houston, TX 77058
Astronaut
Response Time: N/A
Received: N/A

Springer, Jerry
454 N. Columbia Dr. #200
Chicago, IL 60611
Television Personality
Response Time: 17 Days
Received: Signed Photo & TLS

Springer, Robert C.
2101 NASA Rd. 1
Houston, TX 77058
Astronaut
Response Time: N/A
Received: N/A

St. John, Kristoff
7800 Beverly Blvd.
LA, CA 90036
Actor
Response Time: N/A
Received: N/A

Stabenow, Debbie
United States Senate
Washington, DC 20510
Senator
Response Time: N/A
Received: N/A

Stack, Robert
321 St. Pierre Rd.
LA, CA 90077
Actor, Television Personality
Response Time: 54 Days
Received: Signed Photo

Stafford, Michelle
7800 Beverly Blvd.
LA, CA 90036
Actress
Response Time: N/A
Received: N/A

Stafford, Thomas P.
2101 NASA Rd. 1
Houston, TX 77058
Astronaut
Response Time: N/A
Received: N/A

Stallone, Frank
10668 Eastborne #206
LA, CA 90025
Singer
Response Time: 35 Days
Received: Signed Photo

Stallone, Jennifer Flavin
c/o Home Shopping Network
St. Petersburg, FL 33701
Model, Skincare Expert
Response Time: N/A
Received: N/A

Stallone, Sylvester
8800 Sunset Blvd. #214
LA, CA 90069
Actor
Response Time: 8 Years
Received: Signed Photo I Sent

Stallone, Sylvester
270 N. Canon Dr., PMB 1064
BH, CA 90210
Actor
Response Time: 31 Days
Received: Signed Photo

Stang, Arnold
P.O. Box 786
New Canaan, CT 06840
Voice Actor
Response Time: 31 Days
Received: Signed Photo

Stanton, Molly
4024 Radford Ave.
Studio City, CA 91604
Actress
Response Time: N/A
Received: N/A

Stark, Fortney Pete
U.S. House of Representatives
Washington, DC 20515
Politician
Response Time: N/A
Received: N/A

Starr, David
1801 West Int'l. Spdwy. Blvd.
Daytona Beach, FL 32114
Auto Racing Personality
Response Time: 180 Days
Received: Signed Photo

Starr, Kenneth
1001 Pennsylvania Ave. N.W.
Ste. 490-N., Washington, DC 20004
Prosecutor in Clinton/Lewinsky Case
Response Time: 8 Days
Received: SIC

Statler Brothers, The
P.O. Box 2703
Staunton, VA 24402-2703
Music Group
Response Time: 14 Days
Received: Signed Photo

Staubach, Roger
6912 Edelweiss Circle
Dallas, TX 75240
Football Legend
Response Time: 34 Days
Received: Signed Photo

Stearns, Cliff
U.S. House of Representatives
Washington, DC 20515
Politician
Response Time: N/A
Received: N/A

Stefanik, Mike
1801 West Int'l. Spdwy. Blvd.
Daytona Beach, FL 32114
Auto Racing Personality
Response Time: 186 Days
Received: Signed Photo

Stefanyshyn-Piper, Heidemarie M.
2101 NASA Rd. 1
Houston, TX 77058
Astronaut
Response Time: N/A
Received: N/A

Stein, Ben
4549 Via Vienta
Malibu, CA 90265
Actor, Television Personality
Response Time: 32 Days
Received: Signed Photo

Stein, Ben
602 N. Crescent Dr.
BH, CA 90210
Actor, Television Personality
Response Time: 32 Days
Received: Signed Photo

Stenholm, Charles W.
U.S. House of Representatives
Washington, DC 20515
Politician
Response Time: N/A
Received: N/A

Stevens, Brinke
8033 Sunset Blvd. PMB #556
Hollywood, CA 90046
Actress
Response Time: N/A
Received: N/A

Stevens, Carrie
9242 Beverly Blvd.
BH, CA 90210
Playboy Playmate
Response Time: N/A
Received: N/A

Stevens, Connie
426 S. Robertson Blvd.
LA, CA 90048-3908
Actress
Response Time: 46 Days
Received: Signed Photo

Stevens, John Paul
Supreme Court of the United States
Washington, DC 20543
Supreme Court Justice
Response Time: 29 Days
Received: Signed Photo

Stevens, Ray
1707 Grand Ave.
Nashville, TN 37212
Singer
Response Time: 33 Days
Received: Signed Photo

Stevens, Stella
2180 Coldwater Canyon
BH, CA 90210
Actress
Response Time: N/A
Received: N/A

Stevens, Stella
1608 N. Cahuenga Blvd. #649
Hollywood, CA 90028
Actress
Response Time: N/A
Received: N/A

Stevens, Ted
522 Hart Senate Office Bldg.
Washington, DC 20510
Senator
Response Time: N/A
Received: N/A

Stevens, Warren
14155 Magnolia #44
Sherman Oaks, CA 91403
Actor
Response Time: 156 Days
Received: Signed Photo

Stewart, Martha
c/o Martha Stewart Living
11 W. 42nd St., NY, NY 10036
Decorating Expert
Response Time: 20 Days
Received: Signed Photo

Stewart, Paul Anthony
51 W. 52 St.
NY, NY 10019
Actor
Response Time: N/A
Received: N/A

Stewart, Robert L.
2101 NASA Rd. 1
Houston, TX 77058
Astronaut
Response Time: N/A
Received: N/A

Stewart, Shannon
9242 Beverly Blvd.
BH, CA 90210
Playboy Playmate
Response Time: N/A
Received: N/A

Stewart, Tony
1801 West Int'l. Spdwy. Blvd.
Daytona Beach, FL 32114
Auto Racing Personality
Response Time: 157 Days
Received: Signed Photo

Stickney, Timothy D.
56 West 66th St.
NY, NY 10023
Actor
Response Time: N/A
Received: N/A

Stiles, Ryan
4000 Warner Blvd.
Burbank, CA 91522
Actor
Response Time: N/A
Received: N/A

Stiles, Ryan
10201 West Pico Blvd.
LA, CA 90035
Actor
Response Time: N/A
Received: N/A

Sting
2 The Grove, Highgate Village
London N6, England
Singer
Response Time: 21 Days
Received: Signed Photo

Stokes, Suzanne
9242 Beverly Blvd.
BH, CA 90210
Playboy Playmate
Response Time: N/A
Received: N/A

Stone, Doug
P.O. Box 943
Springfield, TN 37172
Singer
Response Time: 44 Days
Received: Signed Photo

Stone, Matt
South Park, c/o Comedy Central
1775 Broadway, NY, NY 10019
Creator, Southpark
Response Time: 50 Days
Received: Signed Photo

Storch, Larry
330 West End Ave.
NY, NY 10023
Actor
Response Time: 8 Days
Received: Signed Photo

Storm, Gale
23831 Blue Hill Bay
Dana Point, CA 92629
Actress
Response Time: 12 Days
Received: Signed Photo

Storms, Kirsten
3000 W. Alameda Ave.
Burbank, CA 91523
Actor
Response Time: N/A
Received: N/A

Strait, George
1000-18 Ave. South
Nashville, TN 37212
Singer
Response Time: 19 Days
Received: Signed Photo

Strait, George
P.O. Box 2119
Hendersonville, TN 37075
Singer
Response Time: N/A
Received: N/A

Strange, Curtis
100 Gulf Club Rd.
Williamsburg, VA 23185
Golfer
Response Time: 37 Days
Received: Signed Photo

Streisand, Barbara
c/o Erlichman, 5670 Wilshire Blvd.
Ste. 2400, LA, CA 90036-5615
Actress, Singer
Response Time: 26 Days
Received: Signed Book I Sent

Strickland, Ted
U.S. House of Representatives
Washington, DC 20515
Politician
Response Time: N/A
Received: N/A

Struthers, Sally
9100 Wilshire Blvd. #1000
BH, CA 90212
Actress
Response Time: 8 Days
Received: SIC

Stuart, Gloria
884 S. Bundy Dr.
LA, CA 90049
Actress
Response Time: 361 Days
Received: SIC

Stuart, Marty
P.O. Box 24180
Nashville, TN 37202
Singer
Response Time: 19 Days
Received: Signed Photo

Stuart, Mary
51 W. 52 St.
NY, NY 10019
Actress
Response Time: N/A
Received: N/A

Stump, Bob
U.S. House of Representatives
Washington, DC 20515
Politician
Response Time: N/A
Received: N/A

Stupak, Bart
U.S. House of Representatives
Washington, DC 20515
Politician
Response Time: N/A
Received: N/A

Sturckow, Frederick W.
2101 NASA Rd. 1
Houston, TX 77058
Astronaut
Response Time: N/A
Received: N/A

Sudduth, Kohl
4000 Warner Blvd.
Burbank, CA 91522
Actor
Response Time: N/A
Received: N/A

Sudduth, Skip
4000 Warner Blvd.
Burbank, CA 91522
Actor
Response Time: N/A
Received: N/A

Sullivan, Kathryn D.
2101 NASA Rd. 1
Houston, TX 77058
Astronaut
Response Time: N/A
Received: N/A

Sullivan, Susan
10201 West Pico Blvd.
Trailer 779, LA, CA 90035
Actress
Response Time: N/A
Received: N/A

Summer, Donna
P.O. Box 16685
BH, CA 90209
Singer
Response Time: 279 Days
Received: Signed Photo

Sundquist, Don
State Capitol
Nashville, TN 37243-0001
Governor
Response Time: N/A
Received: N/A

Sununu, John E.
U.S. House of Representatives
Washington, DC 20515
Politician
Response Time: N/A
Received: N/A

Supernaw, Doug
P.O. Box 998
Olathe, KS 66051
Singer
Response Time: 35 Days
Received: Signed Photo

Sutherland, Kiefer
132 S. Rodeo Dr. #300
BH, CA 90212
Actor
Response Time: 16 Days
Received: Signed Photo

Swaby, Donn
4024 Radford Ave.
Studio City, CA 91604
Actor
Response Time: N/A
Received: N/A

Swanson, Kristy
2934 1/2 Beverly Glen Cir., Ste. 416
LA, CA 90077
Actress
Response Time: 61 Days
Received: Signed Photo

Swanson, Steven R.
2101 NASA Rd. 1
Houston, TX 77058
Astronaut
Response Time: N/A
Received: N/A

Sweeney, Alison
3000 W. Alameda Ave.
Burbank, CA 91523
Actress
Response Time: N/A
Received: N/A

Sweeney, John E.
U.S. House of Representatives
Washington, DC 20515
Politician
Response Time: N/A
Received: N/A

Sweetin, Jodie
6212 Banner Ave.
LA, CA 90038
Actress
Response Time: N/A
Received: N/A

Taft, Bob
77 South High St., 30th Fl.
Columbus, OH 43266-0601
Governor
Response Time: N/A
Received: N/A

Tamblyn, Amber
4151 Prospect Ave.
LA, CA 90027
Actress
Response Time: N/A
Received: N/A

Tancredo, Thomas G.
U.S. House of Representatives
Washington, DC 20515
Politician
Response Time: N/A
Received: N/A

Tash, Shayma
4000 Warner Blvd.
Burbank, CA 91522
Actress
Response Time: N/A
Received: N/A

Tani, Daniel M.
2101 NASA Rd. 1
Houston, TX 77058
Astronaut
Response Time: N/A
Received: N/A

Tauscher, Ellen O.
U.S. House of Representatives
Washington, DC 20515
Politician
Response Time: N/A
Received: N/A

Tanner, John S.
U.S. House of Representatives
Washington, DC 20515
Politician
Response Time: N/A
Received: N/A

Tauzin, W. J. "Billy"
U.S. House of Representatives
Washington, DC 20515
Politician
Response Time: N/A
Received: N/A

Tanner, Joseph R.
2101 NASA Rd. 1
Houston, TX 77058
Astronaut
Response Time: N/A
Received: N/A

Taylor, Charles H.
U.S. House of Representatives
Washington, DC 20515
Politician
Response Time: N/A
Received: N/A

Tarantino, Quentin
151 El Camino Dr.
BH, CA 90212
Actor, Director
Response Time: 91 Days
Received: Signed Photo

Taylor, Elizabeth
P.O. Box 55995
Sherman Oaks, CA 91413
Actress
Response Time: 39 Days
Received: Signed Photo

Taylor, Gene
U.S. House of Representatives
Washington, DC 20515
Politician
Response Time: N/A
Received: N/A

Taylor, Josh
3000 W. Alameda Ave.
Burbank, CA 91523
Actor
Response Time: N/A
Received: N/A

Taylor, Karin
9242 Beverly Blvd.
BH, CA 90210
Playboy Playmate
Response Time: N/A
Received: N/A

Taylor, Paul
1268 East 14th St.
Brooklyn, NY 11230
Actor
Response Time: N/A
Received: N/A

Taylor, Priscilla Lee
9242 Beverly Blvd.
BH, CA 90210
Playboy Playmate
Response Time: N/A
Received: N/A

Taylor, Tiffany
9242 Beverly Blvd.
BH, CA 90210
Playboy Playmate
Response Time: N/A
Received: N/A

Teller, Edward
P.O. Box 808
Livermore, CA 94550
Hydrogen Bomb Creator
Response Time: 30 Days
Received: SIC

Temptations, The
9200 Sunset Blvd.
LA, CA 90069
Music Group
Response Time: 12 Days
Received: Signed Photo

TerBlanche, Esta
320 West 66th St.
NY, NY 10023
Actress
Response Time: N/A
Received: N/A

Terry, Lee
U.S. House of Representatives
Washington, DC 20515
Politician
Response Time: N/A
Received: N/A

Thagard, Norman E.
2101 NASA Rd. 1
Houston, TX 77058
Astronaut
Response Time: N/A
Received: N/A

Theisman, Joe
5912 Leisbury Pike
Falls Church, VA 22041
Football Player
Response Time: 48 Days
Received: SIC

Thiele, Gerhard
2101 NASA Rd. 1
Houston, TX 77058
Astronaut
Response Time: N/A
Received: N/A

Thom, Cristy
9242 Beverly Blvd.
BH, CA 90210
Playboy Playmate
Response Time: N/A
Received: N/A

Thomas, Andrew S. W.
2101 NASA Rd. 1
Houston, TX 77058
Astronaut
Response Time: N/A
Received: N/A

Thomas, B.J.
P.O. Box 1632
Whittier, CA 90609
Singer
Response Time: N/A
Received: N/A

Thomas, Clarence
Supreme Court of the United States
Washington, DC 20543
Supreme Court Justice
Response Time: 25 Days
Received: Signed Photo

Thomas, Craig
109 Hart Senate Office Bldg.
Washington, DC 20510
Senator
Response Time: N/A
Received: N/A

Thomas, Dave
4288 W. Dublin Granville Rd.
Dublin, OH 43017
Founder of Wendy's Restaurant
Response Time: 14 Days
Received: Signed Photo

Thomas, Dave
c/o Wendys International
P.O. Box 256, Dublin, OH 43017
Founder of Wendy's Restaurant
Response Time: 14 Days
Received: Signed Photo

Thomas, Donald A.
2101 NASA Rd. 1
Houston, TX 77058
Astronaut
Response Time: N/A
Received: N/A

Thomas, Lynn
9242 Beverly Blvd.
BH, CA 90210
Playboy Playmate
Response Time: N/A
Received: N/A

Thomas, Thurman
7500 S.W. 30th St.
Davie, FL 33329
Football Player
Response Time: 31 Days
Received: STC

Thomas, William M.
U.S. House of Representatives
Washington, DC 20515
Politician
Response Time: N/A
Received: N/A

Thompson, Bennie G.
U.S. House of Representatives
Washington, DC 20515
Politician
Response Time: N/A
Received: N/A

Thompson, Fred
521 Dirksen Senate Office Bldg.
Washington, DC 20510
Senator
Response Time: N/A
Received: N/A

Thompson, Lea
7966 Woodrow Wilson Dr.
LA, CA 90046-1216
Actress
Response Time: 350 Days
Received: Signed Photo

Thompson, Mike
U.S. House of Representatives
Washington, DC 20515
Politician
Response Time: N/A
Received: N/A

Thompson, Susanna
8660 Hayden Place
Culver City, CA 90232
Actress
Response Time: N/A
Received: N/A

Thompson, Tommy G.
State Capitol
P.O. Box 7863, Madison, WI 53707
Governor
Response Time: N/A
Received: N/A

Thornberry, Mac
U.S. House of Representatives
Washington, DC 20515
Politician
Response Time: N/A
Received: N/A

Thornton, Billy Bob
11777 San Vicente Blvd. #880
LA, CA 90049
Actor
Response Time: N/A
Received: N/A

Thornton, Kathryn C.
2101 NASA Rd. 1
Houston, TX 77058
Astronaut
Response Time: N/A
Received: N/A

Thornton, William E.
2101 NASA Rd. 1
Houston, TX 77058
Astronaut
Response Time: N/A
Received: N/A

Thune, John R.
U.S. House of Representatives
Washington, DC 20515
Politician
Response Time: N/A
Received: N/A

Thuot, Pierre J.
2101 NASA Rd. 1
Houston, TX 77058
Astronaut
Response Time: N/A
Received: N/A

Thurman, Karen L.
U.S. House of Representatives
Washington, DC 20515
Politician
Response Time: N/A
Received: N/A

Thurmond, Strom
217 Russell Senate Office Bldg.
Washington, DC 20510
Senator
Response Time: N/A
Received: N/A

Tiahrt, Todd
U.S. House of Representatives
Washington, DC 20515
Politician
Response Time: N/A
Received: N/A

Tiberi, Patrick J.
U.S. House of Representatives
Washington, DC 20515
Politician
Response Time: N/A
Received: N/A

Tierney, John F.
U.S. House of Representatives
Washington, DC 20515
Politician
Response Time: N/A
Received: N/A

Tierney, Maura
4000 Warner Blvd.
Burbank, CA 91522
Actress
Response Time: N/A
Received: N/A

Tilford, Terrell
51 W. 52 St.
NY, NY 10019
Actor
Response Time: N/A
Received: N/A

Tillis, Mel
P.O. Box 1626
Branson, MO 65615
Singer
Response Time: 12 Days
Received: Signed Photo

Tillis, Pam
P.O. Box 120073
Nashville, TN 37212
Singer
Response Time: 14 Days
Received: Signed Photo - $3

Tippin, Aaron
P.O. Box 121709
Nashville, TN 37212
Singer
Response Time: N/A
Received: N/A

Tognini, Michel
2101 NASA Rd. 1
Houston, TX 77058
Astronaut
Response Time: N/A
Received: N/A

Tognoni, Gina
56 West 66th St.
NY, NY 10023
Acress
Response Time: N/A
Received: N/A

Tolsma, Randy
1801 West Int'l. Spdwy. Blvd.
Daytona Beach, FL 32114
Auto Racing Personality
Response Time: 102 Days
Received: Signed Photo

Tom, David
7800 Beverly Blvd.
LA, CA 90036
Actor
Response Time: N/A
Received: N/A

Tom, Heather
7800 Beverly Blvd.
LA, CA 90036
Actress
Response Time: N/A
Received: N/A

Toomey, Patrick J.
U.S. House of Representatives
Washington, DC 20515
Politician
Response Time: N/A
Received: N/A

Tork, Peter
524 San Anselmo Ave., PMB 102
San Anselmo, CA 94960
Singer
Response Time: 91 Days
Received: Signed Photo

Torkildsen, Justin
7800 Beverly Blvd.
LA, CA 90036
Actor
Response Time: N/A
Received: N/A

Torpey, Erin
56 West 66th St.
NY, NY 10023
Actress
Response Time: N/A
Received: N/A

Torres, Liz
4000 Warner Blvd.
Burbank, CA 91522
Actress
Response Time: N/A
Received: N/A

Torres, Samantha
9242 Beverly Blvd.
BH, CA 90210
Playboy Playmate
Response Time: N/A
Received: N/A

Torricelli, Robert
113 Dirksen Senate Office Bldg.
Washington, DC 20510
Senator
Response Time: N/A
Received: N/A

Toussaint, Lorraine
5555 Melrose Ave.
Hollywood, CA 90038-3197
Actress
Response Time: N/A
Received: N/A

Towers, Constance
4151 Prospect Ave.
LA, CA 90027
Actress
Response Time: N/A
Received: N/A

Townes, Charles H.
University of California
Berkeley, CA 94720
Nobel Prize Winner
Response Time: 185 Days
Received: SIC

Towns, Edolphus
U.S. House of Representatives
Washington, DC 20515
Politician
Response Time: N/A
Received: N/A

Traficant Jr., James A.
U.S. House of Representatives
Washington, DC 20515
Politician
Response Time: N/A
Received: N/A

Travis, Randy
P.O. Box 121712
Nashville, TN 37212
Singer
Response Time: 18 Days
Received: Signed Photo

Travolta, John
1504 Live Oak Ln.
Santa Monica, CA 93105
Actor
Response Time: 18 Days
Received: Signed Photo

Travolta, John
15821 Ventura Blvd. #460
Studio City, CA 91436
Actor
Response Time: 17 Days
Received: Signed Photo

Travolta, John
P.O. Box 3560
Santa Barbara, CA 93130
Actor
Response Time: 29 Days
Received: Signed Photo

Treacy, Jane Rudolph
c/o QVC, 1200 Wilson Dr.
West Chester, PA 19380
QVC Host
Response Time: N/A
Received: N/A

Treadway, Ty
56 West 66th St.
NY, NY 10023
Actor
Response Time: N/A
Received: N/A

Trebek, Alex
10210 W. Washington
Culver City, CA 90232
Television Personality
Response Time: N/A
Received: N/A

Trevino, Lee
1901 W. 47th Place #200
Westwood, KS 66205-1834
Golfer
Response Time: 13 Days
Received: Signed Photo

Trickle, Dick
1801 West Int'l. Spdwy. Blvd.
Daytona Beach, FL 32114
Auto Racing Personality
Response Time: 200 Days
Received: Signed Photo

Tritt, Travis
P.O. Box 2044
Hiram, GA 30141
Singer
Response Time: 136 Days
Received: Signed Photo

Troyer, Verne
18032-C Lenon Dr.
Yorba Linda, CA 92866
Actor
Response Time: 26 Days
Received: Signed Photo

Trudeau, Garry
200 Madison Ave.
NY, NY 10016
Creator, Doonesbury
Response Time: 33 Days
Received: Signed Photo

Truesdale, Yanic
4000 Warner Blvd.
Burbank, CA 91522
Actor
Response Time: N/A
Received: N/A

Truly, Richard H.
2101 NASA Rd. 1
Houston, TX 77058
Astronaut
Response Time: N/A
Received: N/A

Trump, Donald
c/o The Trump Corp.
725 Fifth Ave., NY, NY 10022
Entrepreneur
Response Time: 57 Days
Received: Signed Photo

Trump, Ivana
10 E. 64th St.
NY, NY 10021-7212
Author, Actress, Designer
Response Time: 31 Days
Received: Signed Photo

Tryggvason, Bjarni V.
2101 NASA Rd. 1
Houston, TX 77058
Astronaut
Response Time: N/A
Received: N/A

Tucker, Lynne
c/o QVC, 1200 Wilson Dr.
West Chester, PA 19380
QVC Host
Response Time: N/A
Received: N/A

Tucker, Tanya
109 Wespark Dr.
Ste. 400, Brentwood, TN 37027
Singer
Response Time: 67 Days
Received: Signed Photo

Tucker, Tanya
330 Franklin Rd., Ste. 135A-257
Brentwood, TN 37027
Singer
Response Time: 47 Days
Received: Signed Photo

Turnbull, Charles W.
Government House
St. Thomas, VI 00802
Governor
Response Time: N/A
Received: N/A

Turner, Debbye
Two Ocean Way, Ste. 1000
Atlantic City, NJ 08401
Miss America 1990
Response Time: N/A
Received: N/A

Turner, Jim
U.S. House of Representatives
Washington, DC 20515
Politician
Response Time: N/A
Received: N/A

Turner, Karri
5555 Melrose Ave.
Hollywood, CA 90038-3197
Actress
Response Time: N/A
Received: N/A

Turner, Kathleen
163 Amsterdam Ave.
NY, NY 10023
Actress
Response Time: 110 Days
Received: Signed Photo

Tyler, Buffy
9242 Beverly Blvd.
BH, CA 90210
Playboy Playmate
Response Time: N/A
Received: N/A

Tylo, Hunter
7800 Beverly Blvd.
LA, CA 90036
Actress
Response Time: N/A
Received: N/A

Udall, Mark
U.S. House of Representatives
Washington, DC 20515
Politician
Response Time: N/A
Received: N/A

Udall, Tom
U.S. House of Representatives
Washington, DC 20515
Politician
Response Time: N/A
Received: N/A

Ulrich, Kim Johnston
4024 Radford Ave.
Studio City, CA 91604
Actress
Response Time: N/A
Received: N/A

Underwood, Cecil H.
State Capitol Complex
Charleston, WV 25305-0370
Governor
Response Time: 10 Days
Received: Signed Photo

Underwood, Robert A.
U.S. House of Representatives
Washington, DC 20515
Politician
Response Time: N/A
Received: N/A

Upton, Fred
U.S. House of Representatives
Washington, DC 20515
Politician
Response Time: N/A
Received: N/A

Urban, Keith
P.O. Box 40185
Nashville, TN 37204
Singer
Response Time: 33 Days
Received: Signed Photo

Vail, Justina
5555 Melrose Ave.
Hollywood, CA 90038-3197
Actress
Response Time: N/A
Received: N/A

Van Croft, Nichole
9242 Beverly Blvd.
BH, CA 90210
Playboy Playmate
Response Time: N/A
Received: N/A

Van Der Beek, James
4000 Warner Blvd.
Burbank, CA 91522
Actor
Response Time: N/A
Received: N/A

Van Dyke, Dick
151 El Camino Dr.
BH, CA 90212
Actor
Response Time: N/A
Received: N/A

Van Derbur, Marilyn
Two Ocean Way, Ste. 1000
Atlantic City, NJ 08401
Miss America 1958
Response Time: N/A
Received: N/A

Van Dyke, Dick
23215 Mariposa DeOro
Malibu, CA 90265
Actor
Response Time: N/A
Received: N/A

Van Dien, Casper
3500 W. Olive Ave. #1400
Burbank, CA 91505
Actor
Response Time: 66 Days
Received: Signed Photo

Van Dyke, Dick
5555 Melrose Ave.
Hollywood, CA 90038-3197
Actor
Response Time: N/A
Received: N/A

Van Dien, Casper
5700 Wilshire, Ste. 575
LA, CA 90036
Actor
Response Time: N/A
Received: N/A

Van Dyke, Vonda
Two Ocean Way, Ste. 1000
Atlantic City, NJ 08401
Miss America 1965
Response Time: N/A
Received: N/A

Van Dyke, Barry
5555 Melrose Ave.
Hollywood, CA 90038-3197
Actor
Response Time: N/A
Received: N/A

Van Hoften, James D. A.
2101 NASA Rd. 1
Houston, TX 77058
Astronaut
Response Time: N/A
Received: N/A

Van Wagner, Aaron
3000 W. Alameda Ave.
Burbank, CA 91523
Actor
Response Time: N/A
Received: N/A

Vaughn, Countess
5555 Melrose Ave.
Hollywood, CA 90038-3197
Actress
Response Time: N/A
Received: N/A

Vaughn, Terri J.
4000 Warner Blvd.
Burbank, CA 91522
Actress
Response Time: N/A
Received: N/A

Vega, Makenzie
500 S. Buena Vista St.
Burbank, CA 91521
Actress
Response Time: N/A
Received: N/A

Velazquez, Nydia M.
U.S. House of Representatives
Washington, DC 20515
Politician
Response Time: N/A
Received: N/A

Venable, David
c/o QVC, 1200 Wilson Dr.
West Chester, PA 19380
QVC Host
Response Time: N/A
Received: N/A

Vendela
344 E. 59th St.
NY, NY 10022
Model
Response Time: 68 Days
Received: Signed Photo

Vendela
c/o Ford, 142 Greene St.
NY, NY 10012
Model
Response Time: 125 Days
Received: Signed Photo

Ventura, Jesse
130 State Capitol, 75 Constitution Ave.
St. Paul, MN 55155
Politician, Former Wrestler, Governor
Response Time: N/A
Received: N/A

Ventura, Jesse
5800 85th Ave. N.
Brooklyn Park, MN 55443
Politician, Former Wrestler, Governor
Response Time: 39 Days
Received: Signed Photo

Ventura, Jesse
Citizen Outreach, 130 Capitol Bldg.
St. Paul, MN 55155
Politician, Former Wrestler, Governor
Response Time: 39 Days
Received: Signed Photo

Ver Dorn, Jerry
51 W. 52 St.
NY, NY 10019
Actor
Response Time: N/A
Received: N/A

Vigoda, Abe
8500 Melrose Ave. #208
W. Hollywood, CA 90069
Actor
Response Time: 20 Days
Received: SIC

Vilsack, Tom
State Capitol
Des Moines, IA 50319-0001
Governor
Response Time: N/A
Received: N/A

Vincent, Marjorie
Two Ocean Way, Ste. 1000
Atlantic City, NJ 08401
Miss America 1991
Response Time: N/A
Received: N/A

Visclosky, Peter J.
U.S. House of Representatives
Washington, DC 20515
Politician
Response Time: N/A
Received: N/A

Visnjic, Goran
4000 Warner Blvd.
Burbank, CA 91522
Actor
Response Time: N/A
Received: N/A

Vitter, David
U.S. House of Representatives
Washington, DC 20515
Politician
Response Time: N/A
Received: N/A

Vittori, Roberto
2101 NASA Rd. 1
Houston, TX 77058
Astronaut
Response Time: N/A
Received: N/A

Vogel, Darlene
56 West 66th St.
NY, NY 10023
Actress
Response Time: N/A
Received: N/A

Voinovich, George
317 Hart Senate Office Bldg.
Washington, DC 20510
Senator
Response Time: N/A
Received: N/A

Von Esmarch, Nick
4000 Warner Blvd.
Burbank, CA 91522
Actor
Response Time: N/A
Received: N/A

Von Furstenberg, Diane
c/o Home Shopping Network
St. Petersburg, FL 33701
Fashion Designer
Response Time: N/A
Received: N/A

Von Oy, Jenna
5555 Melrose Ave.
Hollywood, CA 90038-3197
Actress
Response Time: N/A
Received: N/A

Voronina, Irina
9242 Beverly Blvd.
BH, CA 90210
Playboy Playmate
Response Time: N/A
Received: N/A

Voss, James S.
2101 NASA Rd. 1
Houston, TX 77058
Astronaut
Response Time: N/A
Received: N/A

Voss, Janice E.
2101 NASA Rd. 1
Houston, TX 77058
Astronaut
Response Time: N/A
Received: N/A

Vultaggio, Lisa
4151 Prospect Ave.
LA, CA 90027
Actress
Response Time: N/A
Received: N/A

Wagner, Helen
1268 East 14th St.
Brooklyn, NY 11230
Actress
Response Time: N/A
Received: N/A

Wagner, Jack
1134 Alto Loma #115
W. Hollywood, CA 90069
Actor
Response Time: 20 Days
Received: Signed Photo

Wagner, Jack
5700 Wilshire, Ste. 575
LA, CA 90036
Actor
Response Time: N/A
Received: N/A

Wagner, Kristina
4151 Prospect Ave.
LA, CA 90027
Actress
Response Time: N/A
Received: N/A

Wahlberg, Donnie
27 Dudley St.
Robury, MA 02132
Singer
Response Time: N/A
Received: N/A

Wakata, Koichi
2101 NASA Rd. 1
Houston, TX 77058
Astronaut
Response Time: N/A
Received: N/A

Wakelin, Cara
9242 Beverly Blvd.
BH, CA 90210
Playboy Playmate
Response Time: N/A
Received: N/A

Walden, Greg
U.S. House of Representatives
Washington, DC 20515
Politician
Response Time: N/A
Received: N/A

Walheim, Rex J.
2101 NASA Rd. 1
Houston, TX 77058
Astronaut
Response Time: N/A
Received: N/A

Walker, Barbara
Two Ocean Way, Ste. 1000
Atlantic City, NJ 08401
Miss America 1947
Response Time: N/A
Received: N/A

Walker, Clay
1000-18 Ave. South
Nashville, TN 37212
Singer
Response Time: 360 Days
Received: Signed Photo

Walker, Clay
P.O. Box 8125
Gallatin, TN 37066
Singer
Response Time: 52 Days
Received: Signed Photo

Walker, David M.
2101 NASA Rd. 1
Houston, TX 77058
Astronaut
Response Time: N/A
Received: N/A

Walker, Marcy
320 West 66th St.
NY, NY 10023
Actress
Response Time: N/A
Received: N/A

Walker, Mort
61 Studio Court
Stamford, CT 94550
Cartoonist
Response Time: N/A
Received: N/A

Wallace, Kenny
1801 West Int'l. Spdwy. Blvd.
Daytona Beach, FL 32114
Auto Racing Personality
Response Time: 198 Days
Received: Signed Photo

Wallace, Mike
1801 West Int'l. Spdwy. Blvd.
Daytona Beach, FL 32114
Auto Racing Personality
Response Time: 219 Days
Received: Signed Photo

Wallace, Rusty
1801 West Int'l. Spdwy. Blvd.
Daytona Beach, FL 32114
Auto Racing Personality
Response Time: 365 Days
Received: Signed Photo

Walsh, James T.
U.S. House of Representatives
Washington, DC 20515
Politician
Response Time: N/A
Received: N/A

Walton, Jess
7800 Beverly Blvd.
LA, CA 90036
Actress
Response Time: N/A
Received: N/A

Waltrip, Darrell
1801 West Int'l. Spdwy. Blvd.
Daytona Beach, FL 32114
Auto Racing Personality
Response Time: 195 Days
Received: Signed Photo

Waltrip, Michael
1801 West Int'l. Spdwy. Blvd.
Daytona Beach, FL 32114
Auto Racing Personality
Response Time: 248 Days
Received: Signed Photo

Walz, Carl E.
2101 NASA Rd. 1
Houston, TX 77058
Astronaut
Response Time: N/A
Received: N/A

Wamp, Zach
U.S. House of Representatives
Washington, DC 20515
Politician
Response Time: N/A
Received: N/A

Wapner, Joseph
2388 Century Hill
LA, CA 90067
Judge
Response Time: 23 Days
Received: Signed Photo

Ward, Elizabeth
Two Ocean Way, Ste. 1000
Atlantic City, NJ 08401
Miss America 1982
Response Time: N/A
Received: N/A

Ward, Sela
289 S. Robertson Blvd., Ste. 469
BH, CA 90211
Actress
Response Time: 95 Days
Received: Signed Photo

Ward, Sela
8660 Hayden Place
Culver City, CA 90232
Actress
Response Time: N/A
Received: N/A

Ward, Sophie
13 Radnor Walk
London Sw3 4BP, United Kingdom
Actress
Response Time: 36 Days
Received: Signed Photo

Ware, Rick
1801 West Int'l. Spdwy. Blvd.
Daytona Beach, FL 32114
Auto Racing Personality
Response Time: 131 Days
Received: Signed Photo

Wariner, Steve
P.O. Box 1667
Franklin, TN 37065
Singer
Response Time: 11 Days
Received: Signed Photo

Warlock, Billy
c/o Baywatch Productions
510-18th Ave., Honolulu, HI 96816
Actor
Response Time: N/A
Received: N/A

Warlock, Billy
4151 Prospect Ave.
LA, CA 90027
Actor
Response Time: N/A
Received: N/A

Warner, John
225 Russell Senate Office Bldg.
Washington, DC 20510
Senator
Response Time: N/A
Received: N/A

Warren Brothers, The
P.O. Box 120479
Nashville, TN 37212
Music Group
Response Time: N/A
Received: N/A

Warrick, Ruth
320 West 66th St.
NY, NY 10023
Actress
Response Time: N/A
Received: N/A

Washington, Denzel
4701 Sancola
Toluca Lake, CA 91602
Actor
Response Time: N/A
Received: N/A

Wasilewski, Paul
51 W. 52 St.
NY, NY 10019
Actor
Response Time: N/A
Received: N/A

Waters, Maxine
U.S. House of Representatives
Washington, DC 20515
Politician
Response Time: N/A
Received: N/A

Waterston, Sam
1230 Ave. of Americas
NY, NY 10020
Actor
Response Time: N/A
Received: N/A

Watkins, Wes
U.S. House of Representatives
Washington, DC 20515
Politician
Response Time: N/A
Received: N/A

Watson, Alberta
1230 Ave. of Americas
NY, NY 10020
Actress
Response Time: 36 Days
Received: Signed Photo

Watson, Barry
c/o The WB Network, 3701 Oak St.
Bldg. 34R, Burbank, CA 91505
Actor
Response Time: N/A
Received: N/A

Watson, Muse
4737 Lankershim Blvd., Ste. 208
N. Hollywood, CA 91602
Actor
Response Time: 19 Days
Received: Signed Photo

Watson, Tom
1901 W. 47th Place #200
Westwood, KS 66205-1834
Golfer
Response Time: 14 Days
Received: Signed Photo

Watt, Melvin L.
U.S. House of Representatives
Washington, DC 20515
Politician
Response Time: N/A
Received: N/A

Watts Jr., J.C.
U.S. House of Representatives
Washington, DC 20515
Politician
Response Time: N/A
Received: N/A

Waxman, Henry A.
U.S. House of Representatives
Washington, DC 20515
Politician
Response Time: N/A
Received: N/A

Weaver, Dennis
P.O. Box 257
Ridgway, CO 81432-0257
Actor
Response Time: 31 Days
Received: Signed Photo

Weaver, Patty
7800 Beverly Blvd.
LA, CA 90036
Actress
Response Time: N/A
Received: N/A

Weber, Mary E.
2101 NASA Rd. 1
Houston, TX 77058
Astronaut
Response Time: N/A
Received: N/A

Weiner, Anthony D.
U.S. House of Representatives
Washington, DC 20515
Politician
Response Time: N/A
Received: N/A

Weitz, Paul J.
2101 NASA Rd. 1
Houston, TX 77058
Astronaut
Response Time: N/A
Received: N/A

Weldon, Curt
U.S. House of Representatives
Washington, DC 20515
Politician
Response Time: N/A
Received: N/A

Weldon, Dave
U.S. House of Representatives
Washington, DC 20515
Politician
Response Time: N/A
Received: N/A

Weller, Jerry
U.S. House of Representatives
Washington, DC 20515
Politician
Response Time: N/A
Received: N/A

Wells, Dawn
11684 Ventura Blvd. #985
Studio City, CA 91604
Actress
Response Time: 40 Days
Received: Signed Photo - $10

Wells, Dawn
4616 Ledge Ave.
N. Hollywood, CA 91602
Actress
Response Time: N/A
Received: N/A

Wells, Kimberly
c/o Home Shopping Network
St. Petersburg, FL 33701
Home Shopping Network Host
Response Time: N/A
Received: N/A

Wells, Kitty
240 Old Hickory Blvd.
Madison, TN 37115
Singer
Response Time: N/A
Received: N/A

Wells, Sharlene
Two Ocean Way, Ste. 1000
Atlantic City, NJ 08401
Miss America 1985
Response Time: N/A
Received: N/A

Wellstone, Paul
136 Hart Senate Office Bldg.
Washington, DC 20510
Senator
Response Time: N/A
Received: N/A

West, Kimber
9242 Beverly Blvd.
BH, CA 90210
Playboy Playmate
Response Time: N/A
Received: N/A

West, Maura
1268 East 14th St.
Brooklyn, NY 11230
Actress
Response Time: N/A
Received: N/A

West, Shane
8660 Hayden Place
Culver City, CA 90232
Actor
Response Time: N/A
Received: N/A

Westcott, Carrie
9242 Beverly Blvd.
BH, CA 90210
Playboy Playmate
Response Time: N/A
Received: N/A

Westheimer, Dr. Ruth
900 W. 190th St.
NY, NY 10040
Sex Therapist
Response Time: 33 Days
Received: Signed Photo

Westmore, McKenzie
4024 Radford Ave.
Studio City, CA 91604
Actress
Response Time: N/A
Received: N/A

Wetherbee, James D.
2101 NASA Rd. 1
Houston, TX 77058
Astronaut
Response Time: N/A
Received: N/A

Wexler, Robert
U.S. House of Representatives
Washington, DC 20515
Politician
Response Time: N/A
Received: N/A

Whedon, Joss
4000 Warner Blvd.
Burbank, CA 91522
Actor
Response Time: N/A
Received: N/A

Wheeler, Dan
c/o QVC, 1200 Wilson Dr.
West Chester, PA 19380
QVC Host
Response Time: N/A
Received: N/A

Wheelock, Douglas H.
2101 NASA Rd. 1
Houston, TX 77058
Astronaut
Response Time: N/A
Received: N/A

Whelan, Julia
8660 Hayden Place
Culver City, CA 90232
Actress
Response Time: N/A
Received: N/A

White, Betty
P.O. Box 491965
LA, CA 90049
Actress
Response Time: 18 Days
Received: Signed Photo

White, Bryan
Box 120162
Nashville, TN 37212
Singer
Response Time: 15 Days
Received: Signed Photo

White, Lari
P.O. Box 120086
Nashville, TN 37212
Singer
Response Time: 17 Days
Received: Signed Photo

White, Persia
5555 Melrose Ave.
Hollywood, CA 90038-3197
Actress
Response Time: N/A
Received: N/A

White, Vanna
3400 Riverside Dr., 2nd Fl.
Burbank, CA 91505
Television Personality
Response Time: N/A
Received: N/A

White, Vanna
10202 W. Washington Blvd.
Culver City, CA 90232
Television Personality
Response Time: 8 Days
Received: Signed Photo

Whitestone, Heather
Two Ocean Way, Ste. 1000
Atlantic City, NJ 08401
Miss America 1995
Response Time: N/A
Received: N/A

Whitfield, Ed
U.S. House of Representatives
Washington, DC 20515
Politician
Response Time: N/A
Received: N/A

Whitford, Bradley
4000 Warner Blvd.
Burbank, CA 91522
Actor
Response Time: N/A
Received: N/A

Whitman, Christine T.
125 West State St., P.O. Box 001
Trenton, NJ 08625
Governor
Response Time: N/A
Received: N/A

Whitmore, James
4990 Puesta Del Sol
Malibu, CA 90265
Actor
Response Time: 42 Days
Received: Signed Photo

Whitson, Peggy A.
2101 NASA Rd. 1
Houston, TX 77058
Astronaut
Response Time: N/A
Received: N/A

Wicker, Roger F.
U.S. House of Representatives
Washington, DC 20515
Politician
Response Time: N/A
Received: N/A

Widdoes, Kathleen
1268 East 14th St.
Brooklyn, NY 11230
Actress
Response Time: N/A
Received: N/A

Wiest, Dianne
1230 Ave. of Americas
NY, NY 10020
Actress
Response Time: N/A
Received: N/A

Wilcutt, Terrence W.
2101 NASA Rd. 1
Houston, TX 77058
Astronaut
Response Time: N/A
Received: N/A

Wiles, Jason
4000 Warner Blvd.
Burbank, CA 91522
Actor
Response Time: N/A
Received: N/A

Wilkinsons, The
P.O. Box 128365
Nashville, TN 37212
Music Group
Response Time: N/A
Received: N/A

Willey, Walt
320 West 66th St.
NY, NY 10023
Actor
Response Time: N/A
Received: N/A

Williams Jr., Hank
Highway 79 East, Box 1350
Paris, TN 38242
Singer
Response Time: N/A
Received: N/A

Williams, Barry
150 E. 57th St., Apt. 25A
NY, NY 10022-2799
Actor, Singer
Response Time: 17 Days
Received: Signed Photo I Sent

Williams, Chris
4000 Warner Blvd.
Burbank, CA 91522
Actor
Response Time: N/A
Received: N/A

Williams, David R.
2101 NASA Rd. 1
Houston, TX 77058
Astronaut
Response Time: N/A
Received: N/A

Williams, Donald E.
2101 NASA Rd. 1
Houston, TX 77058
Astronaut
Response Time: N/A
Received: N/A

Williams, Greg Allan
c/o Baywatch Productions
510-18th Ave., Honolulu, HI 96816
Actor
Response Time: N/A
Received: N/A

Williams, Harland
500 S. Buena Vista St.
Burbank, CA 91521
Actor
Response Time: N/A
Received: N/A

Williams, Jeffrey N.
2101 NASA Rd. 1
Houston, TX 77058
Astronaut
Response Time: N/A
Received: N/A

Williams, Jet
P.O. Box 177
Hartsville, TN 37074
Singer
Response Time: N/A
Received: N/A

Williams, John
301 Massachusetts Ave.
Boston, MA 02115
Composer
Response Time: 39 Days
Received: Signed Photo

Williams, Kelli
10201 West Pico Blvd.
LA, CA 90035
Actress
Response Time: N/A
Received: N/A

Williams, Leah
c/o QVC, 1200 Wilson Dr.
West Chester, PA 19380
QVC Host
Response Time: N/A
Received: N/A

Williams, Malinda
5555 Melrose Ave.
Hollywood, CA 90038-3197
Actress
Response Time: N/A
Received: N/A

Williams, Michelle
4000 Warner Blvd.
Burbank, CA 91522
Actress
Response Time: N/A
Received: N/A

Williams, Robin
1100 Wall Rd.
Napa, CA 94550
Actor
Response Time: 340 Days
Received: Signed Photo

Williams, Sunita L.
2101 NASA Rd. 1
Houston, TX 77058
Astronaut
Response Time: N/A
Received: N/A

Williams, Tonya Lee
7800 Beverly Blvd.
LA, CA 90036
Actress
Response Time: N/A
Received: N/A

Williams, Van
612 Lighthouse Ave. #275
Pacific Grove, CA 93951
Actor
Response Time: N/A
Received: N/A

Williams, Vanessa
5555 Melrose Ave.
Hollywood, CA 90038-3197
Actress
Response Time: N/A
Received: N/A

Williams, Vanessa
Two Ocean Way, Ste. 1000
Atlantic City, NJ 08401
Miss America 1984, Singer
Response Time: N/A
Received: N/A

Williamson, Fred
10880 Wilshire Blvd. #1101
LA, CA 90024
Actor
Response Time: N/A
Received: N/A

Williamson, Kevin
4000 Warner Blvd.
Burbank, CA 91522
Creator of Dawson's Creek
Response Time: N/A
Received: N/A

Williamson, Kevin
8942 Wilshire Blvd.
BH, CA 90211
Creator of Dawson's Creek
Response Time: N/A
Received: N/A

Wills, Mark
2094 Cobb Parkway
Smyrna, GA 30080
Singer
Response Time: 10 Days
Received: Signed Photo

Wilson, B.A.
1801 West Int'l. Spdwy. Blvd.
Daytona Beach, FL 32114
Auto Racing Personality
Response Time: 99 Days
Received: Signed Photo

Wilson, Brian
15030 Ventura Blvd. #1-710
Sherman Oaks, CA 91403
Singer
Response Time: N/A
Received: N/A

Wilson, Dorien
5555 Melrose Ave.
Hollywood, CA 90038-3197
Actor
Response Time: N/A
Received: N/A

Wilson, Heather
U.S. House of Representatives
Washington, DC 20515
Politician
Response Time: N/A
Received: N/A

Wilson, Marie
4151 Prospect Ave.
LA, CA 90027
Actress
Response Time: N/A
Received: N/A

Wilson, Roger
State Capitol, Room 216
Jefferson City, MO 65101
Governor
Response Time: N/A
Received: N/A

Wilson, Stephanie D.
2101 NASA Rd. 1
Houston, TX 77058
Astronaut
Response Time: N/A
Received: N/A

Wilson, Yvette
5555 Melrose Ave.
Hollywood, CA 90038-3197
Actress
Response Time: N/A
Received: N/A

Winchell, Paul
78845 Golden Reed Dr.
Palm Desert, CA 92211-1843
Voice Actor
Response Time: 19 Days
Received: SIC

Winfrey, Oprah
P.O. Box 909715
Chicago, IL 60690
Television Personality
Response Time: N/A
Received: N/A

Winslet, Kate
31/32 Soho Square
London W1V 5DG, England
Actress
Response Time: 58 Days
Received: Signed Photo

Winslet, Kate
503 The Chambers, Chelsea Harbour
London SW10 OXF, England
Actress
Response Time: 58 Days
Received: Signed Photo

Winston, Hattie
5555 Melrose Ave.
Hollywood, CA 90038-3197
Actress
Response Time: N/A
Received: N/A

Winters, Jonathan
4310 Arcola Ave.
Toluca Lake, CA 91608
Actor, Entertainer
Response Time: 95 Days
Received: Signed Photo

Wisoff, Peter J. K.
2101 NASA Rd. 1
Houston, TX 77058
Astronaut
Response Time: N/A
Received: N/A

Witt, Holly
9242 Beverly Blvd.
BH, CA 90210
Playboy Playmate
Response Time: N/A
Received: N/A

Wolf, David A.
2101 NASA Rd. 1
Houston, TX 77058
Astronaut
Response Time: N/A
Received: N/A

Wolf, Frank R.
U.S. House of Representatives
Washington, DC 20515
Politician
Response Time: N/A
Received: N/A

Wolf, Kathy
c/o Home Shopping Network
St. Petersburg, FL 33701
Home Shopping Network Host
Response Time: N/A
Received: N/A

Womack, Lee Ann
P.O. Box 1096
White House, TN 37188-1096
Singer
Response Time: 12 Days
Received: Signed Photo

Wood, Danny
496 Adams St.
Dorchester, MA 02122
Singer
Response Time: N/A
Received: N/A

Wood, Evan Rachel
8660 Hayden Place
Culver City, CA 90232
Actress
Response Time: N/A
Received: N/A

Wood, Nicole
9242 Beverly Blvd.
BH, CA 90210
Playboy Playmate
Response Time: N/A
Received: N/A

Woodland, Lauren
7800 Beverly Blvd.
LA, CA 90036
Actress
Response Time: N/A
Received: N/A

Woodland, Rich
1801 West Int'l. Spdwy. Blvd.
Daytona Beach, FL 32114
Auto Racing Personality
Response Time: 115 Days
Received: Signed Photo

Woods, Robert S.
56 West 66th St.
NY, NY 10023
Actor
Response Time: N/A
Received: N/A

Woods, Tiger
112 TPC Blvd.
Ponte Verde Beach, FL 32802
Golfer
Response Time: N/A
Received: N/A

Woods, Tiger
1360 East 9th St., Ste. 100
Cleveland , OH 44114
Golfer
Response Time: N/A
Received: N/A

Woods, Tiger
4281 Katella Ave., Ste. 111
Los Alamitos, CA 90720-3541
Golfer
Response Time: N/A
Received: N/A

Woods, Tiger
One Erieview Plaza, Ste. 1300
Cleveland, OH 44114
Golfer
Response Time: N/A
Received: N/A

Woodward III, Neil W.
2101 NASA Rd. 1
Houston, TX 77058
Astronaut
Response Time: N/A
Received: N/A

Woolsey, Lynn C.
U.S. House of Representatives
Washington, DC 20515
Politician
Response Time: N/A
Received: N/A

Wopat, Tom
P.O. Box 128031
Nashville, TN 37212
Actor
Response Time: N/A
Received: N/A

Worden, Alfred M.
2101 NASA Rd. 1
Houston, TX 77058
Astronaut
Response Time: N/A
Received: N/A

Wright, Deanna
4024 Radford Ave.
Studio City, CA 91604
Actress
Response Time: N/A
Received: N/A

Wright, Laura
51 W. 52 St.
NY, NY 10019
Actress
Response Time: N/A
Received: N/A

Wright, Max
300 Television Plaza
Burbank, CA 91505
Actor
Response Time: N/A
Received: N/A

Wright, Michelle
P.O. Box 22953
Nashville, TN 37202
Singer
Response Time: 14 Days
Received: Signed Photo

Wu, David
U.S. House of Representatives
Washington, DC 20515
Politician
Response Time: N/A
Received: N/A

Wyden, Ron
516 Hart Senate Office Bldg.
Washington, DC 20510
Senator
Response Time: N/A
Received: N/A

Wyle, Noah
4000 Warner Blvd.
Burbank, CA 91522
Actor
Response Time: N/A
Received: N/A

Wynn, Albert Russell
U.S. House of Representatives
Washington, DC 20515
Politician
Response Time: N/A
Received: N/A

Yankee Grey
P.O. Box 128371
Nashville, TN 37212
Music Group
Response Time: N/A
Received: N/A

Yankovic, Weird Al
8033 Sunset Blvd.
LA, CA 90046
Actor, Singer
Response Time: 49 Days
Received: Signed Photo

Yarborough, Cale
1801 West Int'l. Spdwy. Blvd.
Daytona Beach, FL 32114
Auto Racing Personality
Response Time: 186 Days
Received: Signed Photo

Yates, Robert
115 Dwelle St.
Charlotte, NC 28208-2929
NASCAR Team Owner
Response Time: 210 Days
Received: STC

Yeager, Chuck
P.O. Box 128
Cedar Ridge, CA 95924
Aviator
Response Time: 14 Days
Received: SIC

Yearwood, Trisha
4636-316 Lebanon Pike
Nashville, TN 37076-1316
Singer
Response Time: N/A
Received: N/A

Yearwood, Trisha
9220 Sunset Blvd. #320
LA, CA 90069
Singer
Response Time: N/A
Received: N/A

Yearwood, Trisha
Box 65
Monticello, GA 31064
Singer
Response Time: 36 Days
Received: Signed Photo

Yearwood, Trisha
P.O. Box 160295
Nashville, TN 37216
Singer
Response Time: N/A
Received: N/A

Yoakam, Dwight
15030 Ventura Blvd. #710
Sherman Oaks, CA 91403
Singer
Response Time: 15 Days
Received: Signed Photo

York, Brittany
9242 Beverly Blvd.
BH, CA 90210
Playboy Playmate
Response Time: N/A
Received: N/A

York, John J.
4151 Prospect Ave.
LA, CA 90027
Actor
Response Time: 29 Days
Received: Signed Photo

Young, Bruce
5555 Melrose Ave.
Hollywood, CA 90038-3197
Actor
Response Time: N/A
Received: N/A

Young, C.W. Bill
U.S. House of Representatives
Washington, DC 20515
Politician
Response Time: N/A
Received: N/A

Young, Dean
235 E. 45th St.
NY, NY 10017
Cartoonist
Response Time: 48 Days
Received: Signed Sketch

Young, Don
U.S. House of Representatives
Washington, DC 20515
Politician
Response Time: N/A
Received: N/A

Young, Jacob
4151 Prospect Ave.
LA, CA 90027
Actor
Response Time: N/A
Received: N/A

Young, John W.
2101 NASA Rd. 1
Houston, TX 77058
Astronaut
Response Time: N/A
Received: N/A

Young, Julianna
9242 Beverly Blvd.
BH, CA 90210
Playboy Playmate
Response Time: N/A
Received: N/A

Young, Sean
11935 Kling St., Ste. 10
Valley Village, CA 91607
Actress
Response Time: 19 Days
Received: Signed Photo

Young, Sean
P.O. Box 20547
Sedona, AZ 86341-0547
Actress
Response Time: N/A
Received: N/A

Young, Steve
4949 Centennial Blvd.
Santa Clara, CA 95054
Football Player
Response Time: 30 Days
Received: Signed Photo

Young, William Allen
5555 Melrose Ave.
Hollywood, CA 90038-3197
Actor
Response Time: N/A
Received: N/A

Yovan, Guy
c/o Home Shopping Network
St. Petersburg, FL 33701
Home Shopping Network Host
Response Time: N/A
Received: N/A

Zacapa, Daniel
5555 Melrose Ave.
Hollywood, CA 90038-3197
Actor
Response Time: N/A
Received: N/A

Zamka, George D.
2101 NASA Rd. 1
Houston, TX 77058
Astronaut
Response Time: N/A
Received: N/A

Zdrok, Victoria Nika
9242 Beverly Blvd.
BH, CA 90210
Playboy Playmate
Response Time: N/A
Received: N/A

Zegers, Kevin
5700 Wilshire, Ste. 575
LA, CA 90036
Actor
Response Time: N/A
Received: N/A

Zeman, Jacklyn
4151 Prospect Ave.
LA, CA 90027
Actress
Response Time: N/A
Received: N/A

Ziering, Nikki
5757 Wilshire Blvd. #206
LA, CA 90036
Television Personality
Response Time: N/A
Received: N/A

Zimmer, Kim
51 W. 52 St.
NY, NY 10019
Actress
Response Time: N/A
Received: N/A

Zoeller, Fuzzy
418 Deer Run Trace
Floyd Knobs, IN 47119

Index

Name		Name		Name	
Bell, Coby	30	Blaney, Dave	35	Brannon, Chad	40
Bell, Lauralee	30	Bledel, Alexis	35	Braugher, Andre	40
Bell, Michelle	30	Bleeth, Yasmine	35	Breaux, John	40
Bellamy Brothers	30	Bliss, Mike	35	Brendon, Nicholas	40
Belushi, James	31	Block, Hunt	36	Brewster, Paget	40
Belzer, Richard	31	Bloom, Brian	36	Breyer, Stephen	40
Benard, Maurice	31	Bloomfield, Michael J.	36	Bridges Jr., Roy D.	41
Benbrook, Liz	31	Blucas, Marc	36	Bridges, Angelica	41
Benedict, Marina	31	Bluford Jr., Guion S.	36	Bridges, Beau	41
Benedicto, Lourdes	31	Blumenauer, Earl	36	Bridges, Elisa	41
Benham, Dorothy	31	Blunt, Roy	36	Bridges, Jeff	41
Bennett, Brad	31	Boatman, Michael	36	Briggs, Randy	41
Bennett, Robert	31	Bobko, Karol J.	36	Brochtrup, Bill	41
Bennett, Tony	31	Bockrath, Tina	36	Broderick, Beth	41
Benson, Johnny	31	Bodine, Brett	36	Broderick, Matthew	41
Bently, Lamont	31	Bodine, Geoffrey	36	Brockovich, Erin	41
Bentsen, Ken	31	Bodine, Todd	36	Bronson, Charles	41
Bereuter, Doug	31	Boehlert, Sherwood L.	36	Brooks & Dunn	41
Bergeron, Marian	32	Boehner, John A.	37	Brooks, Deanna	41
Bergin, Michael	32	Boggs, Wade	37	Brooks, Golden	41
Bergman, Alan	32	Bogush, Elizabeth	37	Brooks, Jason	42
Bergman, Jaime	32	Bolden Jr., Charles F.	37	Brooks, Jim	42
Bergman, Marilyn	32	Bolger, John	37	Brosnan, Pierce	42
Bergman, Peter	32	Bonaduce, Danny	37	Brosnan, Pierce	42
Berkley, Shelley	32	Bond, Christopher	37	Brothers, Joyce	42
Berman, Howard L.	32	Bonet, Lisa	37	Brown Jr., Curtis L.	42
Bernaola, Carol	32	Bonifield, Phil	37	Brown Jr., Henry E.	42
Berra, Yogi	32	Bonilla, Henry	37	Brown, Corrine	42
Berrier, Ed	32	Bonior, David E.	37	Brown, Cynthia Gwyn	42
Berry, Brooke	32	Bonner, Gillian	37	Brown, David M.	42
Berry, John	32	Bono, Mary	37	Brown, Jayne	42
Berry, Marion	32	Boone, Lesley	37	Brown, Mark N.	42
Berry, Tina	33	Booth, Lindy	38	Brown, Ryan	42
Bertinelli, Valerie	33	Boreanaz, David	38	Brown, Sarah	42
Bessey, Joe	33	Borgnine, Ernest	38	Brown, Sherrod	43
Betbeze, Yolande	33	Borgnine, Tova	38	Brown, Susan	43
Beyer, Tanya	33	Boris, Angel	38	Brown, T. Graham	43
Bialik, Mayim	33	Borman, Frank	38	Brownback, Sam	43
Bibb, Leslie	33	Borski, Robert A.	38	Browne, Kale	43
Bickle, Rich	33	Bostwick, Barry	38	Brumbly, Charlie	43
Biden Jr., Joseph	33	Boswell, Leonard L.	38	Bryant, Deborah	43
Biel, Jessica	33	Boucher, Rick	38	Bryant, Ed	43
Biffle, Greg	33	Boudreau, Michelle	38	Bryant, Steve	43
Biggert, Judy	33	Bowden, Bobby	38	Bryggman, Larry	43
Biggs, Richard	33	Bowen, Julie	38	Buchanan, Pat	43
Bilirakis, Michael	33	Bowersox, Bob	38	Buchli, James F.	43
Bingaman, Jeff	34	Bowersox, Kenneth D.	39	Budig, Rebecca	43
Bingham, Traci	34	Boxer, Barbara	39	Buferd, Marilyn	44
Biondi, Matt	34	Boyd, Allen	39	Buffett, Jimmy	44
Bird, Larry	34	Boyd, Stan	39	Bull, John S.	44
Birkelund, Olivia	34	Boyd, Tanya	39	Bulloch, Jeremy	44
Bishop Jr., Sanford D.	34	Boyle, Lara Flynn	39	Bunning, Jim	44
Bishop, Joey	34	BR5-49	39	Burbank, Daniel C.	44
Bishop, Kelly	34	Bracco, Lorraine	39	Burgi, Richard	44
Bissett, Jacqueline	34	Bradberry, Gary	39	Burke, Delta	44
Bjorlin, Nadia	34	Bradley, Bill	39	Burke, Frances	44
Black, Clint	34	Bradley, Kathleen	39	Burnett, Carol	44, 45
Black, Lisa Hartman	34	Bradshaw, Terry	39	Burns, Brooke	45
Black, Lucas	34	Brady Jr., Charles E.	39	Burns, Conrad	45
Blackhawk	35	Brady, Kevin	40	Burr, Richard	45
Blackmon, Edafe	35	Brady, Robert A.	40	Bursch, Daniel W.	45
Blades, Ruben	35	Brady, Wayne	40	Burstyn, Ellen	45
Blagojevich, Rod R.	35	Braeden, Eric	40	Burton, Dan	45
Blaha, John E.	35	Brand, Vance D.	40	Burton, Jeff	45
Blanchard, Rachel	35	Brandenstein, Daniel C.	40	Burton, Lance	45
Blanchard, Tully	35	Brandis, Jonathan	40	Burton, Steve	45
Blanda, George	35	Brandy	40	Burton, Ward	45

Busch, Kurt	45	Carrey, Jim	51	Chretien, Jean-Loup	55
Busey, Gary	45	Carson, Brad	51	Christensen, Donna M.	55
Bush, Barbara	46	Carson, Julia	51	Christensen, Tonja	56
Bush, George	46	Carter, Bobbi Ray	51	Christopher, Robin	56
Bush, George W.	46	Carter, Deana	51	Christopher, William	56
Bush, Laura	46	Carter, Elan	51	Christopher, William	56
Bush, Jeb	46	Carter, Jimmy	51	Cialini, Julie Lynn	56
Butler, Brandon	46	Carter, Nell	51	Cibrian, Eddie	56
Buttons, Red	46	Carter, Rosalyn	51	Clapp, Gordon	56
Buxton, Sarah	46	Cartwright, Lionel	51	Clapton, Eric	56
Buyer, Steve	46	Cartwright, Nancy	51	Clark, Dick	56
Buzzi, Ruth	46	Carvey, Dana	51	Clark, Laurel B.	56
Byrd, Dan	46	Case, Sharon	51	Clark, Marcia	56
Byrd, Robert	46	Cash, Kellye	51	Clark, Roy	56
Byrne, Gabriel	46	Cash, Rosanne	52	Clark, Terri	56
Byrne, Martha	46	Casper, John H.	52	Clarke, Bobby	57
		Cassidy, David	52	Clarke, John	57
C		Cassidy, Joanna	52	Clarke, Jordan	57
		Cast, Tricia	52	Clarke, Julie Anne	57
Cabana, Robert D.	47	Castellaneta, Dan	52	Clary, Robert	57
Cafagna, Ashley	47	Castellanos, John	52	Clatterbuck, Tamara	57
Cagle, Yvonne D.	47	Castle, Michael N.	52	Clay, Wm. Lacy	57
Cain, Dean	47	Cattrall, Kim	52	Clayton, Eva M.	57
Cain, Mick	47	Caulfield, Emme	52	Cleave, Mary L.	57
Caldeiro, Fernando	47	Cavanagh, Thomas	52	Cleland, Max	57
Calderon, Sila M.	47	Cayetano, Benjamin J.	52	Clement, Bob	57
Caldwell, Tracy E.	47	Cedeno, Matt	52	Clennon, David	57
Caliendo, Frank	47	Cedric "The Entertainer"	52	Clervoy, Jean-Francois	57
Callahan, John	47	Cellucci, Argeo Paul	53	Cleveland, Alice	57
Callahan, Sonny	47	Cerf, Vint	53	Clifford, Michael R.	58
Calvert, Ken	48	Cernan, Eugene A.	53	Cline, Kristi	58
Camarda, Charles J.	48	Cerny, Jobe	53	Clinton, Hillary	58
Cameron, James	48	Chabert, Lacey	53	Clyburn, James E.	58
Cameron, Kenneth D.	48	Chabot, Steve	53	Coats, Michael L.	58
Cameron, Kirk	48	Chafee, Lincoln	53	Coble, Howard	58
Cameron-Bure, Candace	48	Chamberlin, Beth	53	Cochran, Anita	58
Camp, Dave	48	Chambliss, Saxby	53	Cochran, Thad	58
Campbell, Ben	48	Chamitoff, Gregory E.	53	Cockrell, Kenneth D.	58
Campbell, Billy	48	Chamorro, Charissa	53	Coe, David Allen	58
Campbell, Glen	48	Chan, Jackie	53	Cohen, Scott	58
Campbell, Larry Joe	48	Chan, Michael Paul	53	Cole, Bradley	58
Campbell, Naomi	48	Chang-Dìaz, Franklin R.	53	Coleman, Catherine G.	58
Cannavale, Bobby	48	Channing, Carol	54	Coles, Kim	58
Cannon, Chris	48	Channing, Stockard	54	Colin, Margaret	59
Cantor, Eric	49	Chanz, Nadine	54	Collins, Eileen M.	59
Cantrell, Cady	49	Chapman, Philip K	54	Collins, Mac	59
Cantwell, Maria	49	Chappell, Crystal	54	Collins, Michael	59
Capito, Shelley Moore	49	Charles, Ray	54	Collins, Phil	59
Capps, Lois	49	Charles, Suzette	54	Collins, Stephen	59
Capriati, Jennifer	49	Charleson, Leslie	54	Collins, Susan	59
Capuano, Michael E.	49	Charvet, David	54	Collinsworth, Kimm	59
Cardin, Benjamin L.	49	Chase, Chevy	54	Comaneci, Nadia	59
Cardwell, Lena	49	Chavez, Nick	54	Combest, Larry	59
Carelli, Rick	49	Chawla, Kalpana	54	Combs, Holly Marie	59
Carey, Drew	49	Checa, Maria	54	Como, Perry	59
Carey, Duane G.	49	Cheli, Maurizio	55	Compton, Stacy	60
Carey, Phil	50	Cheney, Dick	55	Condit, Gary A.	60
Carlson, Gretchen	50	Cheney, Lynn	55	Confederate Railroad	60
Carmack, Kona	50	Cher	55	Conlee, John	60
Carnahan, Jean	50	Chesney, Kenny	55	Conley, Darlene	60
Carney, Art	50	Chestnutt, Mark	55	Conn, Terri	60
Carpenter, Charisma	50	Chiao, Leroy	55	Connelly, Jennifer	60
Carpenter, John	50	Child, Julia	55	Connery, Sean	60
Carpenter, M. Scott	50	Childress, Richard	55	Conrad, Kent	60
Carpenter, Richard	50	Chilton, Kevin P.	55	Consuelos, Mark	60
Carper, Thomas	50	Cho, Margaret	55	Conti, Bill	60
Carr, Gerald P.	50	Chong, Tommy	55	Contreras, Carlos	60
Carrere, Tia	50				

Name	Page
Conway, Tim	60
Conwell, Carolyn	60
Conyers Jr., John	61
Cook, Jason	61
Cook, Rachael Leigh	61
Cook, Terry	61
Cooksey, John	61
Cooley, Dr. Denton	61
Cooper Jr., L. Gordon	61
Cooper, Bette	61
Cooper, Jackie	61
Cooper, Jeanne	61
Copperfield, David	61
Cornett, Leanza	61
Corporal Cajun	61
Corwin, Morena	61
Corzine, Jon	62
Cosby, Bill	62
Costa, Mary	62
Costello, Jerry F.	62
Costner, Kevin	62
Cothran, Shirley	62
Couch, Rich	62
Couric, Katie	62
Couric, Katie	62
Cousino, Tishara Lee	62
Cover, Laura	62
Covey, Richard O.	62
Cox, Archibald	63
Cox, Christopher	63
Cox, Jennifer Elise	63
Cox, Nikki	63
Cox, Ronny	63
Cox-Arquette, Courtney	63
Coyne, William J.	63
Craig, Connie	63
Craig, Jenny	63
Craig, Larry	63
Craig, Yvonne	63
Cramer Jr., Robert E.	63
Crane, Philip M.	63
Crapo, Mike	63
Craven, Ricky	64
Craven, Wes	64
Crawford, Cindy	64
Crawford, Gavin	64
Crawford, Rick	64
Crawley, Sylvia	64
Creamer, Timothy J.	64
Creech, Cassandra	64
Creighton, John O.	64
Cremeans, John	64
Crenna, Richard	64
Crenshaw, Ander	64
Crichton, Michael	64
Crippen, Robert L.	65
Cromwell, James	65
Cronkite, Walter	65
Cross, Joseph	65
Crowell, Judy	65
Crowley, Joseph	65
Crowley, Pat	65
Cruise, Tom	65
Cryer, Jon	65
Cryer, Suzanne	65
Crystal, Jennifer	65
Cubin, Barbara	65

Name	Page
Culberson, John Abney	65
Culbertson Jr., Frank L.	65
Cummings, Elijah E.	66
Cunningham, Randy	66
Cunningham, Walter	66
Curbeam Jr., Robert L.	66
Currie, Nancy J.	66
Curtis, Jamie Lee	66
Curtis, Tony	66
Cusack, Ann	66
Cusack, John	66
Cyrus, Billy Ray	66

D

Name	Page
Dafoe, Willem	67
Dahm, Erica	67
Daley, John Francis	67
Dallenbach, Wally	67
Dalton, Timothy	67
Daly, Tyne	67
Damon, Matt	67
Damon, Stuart	67
Dane, Eric	67
Danes, Claire	67
Dangerfield, Rodney	67
Daniels, Charlie	68
Dano, Linda	68
Danson, Ted	68
Danza, Tony	68
D'Arbanville, Patti	68
Darbo, Patrika	68
Daschle, Thomas	68
Dash, Stacey	68
Dattilo, Bryan	68
Davenport, Lindsay	68
Davidson, Doug	69
Davidson, Eileen	69
Davis Jr., Billy	69
Davis, Neriah	69
Davis, Ann B.	69
Davis, Danny K.	69
Davis, Geena	69
Davis, Gray	69
Davis, Jim	69
Davis, Jo Ann	69
Davis, Josie	69
Davis, Kristin	69
Davis, N. Jan	70
Davis, Susan A.	70
Davis, Thomas M.	70
Davis, Warwick	70
Davison, Bruce	70
Dawber, Pam	70
Day, Doris	70
Dayton, Mark	70
de los Reyes, Kamar	70
de Ravin, Emilie	70
Deal, Nathan	70
Dean, Billy	70
Dean, Howard	70
Dean, Jimmy	70
Deane, Meredith	70
Deas, Justin	71
Deasy, Paul	71
DeBakey, Michael	71
DeCamp, Rosemary	71
DeFazio, Peter A.	71

Name	Page
DeForest, Calvert	71
DeGette, Diana	71
De La Hoya, Oscar	71
De La Hoya, Oscar	71
Delahunt, William D.	71
Delaney, Kim	71
Delany, Dana	71
DeLauro, Rosa L.	71
DeLay, Tom	71
Delfino, Majandra	72
DeLorenzo, Michael	72
DelosSantos, Becky	72
DeLuise, Dom	72
DeLuise, Michael	72
DeMint, Jim	72
Denberg, Lori Beth	72
Dench, Dame Judi	72
Deneuve, Catherine	72
DeNiro, Robert	72
Denisof, Alexis	72
Dennehy, Brian	72
Dennis, Dan	72
Dennison, Jo-Carroll	73
Denver, Bob	73
DePaiva, James	73
DePaiva, Kassie	73
Depardieu, Gerard	73
Dergan, Lisa	73
Dern, Laura	73
D'Errico, Donna	73
Derwin, Mark	73
Desert, Alex	73
Deutsch, Peter	73
Devine, Loretta	73
DeVito, Danny	73, 74
DeWine, Mike	74
Dewitt, Joyce	74
Diamond Rio	74
Diamond, Neil	74
Diamont, Don	74
Diaz-Balart, Lincoln	74
diCesare, Michael	74
Dickens, Jimmy	74
Dickenson, Angie	74
Dicks, Norman D.	74
Dicopoulos, Frank	74
Diffie, Joe	74, 75
Diller, Phyllis	75
Dillon, Kevin	75
Dillon, Mike	75
DiMucci, Dion	75
Dingell, John D.	75
Disney, Roy	75
Ditka, Mike	75
Dixie Chicks, The	75
D'lyn, Shae	75
Dobies, Mark	75
Dobson, Peter	75
Dodd, Christopher	76
Doerr, Bobby	76
Doggett, Lloyd	76
Doherty, Shannen	76
Doi, Takao	76
Dolan, Ellen	76
Dole, Bob	76
Dole, Elizabeth	76
Domeier, Rick	76

Domenici, Pete	76	Ellsworth, Kiko	83	Filner, Bob	89
Domino, Fats	76	Elway, John	83	Fincke, E. Michael	89
Donley, Kimberly	76	Emerson, Jo Ann	83	Finnigan, Jennifer	89
Donnelly, Patricia	76	Emery, Ralph	83	Firth, Peter	89
Donovan, Elisa	76	Emme	83	Fisher, Anna L.	89
Dooley, Calvin M.	77	Engel, Eliot L.	83	Fisher, Carrie	89
Doolittle, John T.	77	England, Anthony W.	83	Fisher, William F.	89
Dorgan, Byron	77	Engle, Joe H.	83	Fitzgerald, Peter	89
Dorman, Samantha	77	Engler, John	83	Flagg, Fannie	89
Dotrice, Roy	77	English, Ellia	83	Flake, Jeff	90
Douglas, Donna	77	English, Phil	83	Flannery, Susan	90
Douglas, Jerry	77	Englund, Robert	83	Fleming, Nancy	90
Doyle, Michael F.	77	Engvall, Bill	84	Fleming, Rhonda	90
Dreier, David	77	Ensign, John	84	Fletcher, Ernie	90
Drescher, Fran	77	Enzi, Mike	84	Fletcher, Maria	90
Dreyfuss, Richard	77	Eplin, Tom	84	Florek, Dann	90
Driggs, Deborah	77	Ericsson, Ulrika	84	Flynt, Larry	90
Drozdova, Inga	78	Eshoo, Anna G.	84	Foale, C. Michael	90
Dubois, Ja'Net	78	Estabrook, Christine	84	Fogelberg, Dan	90
Duffy, Brian	78	Estefan, Gloria	84	Fogleman, Jay	90
Duhamel, Josh	78	Estes, Bob	84	Foley, Scott	90
Dukakis, Michael	78	Etheridge, Bob	84	Foley, Mark	90
Dukakis, Olympia	78	Etheridge, Melissa	84	Folta, Danelle Marie	91
Duke Jr., Charles M.	78	Evans, Andrea	85	Fonda, Jane	91
Dunaway, Faye	78	Evans, Janet	85	Fontaine, Joan	91
Dunbar, Bonnie J.	78	Evans, Josh Ryan	85	Foray, June	91
Dunbar, Rockmond	78	Evans, Lane	85	Forbes, Steve	91
Duncan Jr., John J.	78	Evans, Linda	85	Forbes, Steve	91
Duncan, Christopher B.	78	Evans, Sarah	85	Force, John	91
Dunn, Jennifer	78	Everett, Terry	85	Ford Jr., Harold E.	91
Dunst, Kirsten	78	Everly Brothers	85	Ford, Betty	91
Duplaix, Daphnee Lynn	79	Evernham, Ray	85	Ford, British	91
Dupuis, Roy	79	Evert, Chris	85	Ford, Faith	91
Duque, Pedro	79	Evridge, Melissa	85	Ford, Gerald	91
Durbin, Richard	79	Ewing, Patrick	85	Ford, Judith	92
Dusay, Marj	79	Eyharts, Leopold	85	Foreman, Amanda	92
Duvall, David	79			Foreman, George	92
Duvall, Robert	79	**F**		Foreman, Michael J.	92
Dylan, Bob	79	Fabares, Shelley	87	Forrester, Patrick G.	92
		Fabian, John M.	87	Forsythe, John	92
E		Fabio	87	Forsythe, William	92
Earnhardt Jr., Dale	81	Faison, Donald Adeosun	87	Fossella, Vito	92
Earnhardt, Kerry	81	Faleomavaega, Eni F. H.	87	Fossum, Michael E.	92
Easton, Sheena	81	Falk, Peter	87	Foster, Mike	92
Eastwood, Clint	81	Fargo, Donna	87	Fox, Bernard	92
Ebert, Roger	81	Farr, Sam	87	Fox, Morgan	92
Ebsen, Buddy	81	Farrell, Mike	87	Foxworthy, Jeff	92
Eden, Barbara	81	Farrell, Terry	87	Foxx, Jamie	92
Edwards Jr., Joe F.	81	Fath, Farah	87	Frakes, Jonathan	92
Edwards, Anthony	81	Fattah, Chaka	88	Francis, Genie	93
Edwards, Chet	81	Faustino, David	88	Francks, Don	93
Edwards, John	82	Favre, Brett	88	Frank, Barney	93
Edwards, Tracey	82	Fawcett, Farrah	88	Franken, Al	93
Egan, Susan	82	Fedewa, Tim	88	Franklin, Don	93
Eggert, Nicole	82	Fehr, Brendan	88	Frantz, Adrienne	93
Ehlers, Beth	82	Feingold, Russell	88	Franz, Dennis	93
Ehlers, Vernon J.	82	Feinstein, Dianne	88	Fraser, Brendan	93
Ehrlich Jr., Robert L.	82	Fellows, Ron	88	Freeman, Morgan	93
Eisner, Michael	82	Ferguson, Christopher J.	88	Frelinghuysen, Rodney	93
Eldred, Pam	82	Ferguson, Craig	88	French, Heather	93
Electra, Carmen	82	Ferguson, Matthew	88	Frick, Stephen N.	93
Eleniak, Erika	82	Ferguson, Mike	88	Friedman, Olivia	93
Elfman, Jenna	82	Ferrell, Jami	88	Frist, William	94
Elliott, Alecia	82	Field, Sally	89	Frost, Martin	94
Elliott, Bill	82	Field, Todd	89	Frye, Soleil Moon	94
Elliott, David James	83	Filippo, Fabrizio	89	Fuglesang, Christer	94
Elliott, Patricia	83	Fillion, Nathan	89	Fuller, Jeff	94

Fuller, Victoria Alynette	94	Ginsburg, Nadya	99	Grissom, Steve	104
Fullerton, Charles G.	94	Ginsburg, Ruth Bader	99	Grossman, Leslie	104
Fulton, Eileen	94	Glanville, Jerry	99	Grubb, Kevin	105
Fumero, David	94	Glazer, Eugene Robert	99	Grubb, Wayne	105
Funicello, Annette	94	Gleason, Vanessa	99	Grucci Jr., Felix J.	105
Fuson, Stacy Marie	94	Glendening, Parris N.	99	Grunberg, Greg	105
		Glenn, John	100	Grunsfeld, John M.	105

G

		Glover, Danny	100	Guidoni, Umberto	105
Gabor, Zsa Zsa	95	Goddard, Anna-Marie	100	Guinn, Kenny C.	105
Gaither, Daniele	95	Godin, Tawny	100	Gunn, Jannet	105
Gallagher, David	95	Godwin, Linda M.	100	Gutierrez, Luis V.	105
Gallagher, Kelly	95	Gold, Missy	100	Gutierrez, Sidney M.	105
Gallagher, Peter	95	Goldberg, Bill	100	Gutknecht, Gil	105
Gallagher	95	Goldberg, Whoopi	100	Guy, Jasmine	105
Gallegly, Elton	95	Goldsboro, Bobby	100	G'Vera, Ivan	105
Gammon, James	95	Gomez, Ian	100		
Ganske, Greg	95	Gonzalez, Charles A.	100		
Garces, Paula	95	Gonzalez, Nicholas	101		

H

Gardner, Dale A.	95	Goode Jr., Virgil H.	101	Hackett, Buddy	107
Gardner, Guy S.	95	Gooding Jr., Cuba	101	Hackman, Gene	107
Garfunkel, Art	96	Goodlatte, Bob	101	Hadfield, Chris A.	107
Garlits, Don	96	Gordon Jr., Richard F.	101	Hagel, Charles	107
Garn, Jake	96	Gordon, Bart	101	Haggard, Merle	107
Garneau, Marc	96	Gordon, Jeff	101	Haggerty, Dan	107
Garner, James	96	Gordon, Robby	101	Hagman, Larry	107
Garr, Teri	96	Gorham, Christopher	101	Haig Jr., Alexander	107
Garrett, Maureen	96	Gorie, Dominic L.	101	Haise Jr., Fred W.	107
Garriott, Owen K.	96	Gosdin, Vern	101	Hale, Ron	107
Gates, Bill	96	Goss, Porter J.	101	Hall, Bruce Michael	107
Gaughan, Brendan	96	Goulet, Robert	101, 102	Hall, Deidre	108
Gayheart, Rebecca	96	Goutman, Chris	102	Hall, Irma P.	108
Gayle, Crystal	96	Grabe, Ronald J.	102	Hall, Ralph M.	108
Gaynor, Gloria	96	Graham, Bob	102	Hall, Tony P.	108
Gaynor, Mitzi	96	Graham, Heather	102	Halliwell, Geri	108
Geary, Anthony	97	Graham, Lauren	102	Halsell Jr., James D.	108
Gekas, George W.	97	Graham, Lindsey O.	102	Ham, Kenneth T.	108
Gellar, Sarah Michelle	97	Grahn, Nancy Lee	102	Hamill, Mark	108
Gemar, Charles D.	97	Gramm, Phil	102	Hamilton Jr., Bobby	108
Genet, Sabryn	97	Grammer, Kelsey	102	Hamilton, Bobby	108
George, Jason	97	Granger, Kay	102	Hamilton, George	108
George, Phyllis	97	Grant, Amy	102	Hamilton, Lisa Gay	108
Gephardt, Richard A.	97	Grant, Hugh	102	Hamilton, Marcus	108
Gere, Richard	97	Grassle, Karen	103	Hamilton, Wendy	108
Gering, Galen	97	Grassley, Chuck	103	Hamm, Mia	109
Geringer, Jim	97	Graveline, Duane E.	103	Hammond Jr., L. Blaine	109
Gernhardt, Michael L.	97	Graver, Susan	103	Hanks, Colin	109
Getty, Estelle	97	Graves, Bill	103	Hanna, Jack	109
Getz, John	98	Graves, Sam	103	Hanna, William "Bill"	109
Gibbons, Jim	98	Gray, Billy	103	Hannigan, Alyson	109
Gibbons, Peter	98	Great Divide, The	103	Hansen, James V.	109
Gibbs, Coy	98	Green Day	103	Hansen, Peter	109
Gibbs, J.D.	98	Green, Bill	103	Harbaugh, Gregory J.	109
Gibbs, Joe	98	Green, David	103	Harbour, Vanita	109
Gibbs, Tim	98	Green, Gene	103	Hardin, Melora	109
Gibson, Debbie	98	Green, Jeff	103	Hargitay, Mariska	109
Gibson, Edward G.	98	Green, Mark	103	Harkin, Tom	109
Gibson, Robert L.	98	Green, Mark	104	Harlow, Jade	109
Gibson, Thomas	98	Green, Seth	104	Harman, Jane	110
Gifford, Kathie Lee	98	Greenwood, James C.	104	Harmon, Angie	110
Gil, Maria Luisa	98	Greenwood, Lee	104	Harmon, Winsor	110
Gilchrest, Wayne T.	99	Gregg, Judd	104	Harney, Corinna	110
Gill, Vince	99	Gregory, Frederick D.	104	Harris Jr., Bernard A.	110
Gilley, Mickey	99	Gregory, William G.	104	Harris, Emmylou	110
Gillmor, Paul E.	99	Gretzky, Wayne	104	Harris, Steve	110
Gilman, Benjamin A.	99	Grieco, Richard	104	Harrison, Schae	110
Gilmore III, James S.	99	Griffin, Merv	104	Hart, Holly Joan	110
Gilpin, Peri	99	Griggs, Andy	104	Hart, Melissa A.	110
		Grimes, Camryn	104	Hart, Melissa Joan	110

Name	Page
Hart, Terry J.	110
Hartsfield Jr., Henry W.	110
Harvey, Steve	110
Harvick, Kevin	111
Hasselhoff, David	111
Hastert, J. Dennis	111
Hastings, Alcee L.	111
Hastings, Doc	111
Hastings, Don	111
Hatch, Orrin	111
Hatch, Rich	111
Hatcher, Teri	111
Hauck, Frederick H.	111
Hauer, Rutger	111
Hawkins, Sophie B.	111
Hawley, Steven A.	111
Hayes, Bill	112
Hayes, Reggie	112
Hayes, Robin	112
Hayes, Susan	112
Hays, Kathryn	112
Hayworth, J. D.	112
Head, Anthony Stewart	112
Heatherly, Eric	112
Hedeman, Tuff	112
Hedren, Tippi	112
Hefley, Joel	112
Heft, Robert	112
Heigl, Katherine	112
Helmond, Katherine	112
Helms, Jesse	113
Helms, Susan J.	113
Hemingway, Mariel	113
Henderson, Florence	113
Hendrick, Ricky	113
Hendrickson, Benjamin	113
Henricks, Terence T.	113
Hensel, Karen	113
Hensley, Jimmy	113
Hensley, John C.	113
Hensley, Jon	113
Henslcy, Kelley	113
Henson, Darrin Dewitt	113
Hentrich, Craig	113
Hepcat, Harry	113
Herbst, Rebecca	114
Herger, Wally	114
Herlie, Eileen	114
Herndon, Ty	114
Herring, Lynn	114
Herrington, John B.	114
Herrmann, Edward	114
Hershey, Erin	114
Heston, Charlton	114
Hickland, Catherine	114
Hicks, Catherine	114
Hicks, Catherine	114
Hieb, Richard J.	114
Higginbotham, Joan E.	114
Hilfiger, Tommy	115
Hill, Baron P.	115
Hill, Dule	115
Hill, Faith	115
Hill, Valerie Parr	115
Hilleary, Van	115
Hilliard, Earl F.	115
Hilliard, Patricia C.	115
Hillin, Bobby	115
Hilmers, David C.	115
Hinchey, Maurice D.	115
Hinkle, Marin	115
Hinojosa, Ruben	115
Hire, Kathryn P.	116
Hirsch, Judd	116
Hirschfeld, Al	116
Ho, Don	116
Hobaugh, Charles O.	116
Hobson, David L.	116
Hodge, Kate	116
Hodges, Jim	116
Hoeffel, Joseph M.	116
Hoekstra, Peter	116
Hoeven, John	116
Hoffman, Dustin	116
Hoffman, Jeffrey A.	116
Hogan, Hulk	117
Hogestyn, Drake	117
Holden, Tim	117
Holland, Sean	117
Holland, Tara Dawn	117
Hollenberg, Rich	117
Holliday, Melissa	117
Hollings, Ernest	117
Holmes, Katie	117
Holmes, Scott	117
Holmquest, Donald L.	117
Holt, Rush D.	117
Holyfield, Evander	117
Honda, Michael M.	118
Hooley, Darlene	118
Hootie & The Blowfish	118
Hope, Amanda	118
Hope, Bob	118
Hopkins, Anthony	118
Horn, Chris	118
Horn, Stephen	118
Hornaday, Ron	118
Horne, Lena	118
Hornsby, Bruce	118
Hornsby, Russell	118
Horowitz, Scott J.	118
Horton, Peter	119
Hostetler, Jeff	119
Hostettler, John N.	119
Houghton, Amo	119
Houston, Andy	119
Houston, Anjelica	119
Houston, Marty	119
Howard, Jan	119
Howard, Kyle	119
Howard, Shawn	119
Howard, Traylor	119
Howarth, Roger	119
Howe, Gordie	119
Hoyer, Steny H.	120
Hubbard, Elizabeth	120
Huber, Liza	120
Hubert, Tom	120
Huckabee, Mike	120
Hugh, Sara	120
Hughes, Dan	120
Hughes, Finola	120
Hull, Jane Dee	120
Hulshof, Kenny C.	120
Hunt Jr., James B.	120
Hunter, Duncan	120
Hunter, Kim	120
Hupp, Jana Marie	120
Hurd, Michelle	121
Hurley, Elizabeth	121
Husband, Rick D.	121
Huss, Toby	121
Huston, Anjelica	121
Hutchins, Colleen	121
Hutchinson, Asa	121
Hutchinson, Tim	121
Hutchison, Kay Bailey	121
Hyde, Henry J.	121
Hyde, James	121
Hyder, Brian	121

I

Name	Page
Ice-T	123
Iman	123
Indigo Girls, The	123
Ingle, John	123
Inglebright, Jim	123
Inhofe, James	123
Innes, Laura	123
Inouye, Daniel	123
Inslee, Jay	123
Ireland, Kathy	123
Irizarry, Vincent	123
Irons, Jeremy	123
Irvan, Ernie	124
Irwin, Hale	124
Irwin, Steve	124
Irwin, Terri	124
Isakson, Johnny	124
Israel, Steve	124
Issa, Darrell E.	124
Istook Jr., Ernest J.	124
Ivins, Marsha S.	124

J

Name	Page
Jackson Jr., Jesse L.	125
Jackson, Alan	125
Jackson, Jesse	125
Jackson, John M.	125
Jackson, Joshua	125
Jackson, Samuel L.	125
Jackson, Shar	125
Jackson, Stonewall	125
Jackson-Lee, Sheila	125
James Elliott, David	125
James, Colton	125
James, Dalton	125
James-DeMentri, Pat	126
Janklow, William J.	126
Janney, Allison	126
Jarrett, Dale	126
Jarrett, Dale	126
Jarrett, Jason	126
Jarrett, Ned	126
Jayroe, Jane	126
Jeffcoat, Don	126
Jefferson, William J.	126
Jeffords, James	126
Jeinsen, Elke	126
Jemison, Mae C.	126

Jenkins, Jackie "Butch"	126
Jenkins, William L.	127
Jenner, Bruce	127
Jennings, Peter	127
Jennings, Waylon	127
Jernigan, Tamara E.	127
Jett, Brent W.	127
Joel, Billy	127
Johanns, Mike	127
John, Christopher	127
John, Elton	127
John, Tylyn	127
Johnson, Amy Jo	127
Johnson, Bryce	128
Johnson, Don	128
Johnson, Echo Leta	128
Johnson, Eddie Bernice	128
Johnson, Gary E.	128
Johnson, Gregory C.	128
Johnson, Gregory H.	128
Johnson, Jay	128
Johnson, Jimmie	128
Johnson, Nancy L.	128
Johnson, Nicole	128
Johnson, Rodney Van	128
Johnson, Russell	128
Johnson, Sam	129
Johnson, Tim	129
Johnson, Timothy V.	129
Jolie, Angelina	129
Jones, Bryant	129
Jones, Buckshot	129
Jones, Chipper	129
Jones, Chuck	129
Jones, Davey	129
Jones, George	129
Jones, James Earl	129
Jones, Jill Marie	129
Jones, P.J.	129
Jones, Renee	130
Jones, Stephanie Tubbs	130
Jones, Summer	130
Jones, Tamala	130
Jones, Thomas D.	130
Jones, Tommy Lee	130
Jones, Walter B.	130
Judd, Ashley	130
Judd, Cledus T.	130
Judd, Naomi	130
Judd, Wynonna	130

K

Kamano, Stacy	131
Kanjorski, Paul E.	131
Kapoor, Ravi	131
Kaptur, Marcy	131
Kapture, Mitzi	131
Kasem, Casey	131
Kavandi, Janet L.	131
Kay, Lesli	131
Kaye, Thorsten	131
Kaye, Wendy	131
Kazer, Beau	131
Keating, Frank	132
Keifer, Elizabeth	132
Keller, Jason	132
Keller, Ric	132

Kellerk, Sophie	132
Kelley, Paul	132
Kelly, James M.	132
Kelly, Mark E.	132
Kelly, Michael	132
Kelly, Scott J.	132
Kelly, Sue W.	132
Kempthorne, Dirk	132
Ken L.	132
Kendall, Kerri	132
Kennedy, Anthony	133
Kennedy, Edward	133
Kennedy, Mark R.	133
Kennedy, Mimi	133
Kennedy, Patrick J.	133
Kenseth, Matt	133
Kent, Heather Paige	133
Kepler, Shell	133
Kerns, Brian D.	133
Kerns, Joanna	133
Kerr, Brook	133
Kerrigan, Nancy	133
Kerry, John	133
Kershaw, Sammy	134
Kerwin, Joseph P.	134
Keselowski, Bob	134
Ketchum, Hank	134
Kiel, Richard	134
Kildee, Dale E.	134
Kilpatrick, Carolyn C.	134
Kilrain, Susan L.	134
Kincade, Thomas	134
Kind, Richard	134
Kind, Ron	134
King Jr., Angus S.	134
King, Ben E.	134
King, Carole	134, 135
King, Dave	135
King, Larry	135
King, Perry	135
King, Peter T.	135
King, Rebecca	135
Kingsley, Ben	135
Kingston, Alex	135
Kingston, Jack	135
Kinleys, The	135
Kinney, Kathy	135
Kirby, Andy	135
Kirk, Justin	135
Kirk, Mark Steven	136
Kirk, Pat	136
Kitt, Eartha	136
Kitzhaber, John A.	136
Kleczka, Gerald D.	136
Klemperer, Werner	136
Klugman, Jack	136
Klum, Heidi	136
Knight, Jonathan	136
Knight, Jordan	136
Knight, Michael E.	136
Knollenberg, Joe	136
Knowles, Tony	136
Koch, Ed	137
Kodjoe, Boris	137
Koenig, Walter	137
Kohl, Herb	137
Kolbe, Jim	137

Koontz, Dean	137
Korman, Lindsay	137
Korver, Paul	137
Kosar, Bernie	137
Koslow, Lauren	137
Kozar, Heather	137
Kramer, Steven E.	137
Kravits, Jason	137
Kregel Kevin R.	137
Krumholtz, David	138
Kucinich, Dennis J.	138
Kudrow, Lisa	138
Kurth, Wallace	138
Kwan, Michelle	138
Kyl, Jon	138

L

La Motta, Jake	139
LaBelle, Patti	139
Labonte, Bobby	139
Labonte, Terry	139
Labyorteaux, Patrick	139
LaFalce, John J.	139
Lafayette, John	139
Lago, David	139
LaHood, Ray	139
Lahti, Christine	139
LaJoie, Randy	140
Lake, Ricki	140
Lampson, Nick	140
Landrieu, Mary	140
Lane, Kenneth J.	140
Lang, Katherine Kelly	140
Lange, Artie	140
Langevin, James R.	140
Langley, Neva	140
Lansbury, Angela	140
Lantos, Tom	140
Lapaglia, Jonathan	140
LaPlanche, Rosemary	140
Largent, Steve	140
Larsen, Rick	141
Larson, Jill	141
Larson, John B.	141
LaSalle, Eriq	141
Lascher, David	141
Lasswell, Fred	141
Latham, Tom	141
LaTourette, Steven C.	141
Lau, Michele	141
Laver, Rod	141
Lavin, Linda	141
Lavoie, Jennifer J.	141
Lawler, Jerry	141
Lawler, Patrick	141
Lawlor, Craig	142
Lawrence, Tracy	142
Lawrence, Vicki	142
Lawrence, Wendy B.	142
Lazzaro, Anthony	142
Leach, James A.	142
Leahy, Patrick	142
Leardini, Christina	142
Leary, Denis	142
Leavitt, Michael O.	142
LeBlanc, Christian	142
LeBlanc, Matt	142

McEntire, Reba	158	Miller, George	164	Murtha, John P.	169
McGlynn, Ryan	159	Miller, Nolan	164	Musgrave, Story	169
McGovern, George	159	Miller, Shannon	164	Musgrove, Ronnie	169
McGovern, James P.	159	Miller, Tangi	164	Musial, Stan	169
McGovern, Maureen	159	Miller, Zell	164	Myerson, Bess	169
McGraw, Ali	159	Mills, Billy	164	Myrick, Sue Wilkins	169
McGraw, Tim	159	Mills, Juliet	164		
McGregor, Ewan	159	Ming-Na	164		

N

McHugh, John M.	159	Mink, Patsy T.	164	Nabors, Jim	171
McIlwain, Lena	159	Minnelli, Liza	164	Nadeau, Jerry	171
McInnis, Scott	159	Minner, Ruth Ann	164	Nader, Michael	171
McIntaggart, Peggy	159	Miriam, Jennifer	164	Nadler, Jerrold	171
McIntyre, Joe	159	Mitchell, Beverly	164	Nagel, Steven R.	171
McIntyre, Mike	159	Mitchell, Edgar D.	165	Nagler, Morgan	171
McKellar, Danica	160	Mitchell, James	165	Najimy, Kathy	171
McKeon, Howard P.	160	Mitra, Rhona	165	Napolitano, Grace F.	171
McKinney, Cynthia A.	160	Moakley, John Joseph	165	Neal, Richard E.	171
McKnight, Marian	160	Mobley, Mary Ann	165	Nelson, Ben	171
McLaughlin, Mike	160	Moceanu, Dominique	165	Nelson, Bill	171
McMahon, Linda	160	Mochrie, Colin	165	Nelson, Christen	172
McMahon, Shane	160	Moffett, D.W.	165	Nelson, Craig T.	172
McMahon, Stephanie	160	Mohr, Jay	165	Nelson, George D.	172
McMahon, Vince	160	Mohri, Mamoru	165	Nelson, Willie	172
McMonagle, Donald R.	160	Mollohan, Alan B.	165	Nemechek, Joe	172
McMurray, Jamie	160	Molloy, Irene	165	Nespoli, Paolo	172
McNally, Kerry	160	Moloney, Janel	165	Nethercutt Jr., George R.	172
McNamara, Robert	160	Momoa, Jason	165	Newhart, Bob	172
McNulty, Michael R.	161	Monaco, Kelly Marie	166	Newman, James H.	172
McReynolds, Larry	161	Monaco, Kelly	166	Newman, Michael	172
McVicar, Daniel	161	Mondale, Walter	166	Newman, Robert	172
Mead, Lynda	161	Mo'Nique	166	Newton, Wayne	172, 173
Meade, Carl J.	161	Montalbon, Ricardo	166	Newton-John, Olivia	173
Meehan, Martin T.	161	Montana, Joe	166	Ney, Robert W.	173
Meek, Carrie P.	161	Montgomery Gentry	166	Nichols, Marisol	173
Meeks, Aaron	161	Montgomery, John Michael	166	Nichols, Stephen	173
Meeks, Gregory W.	161	Moore, Barbara	166	Nicholson, Jack	173
Meeuwsen, Terry	161	Moore, Demi	166	Nicklaus, Jack	173
Melini, Angela	161	Moore, Dennis	166	Nickles, Don	173
Mello, Tamara	161	Moore, Dickie	166	Nicollier, Claude	173
Mellons, Ken	161	Moore, Mary Tyler	166	Nielsen, Leslie	173
Melnick, Bruce E.	161	Moore, Roger	167	Nimoy, Leonard	173
Meloni, Christopher	162	Moore, Shemar	167	Nixon, Cynthia	173
Melroy, Pamela A.	162	Moran, Erin	167	No Doubt	174
Melvin, Leland D.	162	Moran, James P.	167	Noguchi, Soichi	174
Mendoza, Alex	162	Moran, Jerry	167	Nolin, Gena Lee	174
Mendoza, Mauricio	162	Moranis, Rick	167	Nolte, Nick	174
Menendez, Robert	162	Morella, Constance A.	167	Nordling, Jeffrey	174
Meriwether, Lee	162	Morgan, Barbara R.	167	Norick, Lance	174
Merkerson, Epatha	162	Morgan, Harry	167	Noriega, Carlos I.	174
Mero, Rena	162	Morgan, Lorrie	167	Norris, Chuck	174
Messina, Jo Dee	162	Morgan, Michele	167	North, Nolan	174
Metcalf, Laurie	162	Morgan, Rob	167	North, Oliver	174
Metcalfe, Jesse	162	Morin, Lee M.	167	Northagen, Callie	174
Mica, John L.	162	Morris, Garrett	168	Northup, Anne M.	174
Michaels, Tammy Lynn	162	Morris, Julianne	168	Norton, Eleanor Holmes	175
Michel, F. Curtis	163	Morrow, Joshua	168	Norwood, Charlie	175
Michele, Michael	163	Mortensen, Viggo	168	Nowak, Lisa M.	175
Michelle, Cara	163	Moss, Ronn	168	Nussle, Jim	175
Mickelson, Phil	163	Mulkey, Chris	168		
Middleton, Mae	163	Mullane, Richard M.	168		

O

Midler, Bette	163	Murkowski, Frank	168	O'Bannon, Frank	177
Mikulski, Barbara	163	Murphy, Eddie	168	Oak Ridge Boys, The	177
Milano, Alyssa	163	Murphy, Kim	168	Oberstar, James L.	177
Millender-McDonald, Juanita	163	Murphy, Lynn	168	Obey, David R.	177
Miller, Christa	163	Murray, Anne	168	O'Brien, Conan	177
Miller, Dan	163	Murray, Joel	168	O'Brien, Parry	177
Miller, Gary G.	163	Murray, Patty	169		

Rainer, Luise	195	Riegel, Eden	200	Runco Jr., Mario	206
Raines, Ron	195	Rigby, Cathy	200	Ru-Paul	206
Raines, Tony	196	Righteous Brothers, The	200	Rush, Bobby L.	206
Ralph, Sheryl Lee	196	Riley, Bob	201	Russell, Keri	206
Ramey, Venus	196	Rimes, LeAnn	201	Russell, Theresa	206
Ramirez, Marisa	196	Ripa, Kelly	201	Russo, Rene	206
Ramos, Luis Antonio	196	Ritch, Michael	201	Ruttman, Joe	206
Ramstad, Jim	196	Ritchie, Sharon	201	Ryan, George H.	206
Randall, Josh	196	Rivers Edge	201	Ryan, Meg	206
Randall, Tony	196	Rivers, Joan	201	Ryan, Mitchell	206
Randolph, Joyce	196	Rivers, Lynn N.	201	Ryan, Nolan	206
Randy Savage	196	Rivers, Melissa	201	Ryan, Paul	207
Rangel, Charles B.	196	Roberts, Cokie	201	Rydell, Bobby	207
Rascal Flatts	196	Roberts, Julia	201, 202	Ryun, Jim	207
Rauch, Paul	196	Roberts, Layla Harvest	202		
Raven, Eddy	196	Roberts, Nora	202		
Ravencroft, Thurl	197	Roberts, Pat	202	**S**	
Raver, Kim	197	Robertson, Lisa	202	Sabato Jr., Antonio	209
Ray J	197	Robertson, Pat	202	Sabo, Martin Olav	209
Ray, Robert W.	197	Robinson, Larry	202	Sadler, Elliott	209
Raye, Collin	197	Robinson, Stephen K.	202	Sadler, William	209
Readdy, William F.	197	Robinson, Wendy Raquel	202	Safer, Morley	209
Reckell, Peter	197	Rockefeller IV, John	202	Sagona, Katie	209
Reddy, Helen	197	Roddy, Rod	202	Sajak, Pat	209
Redford, Robert	197	Roderick, Brande Nicole	202	Sales, Soupy	209
Reed, Jack	197	Roderick, Brande	202	Samuels, Melissa	209
Reeves, Julie	197	Rodriguez, Chi Chi	203	Samuelson, Joan Benoit	209
Reeves, Scott	197	Rodriguez, Ciro D.	203	Sanches, Stacy	210
Reffner, Bryan	197	Roe, Mary Beth	203	Sanchez, Loretta	210
Regula, Ralph	197	Roemer, Tim	203	Sand, Shauna	210
Rehberg, Dennis R.	198	Rogers, Fred	203	Sanders, Bernard	210
Rehnquist, William	198	Rogers, Harold	203	Sanders, Ricky	210
Reid, Francis	198	Rogers, Kenny	203	Sandlin, Max	210
Reid, Harry	198	Rogers, Mike	203	Sands, Lee	210
Reightler Jr., Kenneth S.	198	Rogers, Mimi	203	Santana, Merlin	210
Reilly, James F.	198	Rogers, Suzanne	203	Santerre, Andy	210
Reilly, Patti	198	Rohrabacher, Dana	203	Santiago, Saundra	210
Reiner, Rob	198	Roker, Al	203	Santorum, Rick	210
Reiser, Robbie	198	Rominger, Kent V.	203	Santos, Al	210
Reisman, Garrett E.	198	Roof, Michael	204	Sapp, Carolyn	210
Remar, James	198	Rooney, Mickey	204	Sarandon, Susan	210
Remini, Leah	198	Roper, Tony	204	Sarbanes, Paul	211
Renfrow, Randy	198	Rose, Pete	204	Sarna, Shivan	211
Reno, Janet	198	Ros-Lehtinen, Ileana	204	Saucedo, Michael	211
Retton, Mary Lou	199	Rosman, Mackenzie	204	Sauter, Jay	211
Rex, Simon	199	Ross, Jerry L.	204	Sawyer Brown	211
Reyes, Silvestre	199	Ross, Marion	204	Sawyer, Diane	211
Reynolds, Burt	199	Ross, Mike	204	Sawyer, Elton	211
Reynolds, Debbie	199	Ross, Tracee Ellis	204	Sawyer, Tom	211
Reynolds, James	199	Ross, Tracey	204	Saxton, Jim	211
Reynolds, Ryan	199	Roszell, Jennifer	204	Scales, Crystal	211
Reynolds, Thomas M.	199	Rothman, Steven R.	205	Scalia, Antonin	211
Rhea, Caroline	199	Rotondi, Todd	205	Scanlon, Chris	211
Rice, Anne	199	Roukema, Marge	205	Scarborough, Joe	211
Richards, Brooke	199	Rovero, Jennifer	205	Scarfe, Alan	211
Richards, Denise	199	Rowell, Victoria	205	Schaefer, Laurel	212
Richards, J. August	199	Rowland, John G.	205	Schaffer, Bob	212
Richards, Paul W.	199	Rowlands, Gena	205	Schakowsky, Janice D.	212
Richards, Richard N.	200	Rowling, J.K.	205	Schieler, Nikki	212
Richardson, Cameron	200	Roybal-Allard, Lucille	205	Schiff, Adam B.	212
Richardson, Patricia	200	Royce, Edward R.	205	Schiff, Richard	212
Richardson, Patricia	200	Ruccolo, Richard	205	Schirra Jr., Walter M.	212
Rickles, Don	200	Ruck, Alan	205	Schlatter, Charlie	212
Rickter, Alicia	200	Rudd, Ricky	205	Schlegel, Hans	212
Ricochet	200	Rudie, Evelyn	205	Schmitt, Harrison H.	212
Ride, Sally K.	200	Rue, Sara	206	Schrader, Ken	212
Ridge, Tom	200	Ruivivar, Anthony	206	Schrock, Edward L.	212
				Schroder, Rick	212

Name	Page	Name	Page	Name	Page
Waterston, Sam	247	Wiles, Jason	251	Woodland, Rich	255
Watkins, Wes	248	Wilkinsons, The	251	Woods, Robert S.	255
Watson, Alberta	248	Willey, Walt	251	Woods, Tiger	255
Watson, Barry	248	Williams Jr., Hank	251	Woodward III, Neil W.	255
Watson, Muse	248	Williams, Barry	251	Woolsey, Lynn C.	255
Watson, Tom	248	Williams, Chris	251	Wopat, Tom	255
Watt, Melvin L.	248	Williams, David R.	252	Worden, Alfred M.	255
Watts Jr., J.C.	248	Williams, Donald E.	252	Wright, Deanna	255
Waxman, Henry A.	248	Williams, Greg Allan	252	Wright, Laura	256
Weaver, Dennis	248	Williams, Harland	252	Wright, Max	256
Weaver, Patty	248	Williams, Jeffrey N.	252	Wright, Michelle	256
Weber, Mary E.	248	Williams, Jet	252	Wu, David	256
Weiner, Anthony D.	248	Williams, John	252	Wyden, Ron	256
Weitz, Paul J.	248	Williams, Kelli	252	Wyle, Noah	256
Weldon, Curt	248	Williams, Leah	252	Wynn, Albert Russell	256
Weldon, Dave	249	Williams, Malinda	252		
Weller, Jerry	249	Williams, Michelle	252		
Wells, Dawn	249	Williams, Robin	252		

Name	Page
Wells, Kimberly	249
Wells, Kitty	249
Wells, Sharlene	249
Wellstone, Paul	249
West, Kimber	249
West, Maura	249
West, Shane	249
Westcott, Carrie	249
Westheimer, Dr. Ruth	249
Westmore, McKenzie	249
Wetherbee, James D.	250
Wexler, Robert	250
Whedon, Joss	250
Wheeler, Dan	250
Wheelock, Douglas H.	250
Whelan, Julia	250
White, Betty	250
White, Bryan	250
White, Lari	250
White, Persia	250
White, Vanna	250
Whitestone, Heather	250
Whitfield, Ed	250
Whitford, Bradley	251
Whitman, Christine T.	251
Whitmore, James	251
Whitson, Peggy A.	251
Wicker, Roger F.	251
Widdoes, Kathleen	251
Wiest, Dianne	251
Wilcutt, Terrence W.	251

Name	Page
Williams, Sunita L.	252
Williams, Tonya Lee	252
Williams, Van	253
Williams, Vanessa	253
Williams, Vanessa	253
Williamson, Fred	253
Williamson, Kevin	253
Wills, Mark	253
Wilson, B.A.	253
Wilson, Brian	253
Wilson, Dorien	253
Wilson, Heather	253
Wilson, Marie	253
Wilson, Roger	253
Wilson, Stephanie D.	253
Wilson, Yvette	254
Winchell, Paul	254
Winfrey, Oprah	254
Winslet, Kate	254
Winston, Hattie	254
Winters, Jonathan	254
Wisoff, Peter J. K.	254
Witt, Holly	254
Wolf, David A.	254
Wolf, Frank R.	254
Wolf, Kathy	254
Womack, Lee Ann	254
Wood, Danny	254
Wood, Evan Rachel	255
Wood, Nicole	255
Woodland, Lauren	255

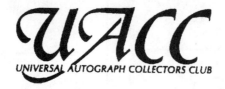

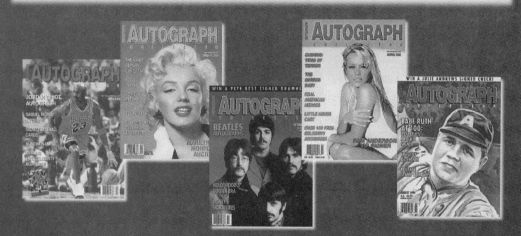

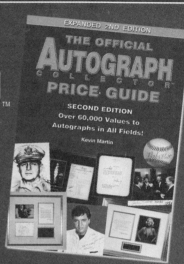
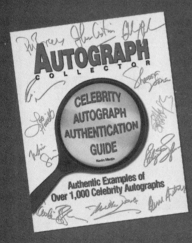

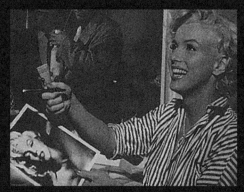